Mr Stephenson's Regret

David Williams

A Wild Wolf Publication

Published by Wild Wolf Publishing in 2012

First print

Many characters and events portrayed are factual, but some incidental details have been amended or conflated for narrative purposes.

ISBN: 978-1-907954-20-7

www.wildwolfpublishing.com

Author's Note

f6

This is a novel, not a history. The true story of George and Robert Stephenson, as far as it is known, is reflected in these pages, but some incidental details have been amended or conflated for narrative purposes. Some scenes and characters are fictional.

I would like to thank the unsung library and museum professionals who have helped me at various times during my research - part of the under-valued, under-resourced but vital public services we need to hold onto in this country. Thanks to Hunter Davies for awakening my interest in the Stephensons, and to Samuel Smiles, their first biographer. Thanks to my son Joe for his usual top-notch editorial job. Special thanks to Wild Wolf for being willing to publish me again, taking the chance in an unfamiliar genre.

This book is dedicated to my wife Paula – we celebrated our ruby wedding anniversary as the novel was taking its final shape. My sympathy for Robert Stephenson's childlessness stems from the love Paula and I have shared for and from our own three children and growing tribe of grandchildren.

I

He could not apprehend this stillness before him.

Death, of course, had presented its calling card frequently enough. Thrice in six years Robert had worn deep mourning: for his stepmother, for his own dear Frances, and now, when most alone, for his father. The women had seemed graceful on the satin pillow, such calm repose a memory and a comfort; he had known them like this in health. George was never still. Not a year ago, prowling with boredom in Robert's Westminster rooms, he had challenged Bidder to a wrestle. Between them they broke so many of the chairs in the outer office that son was moved to send father the joiner's repair bill. Paid promptly and with a cheerful accompanying note. Not a year ago.

The merest movement at his shoulder brought Robert back to the parlour where the coffin lay. Mr Eyre's instinct for punctuality had trumped his carefully-cultivated discretion.

'Of course, yes.'

Robert withdrew to give the cabinet-maker space and privacy to complete his duties. He turned at the door for one last glimpse of his father's folded hands, and so sent Eyre's apprentice into a guilty spasm, caught in the act of positioning the lid for closure. The boy froze, held by his master's glare till Robert quit the room.

In the hallway Eyre's business partner John Robinson waited, idly brushing the nap of his hat. Its weeper trailed almost to the floor. Robinson had a ruddy complexion that spoke more of butcher than draper. Red-skinned cheese to Mr Eyre's chalk. No amount of black crape could solemnify this man's demeanour, though he was not so much blithe as brash. He delivered solicitude with an air of familiarity that seemed to Robert inappropriate and ultimately self-serving.

'Ah, sir, your papa,' he said as Robert came near. 'What a man he was.'

It seemed an innocent enough remark, yet Robert found himself provoked by it. 'Forgive me, Mr Robinson, but I prefer to wait for my father's interment before I discuss his character or achievements in the past tense. I still have him close about me.'

'Of course, I could not agree more.' Robinson failed to repress his smile as he studied the effect of the polishing on his hat. 'The sentiments of our town exactly. We all feel especially close to Mr Stephenson - I refer to the late lamented Mr Stephenson saving your presence, sir - very close indeed at this time.' Robert wanted to say that was not what he meant at all, but the undertaker continued. 'Remarkable how the whole of Chesterfield is closing for the duration, sir. Such is our respect.'

'I saw some notices to the effect.'

'Mmm. From twelve till two. Quite soon now.'

They fell silent, eyes averted, as if listening for the sounds of the town closing beyond the gates of Tapton House. What could be heard instead were the quiet murmurs of funeral guests gathered in the drawing room, waiting the summons to take their respective places in the cortège, and the tap of hammer on nail from the room behind. Robert felt for his waistcoat pocket, recalled he had left his watch wrapped in a handkerchief in his dressing chamber, and looked across to check the time on the longcase clock in the hall. It was stopped, marking the time of his father's death. A nerve quickened in Robert's temple, and he looked quickly away again, to witness Robinson in a frank appraisal of his client's mourning-clothes. Unabashed, the man smiled genially.

'Black Peter's?'

'Pardon me?'

'I imagine they would be your supplier, sir.'

'Jays' of Regent Street.'

'Ah, Jays'. A reputable firm, but I like to think we do as well, sir, in a provincial sort of way.'

'No doubt.'

The undertaker straightened his own cuffs. 'I'll hazard the greater part of this afternoon's procession will bear witness to that fact. I mean, as to their elegance, including the neighbourhood gentry and members of the corporation, not merely the town officers whom we have fitted, so to speak, in common, as becomes the pomp of the occasion.'

Robert winced on his father's behalf at *pomp*, but had no time to voice an opinion before Robinson leaned in to him somewhat to say, 'On which note, I have taken a certain liberty, sir, notwithstanding the letter of your instructions but, I'm sure you'll agree, very much within the spirit of this sombre occasion, to employ a modest band of mutes to precede your father's hearse in suitably sober fashion. Just four, to be precise. It is usual.'

Another of those upstart attempts to make the funeral more elaborate than his client believed necessary. 'I asked for no mutes.'

'Which of course I noted, sir.' Robinson was imperturbable. 'But being privy to the arrangements made by the mayor and the corporation, I felt emboldened... Why, the procession is likely to be three hundred strong.'

6

'Is that not pomp enough, without mutes?'

'My further consideration was for the horses. As you know, they are not so biddable as your locomotive engines. My fear is that the hearse may break off somewhat from the pedestrian traffic, should we not have our trained mourners marching in front to act by way of a check on the progress of the hearse. I believe your father used to do the same with men and flags, when the railways was new.'

Robert could not stop himself rising to the man's impertinence. 'Quite wrong, sir, except where appointed by interfering bodies who thought they knew better. My father dismissed them as entirely unnecessary. Such is the case with your mutes. You may stand them down; I neither wish to see them today, nor tomorrow as an item on my bill.'

'Well, that is a loss,' said Robinson, though whether he meant for the event or for the account was not clear until he risked a final throw. 'I may be a little out of touch with London society, but I'm sure if your poor father could still be present with us he would turn a phrase often employed in our community. Expectation is duty. He appreciated more than most how Tapton and the great houses are looked upon to help define the better...'

'Don't...' Robert's exasperation overflowed into outright aggression. 'Do not, sir, presume to lecture me on my father's opinions. It is clear you knew him very little. I can tell you now, Robinson, that these arguments you have laid before me... If my father had been with us now to hear them, there is every likelihood he would have knocked you down to the floor. I do not speak metaphorically.'

John Robinson had by no means over-estimated the strength of the retinue. By the time the mayor and members of the corporation joined the cortège at Tapton toll-bar, the pedestrian parade between the hearse and the lead mourning carriage bearing Robert and his relatives had grown to more than three hundred. Gentlemen and shopkeepers of the town slow-marched two abreast as they followed the glass-sided hearse. The mourners' silence hallowed the sound of the wheels. Four black horses walked with practised dignity without the benefit of mutes, their black plumes appearing to nod acknowledgement to the onlookers who removed their hats in the traditional gesture of respect as they passed.

Robert could see little of this from behind the blinds of his coach, except for occasional glimpses of the knots of working people gathered to watch at corners, bands of crape fashioned around an arm or hat. The men, he guessed, would be from Clay Cross or Lockorford Colliery;

7

perhaps some from the lime kilns at Ambergate. These, along with the rest of his father's interests, he would have to take on himself now, additions to his own extensive portfolio. The thought wearied him in the circumstances. He sank back into the black leather of his seat, gazed listlessly through the gap afforded by the screen, until one face in the crowd caused him to sit up, even pluck at the blind to stare behind him as the carriage started to climb the hill.

'Somebody you know?' from cousin George opposite, watching him.

'Kit Heppel, I am convinced it was. You remember Kit?'

'I believe I do. Is old Kit still breathing?'

'Unless his ghost has come to pay respect. But surely Kit could not have travelled such a long way to stand and watch the hearse go past.'

George hooked the blind with his finger; looked out at the bystanders. 'Depend on it. Yesterday's train was full. Station master was telling me of folk he had to move on that thought they could do worse than make his waiting room their hotel for the night.' A poignant chuckle. 'One who give him trouble said the railways belonged to his departed friend Mr George Stephenson, and that he would certainly have wanted him to stay at his pleasure.'

'What did the station master do?'

'He was minded to direct him to the house, but thought better of it and sent him on his way. It's no hardship outdoors in this weather.'

'Perhaps that was Kit himself.'

'It would be like Kit, now I think on him.'

Robert was momentarily enlivened by the thought. 'We must look out for old Kit at the church, cousin, invite him to come and take tea with us.'

At Trinity Church Robert soon realised that his hopes of finding Kit were slim among the press of people there. The great and good of the town formed a line along each side of Newbold Lane as the principal mourners passed through their ranks, then followed them through the church doors, their black-edged tickets ready for the ushers. Some of the faithful workforce were allowed in also, while the remainder of the large crowd stood silently in the churchyard and the lane beyond, listening to the last peals of the funeral bell before the service proper began.

Robert was to some degree grateful for this popular show of consideration - he knew how George would have relished it - but he felt his private grief intruded on, not least when the vault beneath the church floor was opened and his father's oak coffin lowered to rest alongside his stepmother's. Robert hesitated at the entrance. His arms opened slightly in what spectators may have interpreted as a motion of prayer or respect, but which in fact sprang from delicacy, as though he wanted to protect his parents from inquisitive eyes. He emptied himself of anguish at that moment; became a cloak. At the end of the service he asked the carriage to return for him and waited until everyone had left before he studied the tablet in solitude.

Almost alone. As he stood by the communion rail he became aware of a figure seated at the back of the church. When he looked up it was with the fond anticipation of seeing Kit Heppel, but the Quaker hat covering the bowed head let him know who was praying there. Robert watched over this silent contemplation, smiled welcome when the man straightened, but made no move to assist his slow progress with walking-stick down the aisle - Edward Pease was as proudly independent as his late partner had been.

Pease nodded his appreciation of the simple inscription on the stone floor. Robert was moved to confess, 'There is to be a commemorative plaque. For the wall, I believe. And perhaps a window.'

'I was dismayed to learn,' said Pease unexpectedly, 'that no petition had been made to the queen.'

'Petition?'

'For thy father's interment inside Westminster Abbey. Why should he not have been laid alongside Thomas Telford?'

'They might have made uncomfortable bed-fellows. There was no harsher critic of his methods of working than Telford. Opposed us on the question of using locomotives for the Liverpool line, and did it with a vengeance; we almost lost our great opportunity.'

'Telford was singing for his supper, that was all - it meant nothing.'

The old man seemed tetchy. Robert had made light of his remarks, but now he saw they were seriously made. 'You surprise me, Edward, condoning such grandness. Do you really feel my father should be in the Abbey?'

Pease clutched Robert by the arm. 'My religion stands no man above another, but for achievement genuinely earned. The two great engineers of their time, Telford and Stephenson. Why is one not given the respect he merits as well as the other? And who was here today?'

'Why, hundreds. Some travelling for miles.' He could feel his elder's bones beneath the fingers at his sleeve.

'Where is Russell? Where is Peel? Is the Duke too busy quelling Chartists? There is no-one here of that ilk, that's my complaint. It is a disgrace.'

Robert was troubled by the idea that he may have been remiss. Perhaps his brain had been overwhelmed by the shock of his father's death - it had not crossed his mind that neither the country's leaders nor the first rank of nobility had applied for representation at the funeral. He felt impelled to put up some defence, but whether on their behalf, his father's or his own he was unsure. 'I'm... My father would have wished for no greater comfort than to be with his true love again, and... for no greater honour than he has received today from the people whose society he cherished, and whose lives he has improved so much.'

'Well said, dear friend,' Pease granted. He relinquished his grip somewhat; maintained hold on Robert's arm for support now, less for emphasis. 'Thou knows I would be the last to deny such simple ends. For all that, I feel thy father's wider contribution has not been acknowledged as it should be, and I see offence in the absence of prime movers.'

Pease poked his walking-stick at the floor with a vestige of irritation as they turned to leave the church. Robert accompanied him in silence until they reached the gate, thoughts racing on the nature of the offence that had so exercised his guest. He surmised that this outburst had much to do with Pease feeling personally slighted by the establishment's apparent indifference to George and his works, as if by implication it degraded his own contribution.

Outside the church gate Robert's carriage was already returned, waiting for him in the sunlight. A servant closed his hand over a small bell that threatened to tinkle at the harness.

'You must come back to the house with me,' Robert said to Pease. 'There are friends present you will not have seen for many a month, I dare say.'

'Pray excuse me that. I'm cold comfort in company. Besides, I have my journey planned. When dost return to London?'

'I travel on the morrow, and have resolved to avoid my office until Monday week.'

'Do I trespass too heavily on propriety should I offer myself as visitor at Gloucester Square on the Second of the Ninth?'

The proposal was warmly received and their parting was affectionate, but Robert was still very much disturbed by what Edward Pease had to say in the church, and he returned to Tapton House in a restless state of mind.

Dinner that evening was an awkward affair, though it was confined to family members in due respect. The fault, Robert thought at first, was that the meal was served in the new style *à la russe*. Consequently the diners had no spread to comment upon and nothing to do but wait for the servants to carry the food in dish by dish and pass around them, constantly appearing at one's elbow to add a helping and further stultify the sporadic conversation. This was presumably an innovation of the new housekeeper; his father had enjoyed the business of carving at the table, always heartily enjoined his guests to take their part in handing around the plentiful side-dishes at each remove.

Soon enough Robert realised it was not the new housekeeper to blame for the inhibited mood, though the fact that Tapton House recently had a vacancy which she filled was germane. Seated at the opposite end of the board to Robert, a blot of black against the scarlet and mahogany, was the third Mrs Stephenson - that is, the widow in her weeds. Six months before, his father had relieved Ellen Gregory of her housekeeper's situation by marrying her, to the surprise of many and the certain consternation of those now around the dining table. Their unease did not spring from class difference - if truth be told the Gregory bloodline was an atom or two purer than the Stephenson - nor much from disappointment over the inheritance; George had told them for years what to expect in his will, and Robert was executor in possession, though of course the widow had to be accommodated. It was simply that they did not care for her, and had failed to appreciate their esteemed relative's attraction for a much younger woman. Those who had met her before his death had found her a baleful presence even in what should have been the first flush of marriage, and now - while strangely devoid of any sign of real grief despite the lock of George's white hair mounted in her mourning-brooch - she cast a deeper pall over proceedings than was called for by convention. Robert had detected an incipient pretentiousness from first meeting, and lately suspected her as the instigator of Robinson's audacious attempts to make the funeral more extravagant than seemly.

After the meal, when the men had their fill of spicy zests and joined the ladies for tea and cakes in the drawing room, the conversation flowed more easily; became quite animated once Mrs Stephenson had retired early to bed. Inevitably it turned on memories of the dear departed and especially his early life, occasioned by Robert relating Aunt Nelly's remark that she had counted ninety windows in this house, being eighty-nine more than George was able to look through as a bairn in their old cottage at Wylam.

11

'It would be like Mam to mention that blessed cottage,' said cousin Meg, 'since she did so every day of her life.' The others laughed, encouraging Meg into affectionate mimicry. 'Aye, one room and eight on us to live an breathe in it. It was turns for this and turns for that. Whose turn to sit nearest the fire. Whose turn to scrub the netty seat. Life was made up of turns them days.'

'Who'd get the crusts off the loaf,' put in another.

'Who'd get the warmest place in the bed. Right in the middle, with Mammy and...'

'Bed! My old man had to mek do wi the shaky-down,' cried George through the laughter; 'Squashed between Uncle George and Uncle Jemmy, wi nowt but a cast-off from the gin horse for a blanket.'

Robert listened, wryly amused at this skit on their elders' attempts to outdo each other in tales of past poverty and hardship. It was an old Stephenson trait to vaunt privation and the way they rose above it; this despite none of them attending school until, at the age of eighteen, George started paying threepence a week from his meagre pitman's wages in return for Robin Cowens teaching him his letters. Robert's surviving cousins knew the stories well enough to lampoon them, but were all too young to have experienced genuine hardship for themselves, as he had early in his life. Not one of them was spoiled, but they had grown up on the fringes of affluence.

The pity of it was that - but for Aunt Anne, still living as far as Robert knew in America - all the children brought up in the Wylam cottage were now dead. Here was their line, here in this room. Who among them would help to provide another Stephenson generation?

After another hour or so the company began to drift off to their beds. When he was at last alone, Robert took a lighted candle and a glass of French brandy, not to his bedroom but to his father's library. There were more models and curios than books. Several plans and sketches lay open still on the large table, as if George had just now left the room and may return to resume his work at any moment. Robert looked about him. In one corner of the room he spied a breeding hutch for rabbits, evidently under repair. On a small table near the window was a tall glass cylinder containing a straightened cucumber, the proud result of one of his father's many horticultural experiments. There was a sectioned drawing of a bee-hive, and a flowing diagram labelled, in a familiar hand, *foriger's dance*, the slight misspelling causing the son's eyes to prick for the first time that day.

Robert moved towards the armchair by the fireplace. As he did so the candlelight shone on a Parian marble bust of Wellington, from his glory days at Waterloo, in pride of place on the mantelshelf. Robert set the candle next to the bust and lingered at the fireplace. The Duke looked past him at something stately and remote; and in truth, though Robert's eyes stayed on the Duke's beaked features, he was no longer really seeing them, for the figure had started a train of thought that took him back to his encounter with Pease in Trinity Church. He drained his glass of brandy, placed the empty glass next to the candle and sat down in his father's usual place. He stared into the empty grate until the study clock chimed once at the quarter-hour. As if that was the signal for him to take a prescription, Robert reached into an inside pocket of his mourning-coat; pulled out a slender silver phial. He shook the vessel absently before uncorking it, and swallowed the contents in one draught. He carefully replaced the phial in his pocket, closed his eyes, and surrendered to the depths of the armchair.

II

He could not recall his mother's face except as an abstract impression, a mere shading in pastels, wraith-like and pallid. His first clear memory was of his father lifting him over a hedge into some woods. He was set down in the long grass while his father straddled the hedge then picked Robert up again in his collier's arms and carried him under the trees. There were just the two of them, certainly, and a distant note that Robert knew later to be the bell from the chapel below the fields, where his mother would be attending service.

George wanted to show him the nest of a song thrush, one couched low enough that he could pull himself up by a sturdy branch and crook Bobby into his left breast to see at close quarters. There were three spotted blue eggs within, the like of which George's own father had shown him years before, and he had remembered always.

What Robert came to remember was the echo of gunfire deeper in the woods, and his father slinking down the trunk to lay his boy carefully at the base before he stole through trees to investigate. Left on his own, Robert soon began to bleat; brought George quickly back to wrap his arms around and hush him, whispering 'Ssh, Bobby, or I'll be bound for the boat, son.' The young pitman concealed himself behind the tree, Robert enveloped by him, swaddled in male musk. He listened intently for the movement of men through the woods. Two spoke near enough for George to detect the tone of their voices - one peremptory, the other obsequious - but not so close as to hear the words. Robert, soothed by the rhythm of his father's heart beating through his back, fell asleep in the warmth of him as they hid, pressed against the trunk.

When he awoke he was at George's hip as his father strode down the hill to join the family at Dolly's Field. This was the place where George in his bachelor days had turned the tables on the bully Ned Nelson, evading his ham-fisted blows and countering with tact and guile. *Brain beats brawn* George said, whenever he told the tale. Robert would come to know this as the picnic field, where all the outdoor feast days were held, as on this Easter Sunday. Practically the whole village was there, now the church and chapel services were over, some with kin who had walked miles from their homes to celebrate the holiday together. Sharing the brief hours of liberation; filling hearts and lungs with the pure swell of it. George had to step aside to make way for the cuddy race starting where the slope turned to flat. Elsewhere he could see children in pairs jarping eggs and in the distance a group running down to the stream, intent on sugar-cupping. His younger sister Anne and another girl were being teased by some youths from the village, but there looked to be no harm in them.

He soon found Fanny sitting on the grass with his parents and sister Nell, but it was Mabel, not his wife, who took her grandson in her lap. George told Old Bob about his near encounter with the gamekeeper. He could afford to laugh about it now that he was safe from the transport ship; brag a little of the defiance he had exhibited by his trespass. While they were talking, Anne ran up to complain to her mother, 'Look how I've lost my shoes that George made. John Nixon has lifted me and pinched them.'

George stood up and lifted Anne too, then let her down gently as she protested, favouring her with a hug. 'He'll gi you them back quick enough for the price of a kiss,' he told her. 'And don't forget you've to lift his hat the morrow.' He released Anne and hunkered down to touch his wife's hand where she rested it over her smock. 'I'm away for a turn at the hoying. Are you all right just yet?' Fanny nodded and he wandered off to join the other young men gathered for the hammer-throwing. Nell took her turn with Robert, waggling her fingers to persuade him to leave the comfort of his granny's lap and walk with her.

'Did you see the sun dance this morning, Bobby?' No answer expected. Nelly was trying to cheer herself up. She had still not got over the disappointment of her betrayal by Daniel Jakes, who'd persuaded her to abandon domestic service in London with the promise of marriage. She had returned home after a long and difficult passage up the coast to find that Jakes had wed someone else. Nell was left with no work, no savings and no lover. Left to walk her infant nephew round the field alone, his fingers stretching to hers, stumbling now and again over her petticoats. All around her she could see couples flirting with each other - even her chit sister Anne had an admirer now - while Nell, just twenty-one, had to play the maiden aunt. Still, Fanny had been thought of as an old maid too, long before George took her up, after his own heartbreak over Betty Hindmarsh.

'Are you wantin to watch your daddy at the hammer?' she asked, privately glad to have Bobby as her pretext for observing the miners at play. Some of them were stripped ready to the waist, as they might be at the coalface. Nelly was more shocked by others lolling on the grass, defying the Sabbath by swigging ale from stone pitchers. George was not among the inebriates, but stood easy, taller than many of his peers but not as thick-set as some, waiting his turn at the sport. When it came he took a firm grip of the sledgehammer, swung it back between his open legs and smoothly forward again, releasing and following the trajectory with outstretched hands as if (were he a more religious man) beseeching the hammer to fly to the heavens. Which it almost did, to judge by the cheers of the spectators. Kit Heppel stepped forward and clapped a hand at his back.

'Not bad for a brakesman, George. Yon's well past the hewers' anyhow.'

'Brain beats brawn, Kit,' from George, inevitably. 'I got the science on it, that's the trick.'

*

Try as he might in adult life, Robert could remember nothing of his mother's condition, or of ever having a baby sister, however briefly. Was he sent to his grandparents during that troubled time? Who could tell him now? Yet he could recall the smell and touch of his father nursing him at table, the feel of the wood under his midget fingers, the turn of a leaf in a book, the scratch of chalk on George's slate as his hold tightened slightly around the boy while he shaped letters in a way so painfully awkward for one who could be touch-delicate within the workings of the smallest mechanical object. Robert could remember his childish excitement as his father entertained him with a contraption he placed in front of them. It had a wooden wheel that he turned to send thick silver liquid running deliciously through glass tubes mounted on the rim. Robert remembered, too, a man as tall as his father come to play with the toy, taking him on his knee in the same way and helping him stretch his hand to reach the wheel and start it spinning. The boy almost falling from the man's careless grasp, and caught up again. The visitor laughed loudly, George joining in. Robert was sure he had never heard his mother laugh like this. He sometimes heard her cough.

He had but one detailed memory of her in their home. He was occupying himself with wooden blocks that George had carved for his enjoyment, building them into a tower on the table before sending them crashing down on the beaten floor. His mother had her back to him; on her knees at the range, trying to coax the fire through the fresh coals by propping the iron bleazer over the grate. As Robert bent to gather up his scattered blocks there was a rushing sound from the flue. His mother pulled away in fright - all but stumbled backwards over the boy. The bleazer fell from the grate and orange flames licked around the opening.

16

'Chimney's on fire!' she shouted; scooped him up, blocks spilling in a ragged line from hearth to doorway. Out in the lane she dizzied him, turning this way and that uncertain as his legs threshed and beat on hers. There was a shriek; not his mother but a neighbour, disgusted at the huge specks of soot falling on her laundry stretched across the hedge to dry. With more presence of mind than Fanny, as soon as she saw flames and thick smoke billowing from the top of the chimney, she ran to the pump with a bucket, then dashed into the cottage to throw water into the fireplace. Fanny put Robert down, rushed to the doorway, pulled up with a painful coughing fit. Two more women emerged from their homes to help. Before long they were even mounting the ridge of the low building to throw buckets of water down the chimney and stop the fire in the flue.

For the rest of the day Robert was left to please himself in the mud outdoors while his mother did her best to soak up the damage inside the cottage. When George came home from his work Fanny all but collapsed in his arms at the threshold. 'Are you needing the doctor again?' he asked; didn't notice at first the chaos of furniture behind her. He comforted his exhausted wife as she told the story to his shoulder, then eased her from him as he stepped inside to inspect the mess for himself.

'Oh, my best clock.'

His prized eight-day clock still hanging on the wall, soot-blackened and stopped. George took it to the table and there and then, still in his dirty work clothes on a sodden seat, he opened the back of the clock and started to poke about at the mechanism inside. He would not move from there until he had the timepiece ticking once more.

*

From that day on, whenever Robert pulled himself up on tiptoe to eye-level with the table, he would find there some neighbour's clock in pieces, or sometimes a pocket watch, or stranger objects he did not know the use of - such things as smoke-jacks and a whirring machine that his father soon planted in his vegetable plot to scare off the crows - as well as the familiar leather and corduroy that George continued to use for making boots and clothes for his friends and family.

Until the morning came when Robert saw that the table had been entirely cleared of this paraphernalia and of his father's tools, to be replaced by a long closed box, made from unvarnished deal. From his infant perspective this box seemed to fill the house, with barely enough room for a boy, much less his daddy, to move around it. He had to crawl underneath to find somewhere to play. Strangely, though, as the morning drew on, the cottage seemed to open up for more and more people, who came through the door and somehow found space around the box to stand silently there, until it became impossible for the room to hold any more and some had to go out into the lane to admit others. There must have been a score of visitors altogether. Several faces Robert did not know, but he recognized his Grandpa Bob and Grandma Mabel, and some of his aunts and uncles, who all seemed to notice him and tilt their heads in the same way, but did not ruffle his hair or sit him down to hear a story as they usually did.

His father stitched a piece of black material around Bobby's sleeve. Some of the adults had them too and others were dressed almost entirely in black. Some of the women wore black hats while the men carried theirs until everyone stepped outside at once and the men put their hats on their heads. The deal box was carried through and placed on the bed of a small cart that waited outside the cottage. A docile pony stood between the shafts with an old man in a black top hat holding its reins. The old man looked so weary, Robert imagined that any moment he'd nod off to sleep and collapse in the road, let his horse go wander. With nothing else to entertain him, the boy stood close by to watch it happen, but the man and the horse stayed perfectly still, until his father broke away from the crowd to stand alongside the cart, his left hand on top of the box. This was the signal for the pony to move, and for the rest of the party to start walking behind. Robert scampered after, trying to keep up with them, but Mrs Lunn, the neighbour who had helped put out the chimney fire, caught him in her arms and took him back to watch at the cottage door as the procession slowly made its way along Paradise Row and down the track that led to the church.

*

He remembered also the day when that same patient pony and that same old man (minus his top hat) took Robert with his Aunt Nelly to visit Newcastle. Nell arrived at the cottage very early in the morning. While George and the driver unloaded some effects from the back of the cart, she marched the boy to the pump, doused his hair and scrubbed his face till it hurt. When he was pronounced spick and span his father strode across and swept him up in his arms, intending at first to swing him onto the back of the cart. Instead, the movement arrested, George held him, smothered his face with kisses until his sister complained, 'I'll have to start all over washing the boy if you don't stop that slaver.'

18

George finally did place Robert tenderly on the cart, and helped Nelly up too. They waited while he locked the cottage door and put the key in a purse which he handed up to Nell. Robert supposed his father would be riding with them, as he had a bag by his side along with his tools, but he simply stood a few moments in front of the cottage to see them off before he started walking in the opposite direction, to work as far as Robert knew.

The boy had never been out of the village. He was thrilled by the adventure of it, and soon absorbed by the sights of the journey, especially when they had left the slag heaps behind and got near to the river. It was a bumpy ride as the little cart's wheels were not adapted to roll along the wagon way. It would in any event have impeded the progress of the larger horses that dragged their heavy loads of coal to the shipping staiths; instead, the travellers followed a badly-made trail alongside. Several times they came close to upending. Once Nell had to climb down to help the old man push the cart out of a rut, bemoaning the ruination of her gloves for the rest of the trip. Robert, though, liked it very well when he was sliding from side to side, twice being caught by his aunt just before he pitched absolutely overboard. His further delight was seeing the collier ships as they waited for their cargo at the wooden staiths, and higher up river the keels with their black square sails, bringing coals under the stone bridge from beyond where the ships could travel, the keelmen seeming to race each other as they guided the boats through the water with their great oars.

Along the quayside the travelling was easier. Nelly was tempted by the stalls selling fish, herbs and bread, but had her orders about the little she had to spend, so did not ask for the cart to stop. Rather it turned up Sandgate towards the heart of the town. Here was the smokiest, most overcrowded part, where more than a dozen alleys, some barely wide enough to allow a stout man access, poured into the main thoroughfare, which was thronged by what Nell pronounced to be a common sort of people who all appeared to be on familiar terms and all engaged in 'a devil's stew of idleness' outside the public houses. Nell was particularly struck by a knot of filthy keelmen playing cards in the street on what looked like an upturned boat. Robert saw them too and clapped his hands for the sake of their colourful blue jackets and yellow waistcoats.

They took their bearings from the lantern spire of the church of St Nicholas and arrived at last at the Bigg Market, where the old man left them after nodding his head several times to show he understood Nelly's instructions to attend on them in front of the concert hall for the return journey. The main provision on offer at the market was oats, but Nell

19

ignored these stalls as well as the goods proffered more or less insistently by the various pedlars with trays round their necks. She had her mind set on the shops, or one in particular.

Passing Sands' Circulating Library, Nell started when she heard her name called; turned with her hand at her breast. She jerked Robert into her skirts as if to save him from kidnap, and from there he saw she was being approached not by ruffians but by a smiling and attractively well-dressed female who had a couple of books under one arm, the other already extended in greeting. Nelly thought just in time to take off her soiled glove before they clasped. She had a warm regard for this young woman, but instinctively deferred to her.

'I was sorry to hear about...' her acquaintance began, then stopped, her eyes meeting the child's as he peeked out from the folds of petticoat.

'Thank you, Miss Hindmarsh. It wasn't unexpected. She rallied a little after... but she was never strong.'

'No.'

The confidence of her initial address, charged with the pleasant surprise of seeing Nell, quickly evaporated, and she became hesitant.

'How is... your brother?'

'Well...' Now it was Nelly's turn to glance down at the boy. 'He was... as you would expect, but lately he has quarrelled with the enginewright Mr Hawthorn. George has always been one to speak his mind.'

Miss Hindmarsh touched Nelly's wrist with concern. 'Has he lost his place?'

Robert contorted his neck to study his aunt, but she held him so close he could not well see past her bosom. She stroked the top of his head as she answered with unconsciously elevated diction. 'Well, a gentleman of his acquaintance, a Mr Trevithick, some weeks ago recommended George for a good position in Scotland, in Montrose, to look after one of Mr Watt's steam engines. In a spinning mill, I believe.'

Far from reassuring, this news seemed to cause Miss Hindmarsh more disquiet. 'Is he to take it?'

'He left this morning.'

'Oh.' Elizabeth Hindmarsh fell silent for a moment, then said, perfunctorily, 'By coach, or water?'

'Shanksy's pony,' from Nell, slipping back into a more comfortable idiom.

'He's *walking* all that way? I mean, Montrose is a long way off, isn't it?' She always felt on surer ground with literature or music than geography. 'And what about little Bobby?'

'He's to stay with me a while. Or rather I'm to stay with him. George hopes to be back within the year. I think he has his sights on America, when he has the money put by.'

'America? Oh.'

Nell recognized in that unguarded response the emotion she herself had felt on her return from London, of hopes dashed, and she moved forward to embrace Miss Hindmarsh again, on equal terms. Robert pulled at her skirt.

'I must go,' Nelly said, breaking away somewhat, though still intimate. 'George has asked me to buy a...' She mouthed *present*, nodded toward the boy. This diversion helped her friend recover herself. She smiled, crouched down to child level. Her books slipped slightly, and she adjusted her hold on them, drawing his attention. She wore a fine silver chain at her wrist, adornment he'd never seen before and wondered at.

'And how do you like Newcastle, Robert?' she asked, lifting his face gently to hers with the touch of a finger. Bashful, he looked beyond her at Aunt Nelly.

'Cat got your tongue?' said Nell. She expected something of him, but he did not know what. He hid his face in her skirts until the women went their separate ways.

For Nelly and Robert it was only a matter of a few paces to the workshop of joiner John Anderson. There Nelly announced who she was and Anderson retired to the back of the shop, returning with an object already wrapped for her collection. 'He purposed to make one himself,' she explained as she paid over the money that George had given her, 'but with affairs to settle, and his child to look after, he lost the time, and he did so want him to have it.' Anderson shrugged indifferently, but Nelly was pleased she had been able to excuse her brother's apparent extravagance.

With the main object of their visit accomplished, Nell felt easy exploring the shops in the Bigg Market. She greatly enjoyed herself at the milliner's where she tried on four or five hats before she salved her conscience by the purchase of a yard of ribbon. While they waited for the return of their driver, Nelly looked over the market stalls with much less interest, tutting over the price of oatmeal. Robert amused himself crawling under and between the tables, until he accidentally knocked over a tower of straw baskets and felt the boot of an angry stallholder. He ran back to Auntie, working up a howl; noticed Miss Hindmarsh hovering, and stopped in his tracks. She had in her hand a penny whistle, bought from a hawker. The boy knocked on Aunt Nelly like a door to make her turn and notice.

'Oh, back again, Miss Hindmarsh?'

'I wish you would call me Betty. May I also be allowed to give a present to Bobby? I could not resist when I heard the tinker play it.'

Robert made swift answer for his aunt, stretching his hand up to the instrument. 'See, he likes music,' said Betty, pleased. 'I knew he must.'

By the time they were halfway home, Nell was far from convinced that *she* liked music so well, not at least the style that Robert was piping incessantly, but she refrained from telling him to stop because she was reluctant to upset the child. As it was, he slept the second half of the journey, despite the pitching and rolling of the cart. He woke at home to sup a little watery porridge. When the table was cleared Aunt Nelly placed on it the parcel they had fetched from Newcastle, and brought the candle near.

'Would you like to open your present now?'

Robert clambered onto his knees on the stool; reached across to rip the flimsy paper. His aunt started to scold him... 'Take more care...' and relented, helped him with the last shreds. There revealed on the table was a beautifully-constructed abacus, with ten rows stretched across the wood frame, and each row with a string of ten brightly-painted wooden beads, inviting to touch. Robert stretched a hand out again and sent the beads spinning, their fresh paint catching the candlelight.

'Daddy!' he shouted in pure excitement, and looked around, then laughed at his own foolishness. Daddy had not come home yet.

III

The widow Stephenson kept to her room while the rest of the family breakfasted, and for the remainder of the day. As each set of relations completed their preparations for leaving, they were afforded brief access to pay their respects before seeking out Robert for a less formal and more effusive parting.

'How could Uncle George have put up with such airs?' asked Meg in a pique when she came down from her appointment.

'I suppose she kept them well in check before my father,' Robert replied. 'Indeed, I once heard him praise her for her discretion. She carried herself softly around him.'

'Pish, nothing compared to your proper stepmam,' said Meg. 'Aunt Betty was ten times she is, and never hoity-toity.'

'Well, perhaps we judge too harshly from ignorance of her true nature,' said Robert reasonably, though he agreed with his cousin, and was alive to every nuance when he made his own appearance in the widow's apartments to bid her farewell. She wasted no time in chafing at his sensibility.

'Do you think it meet, as son and heir, to be seen to leave so hurriedly? Is your business in London so urgent?'

'I have no intention of addressing any business other than the necessities of my father's estate for at least a week,' said Robert.

She sniffed at a black-laced handkerchief. 'And when am I to know what is to become of me?'.

Robert was already impatient despite himself. 'Your husband's wishes were clear. Annual allowance eight hundred pounds, the furniture and plate as listed...'

'I mean as to my continued living at Tapton. Your father's will...'

'That remains to be discussed. The lease is in association with the colliery. The ownership remains with Mr Ricketts. We will have to see.'

Mrs Stephenson fingered her mourning-brooch, her anxiety conspicuous. 'I must write to my brother in Matlock. If I am to be turned out I must throw myself on his mercy, I suppose.'

'Madam, I have no intention of turning you out. I could not turn you out. I merely said that the question of the longer-term tenancy of Tapton House is one to be discussed with Mr Ricketts.'

'As for staying,' she continued, 'that presents its own difficulties. Take it from one uniquely placed to appreciate the cost of upkeep here... I speak only of the household; then there are the gardens and the stables...'

Robert refrained from reminding the lady that it was but recently she earned forty pounds a year all found, or that only one day had passed since her beloved benefactor was interred. He chose instead to terminate the interview. 'Forgive me, but I have a train to meet and cannot stay longer. We will talk further when my... when our grief has abated with time.' With a clip acknowledgement he left, inwardly cursing himself for again letting his annoyance reveal itself so readily, poorly disguised by his strained politeness. His father had been subject to unexpected fits of fury, especially in his later years, but Robert was not normally like him in that respect. The son enjoyed a reputation among friends and employees alike as a patient and even-tempered man, however he might be feeling within. He was too proud to excuse himself easily now on the grounds of his sad loss.

Although Robert had implied that the southbound train was imminent, his sudden departure from the house meant that he had over an hour to wait until it was due. He sent the carriage before him with his bags and walked down the hill in the manner of his father. George had been wont, when meeting guests at the station, to challenge them to a race up the steep path - there was something of the child about him to the last. Robert never had quite the same exuberance for life, but neither did he ever stop wishing for it.

Unlike the mournful silence of the previous afternoon, the town was all bustle, with the shops open again and the market doing a brisk Friday trade. Robert wandered The Shambles unrecognized among the other pedestrians. He was passing Horns' Public House on his approach to the railway station when he got his eye on an ancient who had found a sunny spot at the side of the building and was sitting there quietly on his own.

'Kit Heppel! It *is* you!'

Kit Heppel struggled to his feet as the younger man approached, and made a gesture to his cap, aborted as Robert took his hand in friendship. Kit still wore a band of crape on his sleeve. 'Did you really come all the way from Northumberland to look on at the funeral parade?' Robert asked him.

'Course, aye.'

'I was sure I saw you from my carriage, but lost you again in the crowd. If only I'd known beforehand, you would have been our welcome guest. You could have stayed at the house.'

'Why, I did, Chief. In a manner of speaking.'

'You did?'

'In your father's stables, like. You'll ken old John Wigham?'

'From Benton? The teacher?'

'Well, from farming stock, but he was first to set sums for George, aye. Did you not know your da employed him in the stables here?'

'I did not. I had no idea John was still alive. Or, for that matter...' Robert stopped, slightly flustered. The old man finished his sentence for him, laughing.

'Or for that matter, Kit Heppel? Oh, we'll see a few out yet, happen.' Then it was Kit's turn to feel embarrassment. 'Beg pardon, sir, not meaning to disrespect your father's...'

'Not at all, not at all. Believe me, Kit, you've shown the utmost respect and friendship by coming. Let me make it up to you - will you have a small beer?'

'Thank you, sir, but the train will be in soon. I was just catching some sunshine for the journey.'

'At least let me sit with you until it comes.' Which Robert did, first having made the appropriate arrangements for his luggage and consulted his Bradshaw to find that Kit could expect a homeward train in ten minutes while the one for Derby and the south would be a little longer yet.

'Will this be a Stephenson engine, Chief?'

'Possibly, Kit. Design, at least, if not manufacture. We have some running the Midland.'

Kit shaded his eyes to take in the view of the station in front of him and as much of the line as he could see either side. 'It's a grand thing, the railway, once you're through the pother o making it. George used to boast he would astonish all England one day, and he was right enough. Who would have thought, eh? Half the men we grew up with wouldn't credit the world was round, that's how ignorant they was. Not the vantages, you'd say. But look what Geordie Stephenson done, a pitman same as them. Look what he done.' He looked sideways at Robert squatting beside him. 'Him and his bonny Bobby Shafto.' Robert smiled and studied the ground. 'Geordie Stephenson,' Kit said again, softly to himself, then aloud to Robert, 'Did he ever tell of his giant leap?'

'Leap? No, I don't think so.'

Kit scratched vaguely at his neck as he searched his memory. 'He must have just turned pump-doctor, then - I mind it was at the High Pit and I was sinker still. Between the engine-hour and rope-rolling, we was having us bait - day like today in the sunshine and our backs against the brick-house, cheek by jowl like me and you now. And I mind I said to him, "George, there's this wall behind us and there's that shed wall, facing." He says, "Aye, what o that?" I says, "That's eleven feet. I'll wager you can't make it from here to there with one bound." Do you know what he done, Bobby?'

'I suppose he sprang to the other wall; 'twas a giant leap you said.'

'Ah, but how he managed it is the crack. Your daddy - time I'm on about you're just a bairn yet - your father stands, shakes hisself loose and cons this wall the pair of us been resting at. He figures a way and climbs right to the roof o the brick-house.' As he narrated this part of the tale, Kit stood and Robert looked up, squinting in the sun, to where the old man was pointing to represent the height that George reached on his climb. 'And now,' Kit said, 'Now he makes his giant leap.' Kit's finger tip described a parabola from the imagined jumping-point to the landing on the roof of the imagined shed. 'Eleven feet from that wall to the one anent,' he impressed on his listener. 'Aye, and fifteen feet up.' Reliving the moment, Kit's expression first deepened, then quickened. His eyes were alive in their dark sockets as he turned back to Robert; spoke profoundly, 'Had I won my wager that day, save us, you mun been an orphan twice over and England never been mazed by the railways.' He nodded once and added, 'I never meant to be gambling with un's life, and never did again.'

Robert gazed back at Kit, but was distracted from the present, his mind running on his father's act, and that thought giving way to the memory of an incident from his time in South America. He was about to tell Kit of it when a single bell sounded from the office of the station master.

'Will that be the north train?' said Kit.

'I would think so.'

'By, you can set your watch by the railroad, eh? Not like the old coaches. We're all on London time now.'

Robert walked through the station entrance with Kit, where they joined others jostling for position on the narrow platform. 'Did you bring baggage with you?'

'No. No need of that.' Kit felt about him and said, as if to reassure himself, 'I have my ticket safe.' He found it at last, displaying the slip with some pride to Robert as the train - a Fenton, designed by

Stephenson - drew up to the platform. It seemed to suck the crowd towards it as it clanked and hissed to a stop.

'Come with me to the station agent, Kit. I will have that exchanged for a First Class ticket.'

The old miner seemed thoroughly alarmed by the prospect. 'Oh no, Chief. I've no wish to be seated with gentlefolks, nor them wi me. I'll be more settled in Third. Snug as a pig in pease-straw. Look, it has a roof, even.'

'Aye, it's the law now.' Robert could see there was no persuading Kit, and there was strength in his argument that he would spend a less comfortable journey suffering the offended stares of half a dozen parvenus in a First Class compartment than among his own kind on the wooden boards in Third, however crushed they might be. He did prevail upon Kit to accept his gift of a meat pie bought from a vendor on the platform, to sustain him while he rode.

Robert embraced his companion one last time and saw him off. As the pall lifted from the platform, the celebrated engineer turned towards the waiting room, changed his mind, and stepped back out of the station to bide his time in the sunny place that he and Kit had occupied together.

IV

Steam - or the opportunity to work with it - took George away from his home and his infant son. And steam - or the disastrous consequences from it - brought him back.

In the months between his father's perplexing disappearance and his sudden return Robert grew accustomed to being cared for partly by neighbours and partly by Aunt Nelly, and to his new routines. One involved a weekly visit to Grandma Mabel and Grandpa Bob, who lived near Newburn then. It was a seven mile walk from Killingworth, but the boy and his aunt could stay the night on the shake-down next to the bed if they wished and walk back the next day. Grandma and Nelly would spend the day cleaning, mending and (best of all) baking, while Robert found new places to explore. Darkness brought Grandpa home and the chance of a story of Sinbad the Sailor or Robinson Crusoe, all told out of his head as he held Bobby close so he did not get too fearful when the cannibals came, or the Old Man of the Sea. He told of Boney the Frenchman too, and of Lord Nelson who lately died for England. The child sometimes wondered if his father had gone for a soldier or a sailor, and if he would come back in uniform.

One morning, while the women worked inside, Robert was searching the bushes near the wagon way for a twig that would pass as a soldier's musket. He was bent on guarding Aunt Nell all the way to the colliery – Grandpa had promised a try on top of his fire engine if they should stop there on the way home and bring some fresh-made griddle scones for him to share with his plug man, Joss. The boy was stripping leaves from a broken branch when he heard the creak of the chalder wagon. He scrambled to the top of the scree to watch it go by.

The horse was pulling from the direction of the pit, but there was not the usual load of coal piled high on the wagon behind. Instead there were perhaps half a dozen planks laid across the tub, with two men knelt on top. They seemed to be holding down a third man lying between them. As the cart drew closer Robert saw that the man lying down had a cloth pressed against his face and was squirming on the boards, struggling to get free. The boy's heart hammered against his chest. These other two must be Frenchies, disguised as pitmen, come to attack the English. Robert's grip was tight on the stripped twig, but when the horse stopped at the bottom of the bank he took fright and ran off to the safety of Grandma's cottage.

'Aunt Nell, Boney's come! The Frenchies are here!'

The two women, dusty from their work, emerged together. Mabel locked her arms around Bobby as his aunt went to investigate, armed with nothing but a besom. They heard her anguished cry from beyond the scree. Robert felt his grandma's agitation through his body; every sinew quivered, with Mabel torn between rushing to her daughter's aid and running back into the house to hide away her grandson. She had not moved from the spot when one man's head appeared above the bank-top, followed by another, with Nell in close attendance. As they came nearer, Mabel recognized the man in front. 'It's Bob's marra,' she whispered as if to the child, and pulled him closer to her. He kept his eyes on the burden the men were balancing with difficulty between them on two of the planks from the chalder wagon.

'There's Grandpa.'

The face was still covered, but he knew him by his thick trouser-belt, which Old Bob had once pretended he'd skelp him with for being a scamp. Mabel released her hold on the boy; stumbled across to meet the men bearing her husband.

'He's still alive,' Joss called out to her, and then, half-choked, 'but geet scalded.'

'Scalded?' The old woman clutched at her apron in her anxiety. It was too much for Joss to explain. He buckled, more from the strain of his feelings than the weight he was carrying, and the two women had to help him make the last few yards to the doorway. They cleared a pile of mending from the bed to lie Bob down on it. Fatigued by the ordeal of his journey, the patient no longer struggled. He lay moaning quietly between tortured wakefulness and troubled sleep.

Robert watched from the doorway, ready to bolt if fear overtook him, as his grandmother gently lifted the soiled cotton cloth from Old Bob's face. She gasped to see the red weals underneath. Tears started in the boy's eyes, blinding him from the horror for the moment. It was as if Old Bob had been flayed. Loose shreds of skin hung from him. His eyelids were seared. One huge unbroken blister covered his forehead. They were all dumbstruck, staring at this monstrosity on the bed, until Mabel took control of herself and her kin.

'Heat a needle in the fire,' to Nell. 'Bobby, run to the pump for water.' She knew her man's wounds were well beyond her simple nursing, but she felt she had to try and do something for him. When Robert got back from the pump, half-soaked with spilt water from his frantic running with the bucket, Joss was at the foot of the bed, rocking on his haunches, racked with sobs.

29

'It was my fault, Mabel. I caused it.'

'Don't fret yourself.'

But Joss was determined to take the blame.

'The engine was blocked or summat, I don't know what. Bob crawled inside to fix it, and hollered out to us. I thought he said to try for one more blast, and I shoved the lever across. Twas such a scream he let out.' Joss choked with sobs again so that Mabel had to leave off tending her husband to comfort his friend. Robert stood amazed; he had never seen a grown man cry.

'An accident, is all. God's will.'

'It's a cruel god, Mabel, that bizends your man.'

'Strike you down for blasphemy, Joss Morton,' from Nelly where she knelt at the range, but she averted her eyes out of guilt for speaking so.

Robert and his aunt stayed a night longer than intended. She helped to make her father as comfortable as possible, and debated endlessly with her mother about what might be done. They dared not ask Dr Mitchell to come as they still owed him for his attendance on an ague Mabel suffered in the winter, for which he had no effective remedy. Even without the doctor's confirmation, it was obvious that Old Bob's sight was past saving.

Robert listened to the women's whispered discussions as he lay feigning sleep on the shake-down below his grandfather's bed. 'You mun send for George, that's all you can do now,' Nell was saying. 'None of the others is a deal o use.'

Mabel objected. 'Who's to write for us, and want nothing for it? And what's Geordie to think if he has a shilling to pay for the mail, and having to leave off his work when there's nowt to better him back here?'

'I'll ask Miss Hindmarsh. She won't have to put her own name to the page, so there's nothing forward about it - I'm sure she'll be glad to scribe for us, and freely. As for George, he won't care about a shilling, only about you both, and the chance of seeing Bobby again.'

Robert hid himself under the blanket at the mention of his name, afraid they would look over and find him awake. But they did not - simply continued their anxious conversation in the darkness, until he lost all sense of what they were saying and fell asleep at last.

In the morning, rather than setting off for Killingworth immediately, he and his aunt headed in a different direction, to Black Callerton where Robert had never been. Neither had he ever entered a farmyard, nor seen a door answered by a servant, even if in truth the girl who let them in acted as both scullery-maid and milk-maid, and the only other servant in the house had pigs and chickens to look after as well as the farmer and his human brood. Robert was astonished to find himself in a home where it was possible to move from room to room without finding a different family living in each one, and where there were items recognizable as furniture other than the simple table and wooden chairs that were the limit of his experience to date - including, though he could not name it then, a cottage piano. Elizabeth Hindmarsh was at the instrument, picking her way through a Cramer study when her visitors were shown into the drawing room.

'Nell! How wonderful to see you again, and little Bobby too. Thank you for calling.' Sympathy tempered the brightness of her welcome once Nell explained the purpose of their visit. Old Bob might have been family to Betty, so sad she was to hear of his accident. Soon she was earnestly engaged with Nell at her writing desk composing a letter to George, while Robert was allowed to amuse himself with experimental prods at the keys of the piano. Perhaps it was the discordant sounds that alerted Betty's father, coming in from the yard, to the presence of strangers in the house. As the women bent over their work, the door to the drawing room opened and he poked his head within. Robert, sensing hostility, froze at the keys. Betty glanced around to check on the child, and caught sight of her father. A hint of colour rose in her cheeks. She opened her mouth to excuse the disturbance, but Mr Hindmarsh withdrew immediately, leaving his daughter to contemplate the closed door.

'Do keep playing for me, Bobby, I like it,' she said at last, and smiled encouragement before she turned to resume her letter-writing.

The work done, Betty took both her visitors into the orchard at the back of the house, and invited Robert to hunt in the grass for healthy-looking apples to fill Nell's apron.

'We can't scrump your fruit,' said Nell. 'It's us should be paying you for your help.'

'You are not scrumping, they'll only go to waste. And if it keeps you here a few minutes longer, that's reward enough. I wish you would come often.'

'I don't think your father would approve though, would he? He never cared for Geordie.'

'He refused him, if that's what you mean. Nobody could *dislike* George, could they?'

Nelly demurred, as a sister might. 'Oh, I dunno about that. Ask Ned Nelson. There's a few others - Mr Hawthorn for one - who thinks our George gets above himself. So do I odd times, to say the truth. So does your father, happen.' She touched her friend's elbow. 'You wouldn't have refused him, but?'

'Of course not.'

The boy could feel the gaze of both women on him as he swept at the long grass around the trees with a switch he had picked up. He pretended to be absorbed in his play, but he was also listening carefully, aware of whom they spoke. Betty seemed about to say something, changed her mind, then changed it again. 'We used to meet down here,' she confided.

'In secret?'

'I suppose so. But all in innocence.' She tucked a hand inside Nelly's arm. 'You were in love with someone lately?'

'Loved and left.' They were her own words, but Nell grimaced at the impression they made, and followed up with, 'Not that I would marry Daniel Jakes now, supposing he was free to do it.' She drew herself to her full sixty inches to demonstrate her independence.

Elizabeth Hindmarsh said simply, 'When I lost George I knew I never would wed anyone else.'

*

Robert's father slipped back into his life as quietly as he had stolen away. The morning he came he had already been in the boy's dream, staring up into the branches of an apple tree where Robert was hiding, looking down. When the child roused himself in the half-light, eyes adjusting to the room, he found him seated at the table just as if he had returned from work; indeed he had, though it was more than two hundred miles off and a week of solid walking. George had been there an hour, watching for the moment his son would wake, resisting the temptation to lie alongside him in case he should cause alarm. Perhaps something in Robert's dream had disturbed his sleep, because the first thing he said was, 'Grandpa's eyes is hurt. Uns face is gone all scary.'

'I know, son. I've been to see him. We're going to look after him, but, aren't we? Are you big enough to help now?'

'Yes, sir. But it's a long walk without a carry.'

'We mun let him live near, then, him and Grandma. Would you like that?'

'And Aunt Nelly?'

'Will live with us. We'll be together.'

And so the arrangement was made, though the move and paying off Old Bob's debts cost much of the twenty pounds that George had managed to save from his sojourn in Scotland. The rest he stored behind a loose brick in the fireplace with the hope that one day he could add enough to it to pay his and Bobby's passage to America, *where we'll build steamboats and cross the Great Lakes* he'd tell his child. That dream would have to wait. Not only were his precious savings depleted; his blind and ageing father was now quite unable to sustain Mabel or himself, so the burden rested entirely on George. He fell back on his old occupation as brakesman at a new winning near home. Between shifts and during scarce leisure hours - times when his workmates were generally to be found drinking in the Three Tuns or roaring at dog-fights down the dene - George would be at the cottage table mending a neighbour's clock or making a new pair of shoes for pin money. Meanwhile he'd call out additions and subtractions for Bobby to calculate, with the aid of the abacus at first, later on his old dusty slate as the boy grew in confidence with numbers.

'How many in a dozen?' George asked him one evening.

'Twelve is a dozen. And a half dozen is six.'

'How many dozen in four and twenty?'

'Don't know,' Robert admitted after a while. He swung his legs under his stool and yawned a little. This was the signal for his father to liven up the lesson with a game or some other distraction. George obliged with a song, Nelly joining in as she darned by the fire.

Sing a song of sixpence, a pocketful of rye,
Four-and-twenty blackbirds baked in a pie.
When the pie was opened the birds began to sing;
Oh, wasn't that a dainty dish to set before the king?

'So Bobby, how many dozen blackbirds in the pie? Count them in twelves.'

'I don't have enough fingers.'

'Mark each blackbird on your slate.'

Robert did as he was told, adding a beak and a pair of wings to each mark so it took him several minutes to come up with an answer. 'There's two dozen blackbirds altogether. I think the baker could have made two pies with that many.'

'Do you think so, Bobby?' His father winked at Nelly and leaned forward. 'And how many dozen birds would be in each pie?'

'In... each pie? One, of course. Look.' Robert propped his slate on the table, showed his two rows of markings, and drew a rough circle around each row.

'Very good. But now the baker ull be in bother, won't he?'

33

'Why?'

'Cause he has not used baker's dozens. A baker's dozen is thirteen.'

'What are you talking about?'

'Stop confusing the boy, Geordie,' Nell admonished. 'You've got my head spinning as it is. If you're going to learn him, learn him proper.'

George laughed and reached across the table to ruffle his boy's hair. Robert felt the roughness of hands on his scalp, but it was not unpleasant; nor did he much mind when his father cupped the back of his head into his palm and studied him as if he were contemplating a new design. 'Ah, you're right, Nell. He needs more learning than I can pass on. Better than I got myself. When I were his age I were sharpening picks for pennies.'

'Can I sharpen picks?' Such enthusiasm for the task set his father off laughing again.

'No, you mun sharpen your mind, lad. How would you like to go to school?'

'Where is school? Is it far?'

'Just at Long Benton. Not much more un a mile. And you'll make friends there.' To Nell, 'How much does Tommy Rutter charge a week?'

'Dun rightly know. Not less than thruppence, anyway. Where you going to find that on top of everything else?'

'Wherever I can find things to mend,' said George. 'And bigger than clocks. I've a mind to hawk myself round the Grand Allies. They've got that many pits about here now, there's always engines need fixing, and nary a body with the nous to do it.'

*

While his father tramped from one colliery to another, repairing winding gear and trying to persuade managers he could improve operations for a pittance, Robert took the daily walk across the fields of the glebe farm, past the churchyard where his mother and baby sister lay buried, from West Moor to Long Benton Street and the Rutters' tiny school rooms. Directly under the red-tiled roof, Mrs Rutter taught half a dozen local girls the rudiments of reading, religion and handicrafts. Downstairs Mr Rutter kept a semblance of order over twice as many sons of artisans and shopkeepers, some of whom were not nearly so anxious to learn as their parents were to see their children gain an advantage they generally had not enjoyed for themselves.

When Robert joined the class, it was one more body to crowd onto the long form facing the schoolteacher. He was glad for the boots his daddy had made him, as Mr Rutter's lessons were frequently interrupted by one or other of the bare-footed boys complaining he'd had his toes stamped on under the bench by a well-heeled neighbour, no doubt accidentally. Bobby's toes were not imperilled, but being the newest and smallest pupil he was delegated to sit at one end of the form, and was frequently elbowed off, no doubt accidentally, until he learned to grab onto the sleeve of John Tate next to him whenever he felt himself going. He made a friend of John in that rough and tumble way.

On the whole, Robert preferred his father's teaching, though Mr Rutter was not a cruel task master; he tolerated a degree of boisterous behaviour from boys who were not used to being cooped inside for long periods, and generally reserved his strap for punishing any unkindness they displayed to one another. Most of the learning was done by rote, with the pupils chanting their lessons vigorously, if in bounds set by Mrs Rutter, who often sent one of her girls downstairs to call shrilly over the noise, 'Mistress says you've to pipe down,' or as a last resort would even appear in the doorway herself to level a hard stare at husband and charges alike. Robert was far more wary of her than he was of the master.

The main advantage of the school room over home was the presence of a few well-worn books, some of which had been supplied, on application from Mr Rutter, by the Society for the Promotion of Christian Knowledge. There were the Old and New Testaments, of course; also an *Abridgement of the History of England*, Guy's *British Spelling* and Fisher's *English Grammar*. What Robert liked best was a Bible story of David and Goliath - one of his grandpa's favourites - that had a drawing of David choosing a pebble for his sling as the giant came towards him over the hill, his great chest bulging under burnished plate.

There were conflicting temptations. Robert's inquisitiveness, like his father's, was stimulated as much by what he noticed around him as by conventional education. When harvest came and Aunt Nelly announced she was off to the gleaning, Bobby fell in love with the sound of the word, and begged to go too. George was naturally reluctant to waste the fourpence a week he was paying Mr Rutter, but under a cannonade of pleading he eventually saw there might be a lesson in this for his son.

'You may go, but only to work, not play. I want no skulkin nor shirkin, and you mun stay till the gleaning's done.'

Robert had to pull his sack behind him, being too small to carry it, as he tracked his aunt's footsteps across the field all day, but he was determined to work manfully and by sunset had managed to fill his bag and be paid a penny for it. His father met them at the garden wicket.

'Well, Bobby, how did you come on?'

'Geet well, sir,' holding up his coin like a trophy. 'You mun put this in the brick-hole for America.'

Next day an unseasonably hot sun beat down on already wearied workers. By noon, when they broke off for their bait, Robert was dropping tired. Aunt Nell left him sleeping under the hedgerow, resting his head on the small bump of gleanings in his sack. He stirred in time to half-fill his bag, but when his father asked him that night how he had got on he could only reply, 'Middlin' as he slunk onto his bed.

The third day proved altogether too much for Bobby. There was no respite from the sun, and pickings were scarce on the ground by now. He could not even summon the energy to follow the course of a field mouse that scampered past his fingers as he scraped at the stalks. Sunset found him leaning heavily into his aunt's thigh, one hand clutching at her petticoats to keep him from falling entirely, the other trailing a sack as limp as his aching body. When he saw his father striding down the lane to meet them he made some little effort to straighten up at first, then surrendered completely to his feelings, bursting into tears.

'Oh, Daddy, please let us go to school again.'

George hauled the boy up into his arms and carried him the rest of the way home, leaving till Sunday his sermon on the value of minding to his books. It was a lesson Robert would not forget.

That Sunday was also the day George's friend John Steele came to call. Bodily crippled from a childhood accident on the Pontop tramway, John was mentally strong - one of the few in the region whose practical intelligence matched George's. It was he who had introduced his friend to Richard Trevithick when the eccentric engineer came North to oversee a construction at the Gateshead foundry where John worked. Trevithick had even come personally to talk with George at home while Fanny was still alive, and had amused himself with the earnest collier's prototype of a perpetual motion machine, spinning the wheel of the contraption for baby Robert as he dandled him on his knee. The two men had talked inventions until well after dark. They filled the room with their long legs and their laughter as Trevithick told George the tale of crashing his experimental steam carriage into a Cornish barn, how he'd left it there while he calmed his nerves at a public house, and returned to find both barn and locomotive consumed by fire. *I called it The Puffing Devil,* Trevithick remarked nonchalantly, *And consigned it to the flames.*

'Have you seen Mr Trevithick lately?' George asked as soon as John Steele was settled in his chair. 'I hope he got my letter thankin him for the character he give me in Montrose.'

'Indeed, he read it out to me, George. We spent some considerable time together, trying to get Mr Blackett's engine to work.'

'The railway engine? I've not seen it runnin at Wylam yet.'

'No, and I can tell you now, you never will. It never left Gateshead. In fact it has been pulled asunder for the parts.'

'That is a shame. When Richard spoke of it, I felt sure it could work. I told him, "You'll put every pit horse out to pasture, sir. Stage coaches too, very like, in the fullness of time, and all the ostlers in the country on the parish."'

John chuckled at this notion. 'You're as daft as he is, George. I wish you were right, but we can find no way to harness the power efficiently for a vehicle of that sort. The engines break down at every turn. Besides, the damn things are so heavy they crush any rail you put under them. Even Trevithick has given up now, I believe, since his steam circus failed besides.'

'His steam circus?'

'His *Catch-Me-Who-Can*. Did you not get word of it? Trevithick made a ride of the thing, in London, if you please. A shilling a turn for the leisured classes to spin themselves silly round a track.'

'Oh, do you hear that, Bobby?' The boy was at the hearth trying the effect of stopping the end of his penny-whistle with a coal. '*Catch-Me-Who-Can*. What would you think to a ride on an iron horse?' Robert, his mouth full of pipe, said nothing, but acknowledged his father's attention with a nod, and fell to wondering what an iron horse might feed upon.

'It was less exciting than you imagine,' said John. 'For the most part, all there was to see was broken rails, mechanics trying to fix the fiend, and a line of people wanting their money back. The latest I heard from Trevithick is he has abandoned that idea and turned to all things nautical. You know, steam tugs, that sort of thing.'

George rose, took a pace or two around the room while he reflected on his friend's news. 'I have every respect for Mr Trevithick, John, and I thank you for your help in makin his acquaintance. But can't the man stick to his last for more un five minutes? *Persevere*, that's my motto. Steam boats, though. There is a romance about them. Did I tell you I'm still fixed on America and the Great Lakes?'

'It will be our loss if you go, George.'

'But it seems I must, marra, if I'm to make a better of things. I've had to scraffle a living since I come back from Scotland. I'm not apprentice-served, there's no-one in England will trust us to act as engineer.'

*

The harvest celebrations provided a rare social opportunity for Nell, who had increasingly turned to the Wesleyan Methodists as a comfort since her return from London and her disappointment over Daniel Jakes. As an addition to the usual Harvest Festival, a concert was to be performed on Friday evening by an amateur choir from Newcastle. George, always wary of religious occasions, declined the invitation to accompany her, preferring to stay at home and look after little Bobby while she enjoyed a brief respite from her chores. Nell did not press him further, seemed quite content with the arrangement, and she hummed hymn tunes to herself as she dressed behind the screen. Robert was weaving a mess of cat's cradle round his fingers from a bobbin of strong thread he'd filched while his father repaired a pile of work clothes at the table.

'Nelly, do you want we should walk you to the chapel?' George called to her after a while.

'No need. I'm meeting a party just yon side o the graveyard.'

'Well, don't go cutting through there in the dark, hear me? Follow the outside line of the wall.'

'Yes, brother,' from behind the screen.

'I heard there's redcoats have set up camp on the moor. You mun be careful.'

'I will, George.'

He raised his eyebrows and the boy did likewise, their mute male acknowledgement of the abstraction in her replies and the length of time she was taking over her preparation. When she finally reappeared, George observed the unusual attention she had paid to her wardrobe, and how she had placed a fastening of two artificial cherries in her bonnet. Robert noticed his father's abrupt change from levity to gruffness.

'What frippery have you there?'

'This? Just a brooch I lent off Ann. Don't you like it?'

'Mmm. Not like you to get so bedizened up for church.'

'I'm not bedizened. Just a brooch. Just to mark the harvest...' Her voice trailed away and she seemed to blush under her bonnet. George realised she had been hoping the bright trinket would grace her looks, and immediately rued the remark he had made. Perhaps Nell was setting her cap at some bachelor from the congregation. If so, good luck to her. He

38

kissed her warmly on the cheek to make up for his incivility, and watched her out the door.

'So, Bobby Shafto, just me and you for supper,' he said as he turned back into the room. 'What'll we have?'

'Eggs wi buttered toast.'

George let out a whistle. 'Eggs and buttered toast. Where did you ever get such a meal as that?'

'At Aunt Burn's last week,' said the boy. 'It was *de-licious*. I dun think Auntie Nell knows how to mek it, as we've never had it here.'

George shook his head at the naiveté of the child. Fanny's sister had done well for herself, marrying Joseph Burn of the Red House Farm. There would be eggs and butter aplenty at their house. And fine pork and lamb too, no doubt. George pretended to look around the shelves and slabs before he exclaimed, 'Well, would you believe it. Not an egg nor a pat of butter left in the place. Perhaps we'll come by some tomorrow. Meantime, let's have a crowdie night.'

'We allus have crowdie.'

'Because it's so *de-licious*. Especially with the new milk. Is yon kettle near boiled?' George fetched the basin from the wash stand and soon the two of them were at work preparing their supper. Robert added oatmeal on instruction while his father poured water onto it from the hot kettle, stirring the mixture vigorously.

They settled to the meal they'd made together. Often when they ate at table they could barely get the food down for talking of something that had caught their interest through the day, some phenomenon that may have excited their curiosity. Occasionally, as tonight, they dined in quiet contemplation, as if each were trying to fathom the mystery of the other.

They were washing down their supper with the remainder of the fresh milk when there were two loud thuds at the cottage door. The caller was impatient, renewing the knocking before George had a chance to draw back the bolt, and so heavily it seemed almost an attempt to batter the wood through. The reason it sounded so, as George discovered when he pulled the door open at last, was that the visitor (or intruder) was using the butt of a rifle.

'What's this?' He was shocked to see three fully armed redcoats on his threshold.

'George Stephenson?' from the sergeant at the centre of the group.

'Who wants him?'

'The King. Your king and country.'

39

George glanced within at the boy staring at the soldiers over his mug of milk. He partly closed the door behind him as he stepped forward to remonstrate in a half-whisper, pleading with the officer.

'You cannot press me, you can't. I beg you, sir. My son's mother is dead, and my ain poor father is blind and old. Two families depend on me entirely.'

The recruiting sergeant was unmoved. 'You think we don't hear such stories at every door we knock? You'll be well rewarded for your pains. And we're no press gang, sure - we leave that to the tars. It's a fair ballot of all men that's fit, and you've been drawn, there's an end on it. You join the militia on Monday.'

'The militia?' George spoke with some relief; there was a straw of hope maybe. 'So I can serve at home?'

One of the soldiers sniggered. The sergeant scowled at him, and the man snapped to attention, his chin strap straining as his superior addressed George once more. 'Join Monday, march Tuesday. You're bound for Spain, lad.'

'Is there nowt at all can be done?' Servility was a foreign language to George; he despised himself for it. Shame spread through him as he felt Bobby squeeze by his legs to get a closer look at the men in the doorway, half-hiding behind his father for protection. The sergeant, running his eyes over his new recruit, met the child's, gazing up at him. He watched the freckle-faced boy as he answered the man.

'Unless you can pay another to stand in your stead. Have you money?'

'I'll find it.'

The sergeant spoke to the child directly, made him jump. 'What's your name, boy?'

'Bobby, sir. Robert, I mean.'

'I have a drummer boy not much older than you. How would you like to be a soldier?'

'Don't...' George stifled his protest at the officer's warning glance.

'I'd rather work on the steamboats, if you please. Though the uniform is nice.'

'What, even on this?' The sergeant cocked a thumb at the ludicrously rigid specimen behind, coaxed a giggle from the child. His own features relaxed a tad as he returned to George.

'Monday noon at the Market Cross. Should a man report there and tell me that he's joining in the place of George Stephenson, I won't gainsay him.'

'Thank you, sir.'

The sergeant took a step back, making to leave, but before he did he reached out and, in one sudden, violent movement, ripped a silver button from the tunic of the soldier who had sniggered, and presented it to the boy. 'Keepsake,' he said. He nodded curtly to George and led his men away down the lane.

While Robert scampered back to the table to inspect the silver button closely in the candlelight, his father lingered at the open door. His elbow found the door jamb and he leaned there, as if unable to support his body, long after the recruiting party had faded into the dusk.

When he stirred at last it was to walk to the fireplace. He removed the loose brick from the chimney breast and pulled out the small canvas bag stored behind. He poured coins onto the table and counted them, drawing Robert's attention from his button.

'Are we to go to America?'

'No, no, son. But put your boots on.' He gathered up the coins. 'I need you to come a short way with us now.'

Robert dressed with a sense of adventure; he did not generally go out in the dark. Outside, waiting for his father to lock up, he wondered whether they were going to meet with the soldiers again, and certainly they took the same direction, along the crushed slag path towards town. The grey pit heaps in the distance held secrets behind, perhaps a whole army of enemies waiting. Each shed and privy they passed was suspect. Robert watched every shadow along the way, his right forefinger tensed on an imaginary gun, his silver button in the pocket of his jerkin to show, if challenged, that he belonged to the brotherhood of English soldiery.

The few shops around the market place were closed, but there was one building with flame flickering behind the window, and Robert could hear voices and laughter as they drew near. Perhaps this was where Aunt Nelly had gone. His father pushed open the door, hesitated in a smoky light at the porch. At close quarter the noise was very loud, and harsher too, a din of men discoursing and arguing. Someone yelled, 'Will you come in, or put the damn wood in the hole. There's a draught whistling up me arse.'

George drew Bobby back into the street, hunkered down to his level. 'I have to pop inside, just for a few minutes. I'm going to settle you here...' he lifted his son to a place on the broad window ledge, 'where you can see me and I can see you. Don't take your eyes off us and, if you should have need, knock as loud as you can on the glass. Understand?' The boy nodded, excitement giving way to misery and a little dread. His father studied his expression, chucked him once under the chin to lift his spirits, and left him on the ledge.

41

Peering through the grimy window, Robert could follow his father's progress across the room, watch him move from table to table. George rarely sat down, simply leaned across to speak in the ear of one after another as they supped their ale or sucked at their pipes, listening. Some responded to what he was saying as if it were a great joke, throwing back their shoulders to laugh; others looked serious, mournful even, shaking their heads; a few invited him to take a seat, engaged him in deeper discussion, before they also shook their heads, or pointed out another group he might attempt.

After a while Robert began to feel uncomfortable on the window ledge. His back and neck were sore from holding his position and he had to drum his heels against the wall to stop his feet prickling. When he applied his forehead to the glass it felt hard and cold. An invisible ghost was peering over his shoulder, its mist clouding the glass. An army of spirits collected by stealth in the gloom of the market place, chilling the atmosphere with their cold, dead breath.

He caught the sound of a carriage clipping along the street, and longed to watch out for it, if only to change position, but he had been warned not to take his eyes off his father. Even when the vehicle stopped close enough for him to smell the oil in its lamps he resisted the temptation to look, until he heard a woman's startled voice.

'Bobby?'

It was Auntie Nell. He turned from the window to see her sitting passenger in a one-horse gig. Sitting next to her, holding the reins, was Miss Hindmarsh. She held the horse steady as Nell climbed down to speak with him. His aunt offered to lift him away from the window, but he resisted. 'I mun wait here where Daddy can see.'

'He's inside?' She exchanged glances with Betty. 'And left you here?'

'The soldiers came. Where have you been?'

'The concert, I told you. What soldiers?'

Before the child could answer, the door of the Three Tuns opened and George stepped outside. He was perplexed to find his sister standing with Bobby, but nothing compared to how he felt when he passed the hood of the gig, and discovered who the driver was.

'I did not know you meant to go out, George,' said Nelly, rounding her vowels. 'If you had told me I would have stayed to look after the bairn.'

'I had no intention of going out. I'm not one to frequent these places, you know that.' This last was aimed as much at Elizabeth as Nell. He could think of nothing else to say for the moment, and all three adults fell into an uncomfortable silence, looking and not looking at each other. In the gap Robert seemed to hear the ghost army depart, murmuring. The horse shivered in its traces. Nelly was the first to speak again.

'See who I met at the church, George. Betty... Miss Hindmarsh has been singing with the Newcastle choir. She offered to bring me home.'

'Hello, George.' Betty's greeting was deliberately warm, reassuring. 'I'm sorry we don't have room for everyone, but perhaps Bobby would like to ride with us.'

'Yes, please.' He lifted his arms out, willing his father to swing him from window-sill to carriage.

'Wait,' said George. 'I've summat to say.' He gathered himself. 'I don't want you driving off thinking bad of us.'

'I don't...'

'No, listen. I been drawn for the militia. I'm down for soldiering in Spain.'

Nell's fingers came up to her mouth, and slowly down again as she said in sincere bewilderment, 'More bad news, more bad news. Lord, what's our family done to deserve this?'

Robert, alerted by her tone, paid attention now to the words more than his own senses. What had Daddy said about Spain? Was he leaving them again?

His father seemed to answer his thoughts directly. 'I may not... Don't fancy I'm feared o going, I'd be proud to, but for responsibilities here...'

Betty, too, attended carefully. She watched the set of his jaw as he talked, saw how his eyes eluded her as he said, 'I've found a feller the night who'd serve in my stead. But he's asking more un I can give him in my... present condition.'

'How much more?'

'That's not your affair, Liz.' It was not that he meant to sound rude; his independent disposition made him speak so. For her part Betty was trying to hold down her distress with a show of practicality.

'It's just... Perhaps I could lend you the money.'

'No.'

'Where's the harm in that? Better than some cent per center.'

George reached up to touch her gloved hand where it rested on the rein. 'I treasure your generosity. Don't think I don't. Your father, though, has called us a penniless pitman, an I'm not about to hand him proof on it. No, I've... an idea where I can lend what I need.' He did not elaborate, did not want to admit to his ex-sweetheart that he planned to apply to his dead wife's sister for aid. He had to trust that Farmer Burn would not divulge the information to Farmer Hindmarsh, or his rejection of Betty's kind offer would have been to no avail.

*

George had good reason, in these days, to recall the myth of Sisyphus (one in Old Bob's repository of classical tales) whom the gods punished for trying to escape the underworld, condemning him to the ceaseless task of pushing a boulder up a mountainside only to see it tumble down again. Having escaped the clutches of the army through the funding of a substitute, he found himself once again without reserves, and indebted to the tune of seven pounds to his brother-in-law. By dint of hard work in the foothills of artisanship, he nevertheless kept his family's needs simply supplied, and persisted with Robert's elementary education. He added to this where he could in the areas of practical knowledge, often letting his son sit with him as he took apart and rebuilt all manner of machinery, treating him, even at that tender age, almost as an apprentice.

Was it wholly George's fault that he led the boy once more into danger by trespass, or was Robert as much to blame for a childish willingness to follow him (pleaded to) for the sake of ventures and inventions that fascinated them both? The plain fact is, a year on from their encounter with the soldiers, the two of them stole under cover of night to the lake at Gosforth Park to test a new device. The prospect of fresh fish for the table was an added incentive.

Of course they kept well away from Gosforth Hall, but that brought its own difficulties, for this side of the lake was wild with wood and marshy ground. Struggling to keep up in the darkness, Robert was forever tripping over exposed roots and stepping into knee-length potholes, ankle-deep for George.

'Ssh!'

'I can't see where I'm going.'

Their only source of light was within a flask wrapped in sacking, for good reason; that was the object of the experiment.

'Keep close. Hold onto my coat.'

Somewhere ahead, a soft deep splash.

'What was that?'

'Cormorant, most like. It's not just us catching fish in the dark.' And a minute later, 'Here, here's the edge.' He squatted at the base of a tree overhanging the waters of the lake. 'Kneel next to me. Is the bank sound under you?'

'I think so.'

George set the sack down carefully between them; produced a length of twine from his pocket. He tied one end by touch to the neck of the glass flask in the bag, tested it for strength, and played more twine out from the ball in his hand. He stood erect, reached for the nearest branch, pulled at it with a low grunt of effort and swung his long legs up into the tree. It swayed significantly with his weight as he struggled to slot the ball of twine through the crook of the overhanging branch. Robert watched in expectation of calamity, and jumped with the soft shock of the twine lobbed back at him on the bank. He managed to recover just in time to grab the string before it plopped into the lake; gathered it into him as his father landed alongside.

'Got it?'

'Yes.'

'Good lad. Now, your task is to hold the line tight while we swing the vessel ower the water.'

Delicately, George removed the sacking from the flask as if from the cage of a timorous bird. He drained off some water contained within, leaving a moist, waxy substance in the bottom. Setting the flask straight on the bank he felt in his pocket for a paper of powder, which he emptied into the vessel like an alchemist at work. Robert took up the slack of the twine as his father stood with his flask and held it steady by the base.

'Now gently, pull.'

The boy pulled down upon the twine. As the line tightened, George lifted the jar to the edge of the bank and, again as it were a bird, opened his palms to liberate it. The flask swung slowly over the water, turning a little beneath the branch.

'Watch, Rob.'

They could see the green glow of phosphorus like a firefly captured in the bottle. They sat, waiting, barely breathing. From the other side of the lake an owl hooted. The flask spun one way, then another, stopped; and the magic started. A quick tongue of orange flame flickered inside the jar, disappeared, then came again, stronger and brighter. Spontaneous combustion. Some bird took wing through the trees in alarm. The genie flame burned more intense. Fumes poured from the funnel of the flask and the child's eyes went to the twine, fearing it would snap in the heat. Back again to the glass as another flame ignited, white this time, and brighter than before. His father excited beside him.

'That's the magnesia going. Dip now, Bobby.'

Robert played out twine until the vessel touched the surface of the water, paused, and played out more. The flask dipped under the

45

surface. His father dropped to his knees on the edge of the bank; leaned forward.

'Look,' he said, though the boy was looking intently and marvelling at what he saw. Instead of dowsing the flame, the water seemed to feed it. The jar was a ball of white light inside the lake.

'See, see them coming?'

What they could both see clearly in the illuminated water were fish, dozens of them, attracted or dazed by the light, swimming here and there in confusion. George gripped a tussock on the bank with one firm hand, leaned out almost to the point of toppling in, and plunged his free hand swift and deep into the water. Out again as quick, and then he was scrabbling for something on the bank, something that flopped wildly at Robert's feet.

'Here, Dad!'

'Where?' He felt around. 'Damned if I can see it in the dark. Haul the light out there.' Robert hoisted the lamp out of the water. The bank was illuminated briefly by the glow, but it was fading now. George searched to no avail. 'Aggh, he must have slipped back in the water.'

'Mun we try once more?'

'Too late, the stuff is all used up.'

They watched while the flame subsided in the jar. As it slowly died George relaxed, leaned back, propped his elbows on the bank. ' Oh, but it worked, did it not, as I said it would?' He squinted up at the boy and laughed. 'Bobby, lad, I'm a better engineer than a poacher.'

'Aye, and a noisy one at that.' The voice came harshly from behind.

Shock caused Robert to let go of the string. Their flask escaped into the water; he had an urge to follow it. George sprang to his feet, placed his bulk between his son and the gamekeeper standing higher up the bank. For a second all three were frozen in position, staring at each other, then George pushed at Robert's shoulder, a signal for him to run away, but the child dared not move without him.

'Together, go!' George shouted, and they made a dash for it, running diagonally up the bank to evade capture. The gamekeeper was overweight - would have lost them had Robert not stepped into a rabbit hole and turned an ankle. His father stopped when he heard the cry, but the keeper was first to the boy, snatching a fistful of his jerkin. Robert fought like a trapped animal to get free.

'Don't you bite me, brat. I'll see you hanged.'

'Daddy!'

46

'Let him loose,' George warned, 'or I'll rip your head off.' He meant it too.

'No, no. See this gaff?' The steward produced a wicked blade from inside his coat. 'One step more, and his throat's cut.'

'Daddy!'

'One step!'

'All right, all right.' George showed palms to the man. 'We meant no mischief.'

The keeper took a fresh hold of Robert's collar, dragged him up and made him stand, be it only on one leg for the pain in the other. 'We'll see what Mr Brandling has to say about that. You'll be rolled for the next transport, I'll wager. That's if you catch him in a good mood. Walk on ahead. We're going up to the house.'

George could see the pain Robert was in from his ankle. 'I'll carry my lad.'

'Oh aye, spirit him off into the night. Not likely. The whelp walks with me. He'll live, for now anyway. Move on.'

George had no choice but to walk a few yards in front as a prisoner unchained, leading the way to whatever fate awaited at the hands of Mr Brandling at Gosforth Hall, his son half-dragged and limping behind.

The grass gave way to gravel, and then they were in the shadow of the Hall itself. The gamekeeper gestured not to the main building but to some darkened stables across the yard, where he roughly pushed his prisoners in and bolted the door from the outside. They could not see an inch in front of their faces, but could feel and smell dirty straw underfoot, and heard the restlessness of the horses in their stalls, alarmed by the presence of strangers. Perhaps the horses could smell fear too, and may have heard the boy blubber a little. George reached for Robert's shoulder in the dark and drew him close. They stood in a pitiable embrace for several minutes, until they heard the rattle of the bolts outside, and the door re-opened. Two figures blocked the entrance, one with a lit lantern. The other spoke first.

'Thank you, Mr Dunning. Bring them to the light. Let's see what you have bagged.' His voice had not the natural burr of the men Robert was used to; it was crisp, fairly bounced off the stable walls. George kept his arm around the boy and - rather than be disclosed as cornered quarry - stepped forward into the pool of light made by the candle. He would have been taller than the gentleman had his protective stance not given him a slight stoop. He was restrained, respectful even, under Mr Brandling's examination, and silent until spoken to.

'So, fellow. Who might you be, and what the devil are you doing on my land?'

'Name of George Stephenson, sir. This is my son, Robert.' Paused before he added, 'We're honest folk, Squire.'

Dunning, in charge of the light, snorted on his master's behalf. 'An honest poacher. That's a new one on me, Mr Brandling.'

'I'm not a poacher, I'm a hard-working man; any soul round here ud vouch for that.'

'A collier?' from the squire, a coal-owner himself.

'Brakesman at Killingworth lately, sir; a contractor now, and bent on improvement.'

'What about your boy? Have you put him to work?'

George smoothed his hand over the top of Robert's head as if to draw Mr Brandling's attention to his cranial capacity while he answered. 'No, I aim higher for him, sir. He's at Mr Rutter's every day, though it costs us fourpence a week to send him. The man ull tell you himself, our Bobby's the brightest pin he's ever had.'

Brandling inspected the specimen before him with a certain air of scepticism. 'Hmm. An education paid for by selling my game, no doubt.'

'No, sir, paid for by making shoes mostly, for my neighbours, or fixing clocks, that sort o thing. Whatever extra I can turn my hand to.'

'Well, you'll be welcomed in Australia,' said Brandling drily. 'I'm sure your skills will come as a great boon to the colony.'

'Are we to be transported, Father? What will Auntie Nell do then? How will Gran and Grandpa manage without us?'

'Ssh, Bobby.' These questions lacerated him. His head dropped as he felt his own foolishness exposed. Mr Brandling added salt to the wounds.

'Your father should have thought of that before he brought you night fishing, boy.'

George tried to defend himself. 'You've a big lake and a great deal of land, Squire.'

'Are you a Jacobin, man? Would you deprive me of it?'

'No, sir, I just meant... I didn't expect to be catched.' Dunning snorted again, possibly to draw attention to his superior wiles, and George gave him a glance of contempt as he continued, 'Mebbes if I was a real poacher I wouldn've been. We was just... experimenting, is all.'

'Experimenting?'

'With our lamp. It shines underwater and attracts the fish.'

Mr Brandling's curiosity was pricked. 'How the devil does it do that?'

48

'Not much in the construction, Squire. Just a big glass jar, really. It's mainly the science inside it. There's two tricks; first, the phosphorus...'

'Phosphorus? How did you obtain that stuff?'

Both men had become animated by the discussion, but there was a tinge of embarrassment in George's response. 'Well... you may not wish to know that, sir.'

'You mean you stole it?'

'No, no. Not at all. It's very much my own. Er, made from boiling my own waters, that is.'

Brandling was astonished. 'Your own... Your urine?'

Robert could vouch for that – the smell was in his nostrils yet, and the cottage still reeked of it despite Aunt Nelly's best efforts.

'I said you might not want to know...' still diffident but George's voice had lost its strain, making his explanation, and even Dunning's face betrayed a flicker of amusement before he turned aside to conceal it from the prisoners. Mr Brandling's mind was active on the lamp.

'So, the phosphorus provides ignition as it were... but that could not be sustained underwater.'

'Magnesia powder, lit by the phosphorus afore it's doused – that ull burn in water, and so it did, fierce an all, eh, Bobby?'

'Yes, Dad.' (Were they not to be transported after all?)

'I must see this remarkable lamp,' said Mr Brandling.

'Oh.' Robert's hopes sank. 'I dropped it in the lake when we was shouted at.'

He expected at least a tirade from Mr Brandling, but what the squire did instead was laugh – loud and hearty. And George laughed with him. Their eyes shone in the light cast by Mr Dunning's lantern. The boy knew then they were safe.

He was under orders to keep the fact of their capture and temporary imprisonment from Aunt Nell; told it was for the sake of her worrying, but Robert suspected it was more that his father did not care to feel the lash of her tongue for taking such a risk, especially as they had no fresh fish to show for it. George had, though, to make up some story about a chance meeting to explain his commission of a new pair of riding boots for the squire. In reality the work had been offered as a form of reparation for their trespass, and Robert observed his father almost melt in private relief when the proposal was accepted. Fulfilling it meant that the next time they walked into the grounds of Gosforth Hall (Robert's ankle almost mended) they were headed not for the stables, but to the front entrance, with a package to deliver. They had not made it as far as

49

the stone steps when they heard Dunning's voice at their backs once more.

'Hey! Come away from there. Get off out of it!'

George did not break stride, calling over his shoulder, 'I'm here to see Mr Brandling. I've got new boots for him,' and when Dunning barrelled across the courtyard to grab him by the elbow it was only the boy clutching at his father's free hand that prevented him from swinging at the steward.

'It's you, is it?' said Dunning, with that old look of disdain. 'Don't you know your place? Tradesmen's entrance round the back.'

'It's my intent to deliver in person.'

'Mind your lip and hand em over. I'll see the squire gets em.'

'I said, I intend to deliver in person.'

'And I said, hand em over.'

The stand-off between the two could only end in a brawl. Robert moved in close to George's side, not so much for his own protection as to inhibit both men from starting the fight. He had no doubt of his father's physical superiority, but also had cause to remember the gaff handy at Dunning's belt. While the two men smouldered at each other, eyes locked, there was movement at the gate, and the clip of hooves over gravel.

'What's the to-do, Dunning?' The squire, returned from a ride. 'Ah, it's Mr Make-Water, Professor Phosphorus. Here for more fish?'

'No, sir. Brought the boots I promised.'

'First-rate.'

Mr Brandling dismounted. Dunning stepped forward to make complaint, but his master spoke over him. 'Stable the horse, Dunning, there's a good chap. Here, er... what's your name again?'

'George Stephenson, Squire.'

'Quite right. Come, Stephenson, you and your boy sit over here while I try these on.'

The gamekeeper, in high dudgeon, led the horse away. The Stephensons sat on the steps of Gosforth Hall with Mr Brandling trying his boots for size.

'I say, these look the crack.' He paraded a little across the courtyard, looking down at his new boots with evident satisfaction.

'Aye. I spent a deal of time on em.'

'Splendid. Something to cheer me up after Monday's news. Did you hear? Ninety-two perished, men and boys.'

'Ninety-two. That's some loss,' George agreed. 'Was it Spain or Portugal?'

'Spain or Portugal?'

'The battle.'

The squire's hand fluttered. 'No, no, this wasn't Boney's doing. Nor was it abroad, but just over the Tyne here, at Felling Colliery. A family interest too – most disturbing.'

George showed more concern for this news than he would have for any battle. 'What – a fall?'

'An explosion. Fire-damp.' Brandling looked down at his boots again. 'Wouldn't you know, this fit is perfect. Well done, Mr Make-Water.'

'It's the bane of a pitman's life, that gas.'

'And the owners', I assure you. A high risk business for all parties. Be sure to take care of yourself while you're working, Stephenson. We wouldn't want to waste a talent like yours.'

This was the opportunity George had been waiting for, if he could lead the conversation in the right direction. He began with, 'The country may have to do without me before long, Mr Brandling. Thing is, of necessity, I'm fixed for America and the Great Lakes once I've put enough by.'

'Emigration, is it? Another high risk business.'

'Seems I have to but... if I'm to get on. I can get nothing in England, and I have to pin my hopes on the new steamboats over there. They're on the Mississippi now, and the Lakes is next, according to Trevithick.'

'Trevithick the Cornishman? I've read about his contraptions in *The Monthly Visitor*. Are you a proselyte for steam?'

'Aye, since he came to see us.'

Mr Brandling stared at George, unsure what to make of him. 'Richard Trevithick came to see you?'

'When he was up north, aye. He'd heard of my work on perpetual motion and wanted to see...'

Brandling clapped his hands and laughed like someone appreciating the antics of Mr Punch. 'Don't tell me you have discovered the secret of perpetual motion.'

George was a little put out by this reaction: 'Well, no, I've all but abandoned it except as a toy for the lad, but Mr Trevithick was very interested...'

'I'm sure he was, I'm sure he was,' said Brandling, evidently a gentleman without much time for listening to other people's speeches. 'You are a fascinating chap, George Stephenson, you really are. You will be a man of means one day, I'm sure of that. Which reminds me, I must pay you for my splendid new boots.'

'I made em as a gift, Squire – well, as a thankyou for not shipping us off to Australia.'

'No steamboats there, eh? Nevertheless I insist on paying you for your work.'

Robert sincerely hoped he would, remembering what Aunt Nelly had said only the other day about prices going up because of the wars, but his father insisted, 'No, it was a boon job. Don't make me break my promise, sir.'

Which Mr Brandling did not, and all they came away with in the end was his good wishes. Young as he was still, Robert knew that his father had hoped for more, and more than payment for the boots. He could tell from his dejected air on the long walk home that George was feeling it most particularly to have his expectations dashed yet again.

*

Father and son continued to pursue their mutual love of nature. In the spring they tamed a blackbird, or rather it cultivated their friendship, constantly flying about the cottage and landing in their small patch of garden. To George's amusement, the blackbird used his mechanical scarecrow as a convenient perch. Twice it came to Robert's finger to be fed, and before long it had found a tiny hole in the eaves, allowing it to squeeze into the cottage itself and nestle in a nook just behind the front door. George had the idea of making it a home there, and had a square of glass cut to the right size to contain the bird and permit it to be observed from inside. The boy could hardly wait for the putty to set before he was dragging his father to the garden gate to watch for Blackie flying home.

While they waited, George spied Kit Heppel returning from his place at the new winning. He called him over. 'Well, marra, have you got to the bottom of the High Pit yet?'

'Geordie, man, they've been sinking it a twelvemonth, and by my rating they'll be on till Doomsday. The men are allus flooded out.'

'I had a good look at that Newcomen when I was over last. There's no reason it shouldn't be up to the job. That is, if it's fit up right.'

'You reckon it's not?'

'I don't reckon, I know. I told McCree as much, but he'd nowt to learn from a brakesman, he said.'

'McCree wouldn't tek a lesson from Moses.' Kit spat on the ground. 'So you think you can crack it?'

Robert was searching the skies as they talked, and at once tugged at his father's sleeve. 'Look, there's Blackie!' The men broke off from their talk to watch as the bird landed on the roof of the cottage, cocked its head on one side, then dived into the gap between the eaves. A moment later it reappeared at the hole, perhaps to congratulate the builders, before vanishing again. George's pride in his latest achievement rendered him bold in his answer to Kit.

'I could make her draw and send you all to the bottom in a week.'

That Sunday Ralph Dodds, the head viewer, deliberately sought out George on the path from chapel, where he waited for his sister and his son. 'Well, Geordie, they tell me you think you can put our blighted pump to rights.'

'Oh aye, sir, certain sure. But McCree won't let the dog see the rabbit.'

'He says you have no experience to bring.'

'McCree needs his lugs washed out. There's a mill in Montrose was plagued wi silting till I was sent for - now it's got the smoothest engine in Scotland. Mr Bell up there could furnish a character...'

'No time for that. I'll give you a fair trial, soon as you like. We're clean drowned out and cannot get a step further. It's had every Alliance engineer beat. If you succeed where they've failed, depend on it, I'll make you a man for life.'

Behind the overseer's shoulder George could see little Bobby running ahead of his aunt towards him. He kept his eyes on the boy as he answered the man. 'You'll not be let down, Mr Dodds.' Then, almost as an afterthought, 'The hands, though, must either be all Whigs or all Tories - I'll want my own party in, without interference.'

If Dodds was surprised by the effrontery of the hireling, he did not let him see it; simply nodded, setting his seal on the bargain, and tipped his hat to Nelly as he strolled back to where his family were waiting for him at their carriage.

George had his crew ready by Tuesday morning. They were gathered by the cottage gate as Robert left for school, and marched together to High Pit Colliery, where they entered the yard to the kind of silence generally reserved for blacklegs. Dick McCree stood at the head of his fitters next to the Newcomen engine, his arms folded, watching their approach. When George reached him at the head of the group McCree said, 'I spect you got all your own tools, since you'll brook no interference.'

'I've got all I need here. You and your men better find summat else to do, less you're here for the learning.'

53

After that the Stephenson set were left entirely on their own to strip down the engine and lay it out in pieces across the yard. About noon, Mr Dodds came out of his office to inspect the progress of the works. 'Have you found what's wrong yet?'

'This engine is sound. The fault's in the application.' George pointed out for Dodds the parts that had been wrongly assembled by McCree and his men. 'You've got a cistern that's been placed too low, an injection cock only half the width it should be... Properly fitted, that boiler could bear twice the pressure that's been put on it and not feel the strain.'

'The proof of the pudding... When will it be ready to try?'

'I promised you could send your men to the bottom by the end of the week. Keep faith with it.'

'McCree claims that's gab. He wagers you'll not have this lot back in one piece by Saturday louse.'

'To return your quote, Mr Dodds, the proof o the puddin...'

The next day, about the hour George and his team were making preparations for restoring the pump to full working order, his son was leaning against a tree outside Mr Rutters' school house, bartering with John Tate for a share of one another's rations.

'If I give you the gowk off my apple, will you give us a bite off your pie?'

'Only if it's a big gowk.'

'Only if it's a big bite.'

Negotiations complete, they ate and chatted as others played around them.

'Did you push Tommy Addison off the form this mornin?' Robert asked.

'I did not. He fell arsy-varsy off the end. There's too many of us on that spelky bench.'

They snorted and larked as boys do, pushing their shoulders against each other in a parody of their daily struggle to stay on the school furniture. 'Anyway,' said John, 'there'll be one less if your dad fixes that pump at the High Pit. Mebbes more than one.'

'How is that?'

'My dad says it'll be like a new winnin if they can get to the bottom. They'll be wanting more men. An I'm to be a trapper.'

'You mean, trapping animals?' from Robert, not comprehending.

'Oh, you're like this gowk, you. On the trap doors. All the younguns start there, or as corf-batter. Or on the puttin if you're strong enough for the tubs.'

'Will you like that?'

'It's fourpence a day,' said John. 'An not having to learn your tables.'

Robert thought about this. 'I'd like the fourpence.'

'Who wouldn't? I hope your dad gets that pump to work. Everybody does.'

At the High Pit Colliery, however, George's confidence took a severe knock when the time came to reconstruct the Newcomen engine. One of the three regulator valves was missing.

'I cannot understand it, George,' said Kit. 'I took care wi my inventory, like you asked. Everything was properly marked and accounted for. There was definitely three valves laid out here yesterday.'

'There's just two now,' said George. 'We canna get it to work without all three.' He picked one of the remaining valves from the ground, and studied it closely. 'It's an intricate little piece an all.'

'Mebbes you should ask McCree if he has a spare. Or to use his workshop, see if we can fashion summat that ull serve the purpose till you can replace the valve properly.'

The workshop was just across the yard, with the engineer in the doorway, watching from a distance. Perhaps McCree was waiting for such a request.

'I'm asking McCree for nowt,' said George. 'Listen, Kit, can you see to the rest of the assembly while I slip away an deal wi this? Other than the valve, it's just more or less tightening up to do.'

'Nae bother,' said Kit. 'Speed well.'

Late that afternoon, unaware his father was walking south-east along the narrow path that led through the churchyard, Robert was taking the same path north-west to home. George was encumbered by the mechanical scarecrow he had uprooted from their garden, as well as another device in his right hand and his bag of tools across the shoulder. Robert had for company Johnny Tate, who was swishing at the tombstones with a branch he'd picked up. 'Die. Die.'

'They're dead already,' said Robert, meaning the people in the graves.

'No, these are soldiers left on the battlefield, up to the knees in dead bodies. My job is to finish them off.' He halted Robert on the path

55

and pointed with his branch to an oak a little way ahead of them. 'What would you do if there was Frenchies hidden behind that tree?'

'I'd run by so fast they wouldn't have time to catch us.'

'Then you'd be dead,' John announced, 'for one of em has a musket, and he'd shoot you in the back.'

Robert shaded his eyes from the low sun to consider the tree more carefully. It was perfectly placed for a surprise attack, commanding a view of the path. He wondered what he would do if there were indeed soldiers hiding there. Perhaps he could skirt round, dashing between tombstones to protect himself from the soldier's fire; but he dare not run across the graves. 'What would you do?' he asked.

'Me? I would take a cobble and hoy it in the tree.' John picked up a small stone from the edge of the path to demonstrate. He threw it high into the branches of the oak. 'The Frenchies look up, mizzled by the noise, an I sneak round the back of the tree an run them through with this. Die! Die!'

Robert laughed at his exuberance. 'With a branch?'

'With a sword. Charge!' Johnny put his head down and ran full-pelt along the path, holding out his sword, just as George appeared from the other side of the oak.

'What's this, an ambush?' said George in mock alarm, thrusting out his iron man like a shield as he side-stepped the attack.

'Dad!' Robert called out in surprise, and ran up to him, eagerly. 'I can carry summat. Where are you going with the flay-craw?'

'To the smithy. I need some of his metal to make one o these.'

He showed the valve, and Robert inspected it as closely as his father had done in the colliery yard. 'Let me help.' But he was turned down.

'You mun go home and keep company with Aunt Nell. It'll be dark afore I'm done.'

He was wrong in his estimate; the work took him much longer. Robert stayed up to wait for him as long as Aunt Nelly would let him, and an hour or so more in his bed before sleep won the battle. Anyone who was abroad in Long Benton that night would have seen a glow from the forge behind the village. It could still be seen when the knocker-up was rapping his pole on the doors marked with a *3* to wake the men on fore-shift. Morning had long since broken by the time George emerged from the smithy with the piece he had made. He walked past his own home, where his son and his sister were just stirring, and straight on to Killingworth High Pit to complete his repairs to the pump.

Robert was present for the trial of the engine at five o' clock in the afternoon. Indeed it seemed that half the males in the community were there, including McCree and his fellow engineers along with the rest of the workforce, who were unable to get at the coal face as the pit was again full of flood water. A public execution would hardly have drawn a larger crowd. Ralph Dodds presided. Kit Heppel had his hand on the lever of George's new-made regulator valve, waiting for instruction.

'Start her at five pound and build her up to ten, Kit,' said George.

Dick McCree stepped forward, apoplectic. 'Are you stark mad, Stephenson? Smeaton, who made this, warned the pressure should never be took beyond five pounds. Newcomen himself set the limit.'

'Are you certain the pump will stand it?' Dodds asked George.

'Aye. It'll bounce in the house, but it's sturdy enough to hold.'

'Then you can have your head.'

McCree protested. 'It's bound to blow, I'm warning you. Everybody stand right off.'

There was small movement from the crowd on McCree's say-so but, when the engine started and Kit pushed the valve open, everyone scuttled back by instinct with the shock of the noise, including Robert despite himself. It was like a monster roused. Steam belched, chains clanked, there was a sound like a giant hammer on an anvil, and the pipes attached to the pump bucked alarmingly with the force of the water rushing through. Dodds grabbed George's elbow.

'Bounce in the house! She's like to knock the house down! She's worse than she was. Turn it off!'

'Leave it be. Trust us, it'll draw.' Even as he said so, George caught Robert's eye in the crowd, and winked reassurance. Robert clenched his hands behind his back, resisting with an effort the temptation to clamp them on his ears against the hellish din. He crossed his fingers, and even prayed a little under his breath, as Aunt Nelly would.

Gradually the pipes ceased writhing, settled with ferocious intent like a serpent to its meal, and seemed to suck the water in great inhalations as the piston rose and fell in the cylinder. The tremendous noise continued, but now there was a controlling majesty about the movement of the pump, and the satisfying sound of flood water gushing by gallons into the wells. Robert ventured forward to stand beside his father and watch the monster working under new mastery. Kit came to clutch George's arm. 'She's drawin, Geordie. You've got her drawin, marra.'

'Thank God for that, Kit,' said his friend under his breath. 'I was sweatin on it. First few minutes, I were sure she were gonna blow.'

57

By ten o' clock at night, when George belatedly minded Bobby's presence among the handful of spectators remaining, the water in the pit was lower than it had ever been before, and they could both return home for an overdue rest.

The pump continued its work ceaselessly over the next two days, so that by Friday afternoon George was able to act in an honorary capacity in sending a cage full of men to commence work at the very bottom of the shaft. It happened to be his last ever duty as a brakesman, for when he climbed down from his position he found Ralph Dodds at the foot of the ladder.

'The owners are well pleased with your work, George. I have ten pounds to give you.'

'Ten pound. I don't mind telling you, sir, that's more un I ever earned for a week's work. Nor from one quarter day to the next.'

'Didn't I say I'd make you a man for life, if you succeeded?'

'Aye. Ten pound will go a long way to that end. Twill clear all my debts, anyroad.'

'There's more,' said Dodds. He paused, maybe for effect or to weigh up his man before he said, 'I hear you've made the acquaintance of one of our owners, Mr Brandling.'

'I know him, aye. What of it?' George was wary; he'd had trouble from previous bosses over what they saw as his come-uppance.

'Only the master's given me full backing for summat I'm wanting to do,' said Dodds. 'I'm to take you on as my enginewright, while the sinking continues. A hundred pounds a year. You'll have tenure for a twelvemonth, at least. What do you have to say to that?'

George stared as if he was watching the man's words take visible shape in front of his eyes. Finally, breathless, he answered. 'I say you're right, Mr Dodds. I am made for life.'

Sunday morning began at the Stephenson cottage with eggs on richly buttered toast. After breakfast, Nell made her way to church (still wearing, Robert had observed, her brooch of cherries) while man and boy walked over to the colliery. There was no work for George that day - he did not give more than a cursory glance to the Newcomen pump as they passed - but he had an appointment at the stables. Tommy Mitcheson, the bank horse-keeper, was waiting to hand over the dun galloway that came with George's new position. The keeper was, it must be said, a little surly.

'Mind what you do wi this beast. He's renty, but he's little - more fit as a pack horse than a gallop - but you'll not heed what I say. Set such fellers as you on horseback and you'll ride like the divil.'

'Whisht, Tommy, I'm St Francis himself with animals. What do you reckon to him, son?'

Robert reached out to trace his finger along a faint stripe that ran down the horse's back; felt a tingle down his own spine as if some invisible being was doing the like to him. 'He's perfect. What's his name?'

Tommy answered from underneath the horse, where he was tightening its girth. 'Squire, I call im, but you name im what you like. Meks no odds to me.' He was, it must be supposed, less than enthralled by brakesman Geordie's sudden elevation.

'We'll clepe him Bobby,' said George to the boy. 'There y'are. You've got summat called after you.'

Once the new-named Bobby had Mitcheson's oldest, most worn-out saddle fastened securely, George hoisted his son to sit between his legs. They jogged out of the yard and were soon enjoying a fast trot by the open fields.

'Should we show him to Aunt Nelly?' Robert's voice was all vibration, his eyes streaming in the wind.

'Soon enough. We've first to call on your Aunt and Uncle Burn.'

The Great North Road lay across the track to the Red House Farm. They paused a moment to look along it. For Robert it was interesting in itself, the only turnpike road in his limited experience to date. His father's mind was on his hard walk to Montrose and the stagecoaches that had rattled by occasionally, their occupants trying to maintain a steady stare as if they thought him some footpad who might at any moment leap up and rob them of their valuables. Once, he'd come upon a coach with a broken axle, and stopped to help, but neither the driver nor his passengers gave consideration to the possibility of their rescuer riding gratis for even a short stage in return. He still carried with him the memory of the restored vehicle disappearing into the distance while he resumed his long walk. How the incident had redoubled his determination. One foot in front of another - that became his mantra. 'Aye, Bobby,' he said now, as if he had been sharing these thoughts with the boy, 'We Stephensons can shift for ourselves, eh? Aye, better un most. We persevere.' Robert turned the word around in his head, wondering about its meaning: *persevere* - it had the sound of something from a tale of King Arthur.

At the end of the lane that led to the farm they met with the Burns' carriage, just returned from morning service. If George had

59

expected to surprise them by his appearance like a gentleman on a mount, it was he who was surprised to find that Joseph Burn knew all about his triumph at the High Pit - it had been the talk of the mart on Saturday.

'Then you know I'm well able to pay off my debt to you. And I've rode over on purpose to do it.'

'No need to break the Sabbath for that, George. There's nothing spoiling. Come back on a business day.'

'Come back any day.' This from Fanny's sister, Ann. 'We never see enough of you, George, or of little Bobby.'

'Enough to give him fine tastes in dining,' and George told them of Bobby's innocent request for eggs and butter, without the shame he would have felt only a week ago. That led to Ann insisting they come in to sup something before their ride back home. Across the table she raised the question that had been preying on her mind for some time.

'Have you never thought of remarrying, George?'

'Oh...' and now George did betray some awkwardness.

'I mean for Bobby's sake, as much as anything.'

'We rub along all right, us two, with Nelly's help.'

'But you may not have her always,' Ann pressed him. 'She may want to marry herself someday. May be sooner rather than later.'

'Have you heard summat?'

'Not of any consequence. But it might happen. Then what?'

George shifted under her interrogation, but something in him welcomed the conversation. It was almost as if, through her sister, his dead wife was giving him permission to entertain certain feelings again.

'I've no time for courtin and such...' he started to say, but Ann seemed to be listening to his thoughts rather than his speech.

'Do you ever see anything of Betty Hindmarsh? You were sweet on her one time, weren't you?'

'That was long ago.'

'I remember watching her dance at the country fair one summer. She had on the daintiest pair of shoes that you made for her. I coveted em for myself.'

Joseph, who had been conspiring with Robert to feed his dog scraps from the table, suddenly said, 'Twas Thomas Hindmarsh told us at the mart about your success with the pump.'

'Hindmarsh?' George was genuinely surprised. 'Where's he wit of it?'

'I have no notion. But he come across quite proud. Whether to know of the deed, or you, I couldn't rightly say.'

Nothing more was said on the subject, but when George and Robert had taken their leave and trotted Bobby up the track away from the farm, George hesitated at the place where one path crossed another. East was Killingworth. West and a little south lay Black Callerton. Perhaps there was still time for a short visit. As he considered this, the horse standing obediently, George felt his son turn in the saddle.

'Do we have to take Bobby straight back to the stables? I know Aunt Nell would like to see him. And so would Granny Mabel. And Grandpa could feel his mane.'

Robert remembered later the smile on his father's face as he looked back and up at him, for it seemed to emerge gradually from within, as if he'd been warming it in his heart before he gave it to the boy. After a moment's silence he said, 'Course they mun see him. Yes, course they must.' He flicked at Bobby's reins and they headed in the direction of home.

V

The North Midland train to Derby was on time. The businessman in Robert might have preferred to see it fuller than it was, but for his comfort he was pleased to find that his First Class compartment, built to accommodate six, had just two other men occupying it when he boarded. They nodded courteously as he stepped in, each silently assessing him for likely rank and station from the clues offered by his dress and manner. Robert, it must be admitted, did the same.

The older gentleman in the far corner of the carriage was as soberly suited as Robert in his mourning, with a dark double-breasted Prince Albert coat and wearing his top hat despite the heat, though it meant he had to sit well forward in his place, with his hands folded over the knob of his cane. His collar was high, and he perched so trim and perpendicular that Robert suspected he was one of those who had not yet abandoned the former fashion of the corset. The man nearest the doorway was a more relaxed passenger and more flamboyantly dressed, with wide lapels to his jacket, open to reveal a broad-checked waistcoat and a yellow silk cravat worn in bow tie style. He wore elastic-sided boots that he withdrew good-naturedly from where they were parked on the opposite seat, to allow Robert access. As he did so he glanced out of the window towards the platform.

'Ah, we're in Chesterfield. Tell me, friend, has the famous spire straightened up yet?'

'No,' Robert replied. 'As crooked as ever.'

'It still awaits a virgin through its doorway, then.' He checked his leer when he saw that Robert, who had heard the joke many times in masculine company, remained unmoved, but he failed to notice the shadow of contempt on the old gentleman's face, and continued conversational. 'I got wind of George Stephenson's... Hasn't he just been buried there?'

'Well, no, in... In Holy Trinity.' Robert was used to hearing his father's name mentioned in public, but the altered context dried his throat as he essayed a response.

'Oh, were you witness?'

'Yes.' He would have disclosed his kinship next, but the dandy was more interested in his own perspective than Robert's.

'Do you know, I damn near stopped off myself on the way up - pay respects - but I would have missed the meeting at York. Damn wish I had - would have saved me money.' From this and his general demeanour, Robert supposed him to be a gambler rather than a man of business, and the meeting he referred to, the Ebor at York racecourse. This was confirmed as he went on. 'Capital fellow, Stephenson. Father of the Railways, what? Changed all our lives. Example: horse racing - that's my ticket. Are you a sporting chap?'

'No.'

'Take my word for it, changed out of all recognition. Example - from the meeting I've just left: Gimcrack Stakes. Damn fine race for two-year-olds. Six furlongs. Could you have seen that a few years ago? No. Why? The railways. I rest my case.'

'I'm partly with your reasoning,' said Robert, somewhat buffeted by the man's style. 'You mean travelling to meetings...'

'On the nose, friend. Both man and beast. More meetings, more people, more races - but there's more to it than that. Before the trains, how did the owners move their horses from one meeting to another? Why, they walked them, of course. Let's say, Goodwood to Epsom, there's four days. On to Newmarket, another seven. And you're supposing the horse has the stamina to make it. Not at two years old, that's certain, nor three. So it's four years and over, running the longer races. And who's there to watch them? Not me, less it be inside a dozen miles. Now, we come from all over, and what a spectacle it is. A full card of races, long and short distance, wide range of fit animals, ready to race. Good for punters. Good for business. I rest my case.'

'Railways good for business... Balderdash.' This from the gentleman in the corner, speaking for the first time, and in very ill humour.

'Respectfully, sir, I won't give way on that point. Capital business, in all manner of ways. Progress... untethered, as it were... No more limited to the speed a horse can go. I take my hat off to Mr Stephenson - in fact, I have already, it's so damned hot.' The gambler winked at Robert. 'One of society's great benefactors. Look how folk of all degree can get so easily about now. Great equaliser, the railway.'

'As for that,' replied the old man sourly, 'I'm with Wellington. What good is served by the lower orders wandering uselessly about the country? And for equality - would you wish to be shut up in a carriage with a madman, or a diseased person? I think not. But to return to business, sir. Whose interest has been fed by the mushroom growth of the railways? Why, it turns out, none but the engineers and the lawyers. And of course that great Yorkshire windbag, Hudson.'

'The Railway King,' the dandy declaimed, borrowing the nomenclature favoured by the newspapers.

'The Railway Knave, I'd call him. He puffed up the Mania and hoodwinked honest investors. I myself lost...' The speaker made a vague gesture to indicate some significant sum, managing at the same time subtly to convey that he was far from impoverished by the loss. 'Oh, but now the full extent of his crookery is to be exposed at last.'

Robert had been uncomfortable from the first mention of George Hudson. The magnate's long association with the Stephensons was well known - paraded by Hudson - and Robert in particular could be called close. The connection had gained him his Whitby seat. He would privately admit, too, that he owed Hudson for his escape from his luckless involvement with the Stanhope and Tyne. When he accepted a shareholding in lieu of fee for his services, Robert had failed to appreciate the extent of the financial responsibility he was taking on, until the company went bankrupt and he was left as the only shareholder with any assets. Hudson had come to his rescue, bundling the Stanhope and Tyne with other minor lines to create the Newcastle and Darlington route, thus relieving Robert of a potentially ruinous liability. Thank God then for the Railway King. There were many who did not like his methods, but most acknowledged the presiding genius as well as the volcanic energy behind the astonishing growth of the railways since *Rocket* first was stoked. Robert was inclined to consider Hudson a visionary. Things had been sticky here and there, but they could never have achieved so much without him. He had reminded his father of this only weeks ago when George was in high dudgeon at Newby Park... but had they supped with the Devil?

'You interest me, sir,' Robert managed to say at last, when the gentleman's ire seemed exhausted and he had turned his gaze on the passing scenery. 'I have not kept quite up to date these last few days. What exposure do you refer to?'

The old man studied him with one eye as if, having spent himself on one unworthy fellow-passenger, he was weighing up whether the other merited further expenditure of his precious breath. He must have been satisfied for quality as he leaned forward to say, almost *sotto voce*, 'Nothing has yet appeared in the newspapers to my knowledge but, mark my words, when Smith's pamphlet is fully out, the fat ox will be roasted.'

'Please pardon my ignorance, but who is Smith and what is his pamphlet?'

'Count him a friend of mine,' said the gentleman. The lift of his chin signalled pride in the acquaintance. 'Hudson has reason to know

Arthur Smith. Oh yes, and to fear him - he has been on his tail for quite some time - a champion of the uncorrupted shareholders. His pamphlet, lately published, is *The Bubble of the Age*. Do you have railway stock, sir? If so, I recommend you read it.'

'What does the pamphlet have to say of Hudson?'

'Oh, that he is a miracle of our times - or so he seems in his presentation of accounts that boast of profits which when examined look very much like losses, while Hudson bribes the shareholders with their own money, paying dividends out of capital instead of revenue. In fine, that Hudson is nothing but an embezzler and a fraud.'

There was a hearty laugh from the opposite end of the compartment. 'More fool the speculators he gulled,' said the gambler. 'They'd do better to invest their money at the turf. Ah, no, perhaps they should keep away, they could not resist being duped at the three-card trick.'

Robert could not share in the amusement. He sank into his seat with a sickening sense of guilt by association. Just four days before, at a hastily-arranged conference between his father's death and the funeral, George's solicitor Thomas Morris had predicted that the combined family fortunes were likely to make Robert Stephenson the first engineer millionaire. If Hudson was to be dragged through the mire, as now seemed likely, were the detractors going to question the Stephensons' probity too? That would be entirely unjust.

His torment, though, went deeper than that, rooted in something more personal and intense. It stemmed from his sure knowledge that his father's long relationship with George Hudson had survived as long as it did only because Robert had acted as the developer's chief apologist. Over the past few months in particular his father had privately expressed grave doubts about Hudson's honesty and motive. During Robert's meeting with Morris, the solicitor had also shown him a letter lately received from George. His father had written, *Hudson has become too great a man for me now. I am not at all satisfied at the way the Newcastle & Berwick has been carried on, and I do not intend to take any more active part in it. I have made Hudson a rich man, but he will very soon care for nobody except he can get money by them.* Reading that correspondence then, and remembering it now, Robert was all too painfully aware how it was he who had defended Hudson to the last.

VI

All Robert really knew of Dr Bruce's Academy was that it was to be found in Percy Street, and that he was to be there by eight thirty. He had plied his father with questions about the school beforehand, but soon found that George knew little more than he did - only that this was the place where he could stretch himself as a scholar, now that he had outgrown Mr Rutter's capacity to teach him. George had ventured to ask advice from Squire Brandling, whom he often had to report to in the course of his work. Mr Brandling asked whether he wanted a classical education for his son, or something of a more liberal nature.

'To speak truthfully, sir, I'm not right certain of the difference. When you say classical...'

'I mean Greek, Latin, that sort of thing. If that's what you wish, I'd recommend the Royal Grammar School in Newcastle. Lord Eldon himself went there in his early years and, I believe, Lord Collingwood. An excellent establishment.'

'Oh, I'm not sure Greek or Latin or any of that high learning would answer, not for folks of our stamp...' George was as much put off by the thought of future peers of the realm commanding undue attention as by the nature of the syllabus. 'Something more of practical application might suit better.'

'In that case, John Bruce is your man. An antiquarian scholar himself, but his school is modern in its character. And cheaper too, if cost is a consideration. I'm sure Robert's education would profit under Bruce. He'll come on in leaps and bounds there. Make plenty of friends too, no doubt. And have you thought of enrolling him as a reading member of the Literary and Philosophical Society? There is a very good library there, open til ten in the evening.'

'I know nothing of it.'

'Let me put in a word. It provides manna for the curious appetite.'

'Well, I hope to feed off some of it myself, sir.'

George had little enough time to broaden his own education, being supervising engineer now for all the Grand Alliance collieries, but he hoped to imbibe something of Robert's learning along the way. 'I mean to squeeze every ounce of the forty pounds I'm paying out to Bruce,' he joked to John Steele after the arrangement was made.

Robert had risen particularly early, expecting to walk the five miles to Newcastle, but he had a surprise waiting. Outside the door of the cottage (which George was extending to accommodate his parents) he found Old Bob stationed, cradling the muzzle of a donkey that was to be Robert's own. 'He feels a real blood, this cuddy,' the blind man assured his grandson. 'A real, genuine blood.'

Robert spent the first half of the journey pleasantly enough, musing on what he should call his cuddy. Perhaps Copenhagen, to mark the news of England's great victory at Waterloo - but the Iron Duke would not be flattered to have a donkey named for his horse. Besides, the creature was said to have kicked his master when he dismounted; Robert did not want to risk investing a spirit of malice with the name. The boy soon lost this train of thought, his uneasiness growing as he came to the outskirts of town. By the time he'd made his way to the end of busy Northumberland Street - a little late through first mistaking the Orphan House for the building he was looking for - he was as nervous as any new pupil expected to be.

At this time of the year, however, Robert was the only fresh arrival. The other boys watched with interest and some amusement through the windows of the writing room as he rode through the wrought iron gate in front of the school and searched for somewhere to tether his donkey. In his home-made corduroy trousers and blue coat-jacket, carrying the bait of rye bread and cheese that Nelly had put up for him, he cut a distinct figure from the bulk of the students. There were modest eruptions of laughter for the noise of his iron-plated soles ringing along the stone-flagged corridor, abruptly cut off as the door swung open to reveal Dr Bruce himself alongside the stranger. The class stood in a show of respect.

'Do sit down, boys,'

The headmaster ushered Robert in front of the assembly.

'We have a new pupil to welcome today. Perhaps some of you know Master Robert Stephenson?' No-one spoke up; all silently appraising the donkey boy at close quarters. Dr Bruce addressed a youth who sat near the back of the room. 'Thomas Buddle? I believe your uncle and Stephenson's father have worked together.'

The name meant something to Robert – John Buddle, viewer at Wallsend Colliery; that must be the uncle. One or two faces turned to Thomas Buddle, who glared almost mutinous at the master, and shook his head. A shadow fell across Dr Bruce's characteristic geniality, until his eyes lit on an empty seat.

'Ah, I see a place by young Hancock. Perhaps you would like to billet there for now.'

Robert was wafted considerately to the vacant half of a hinge-top desk where a boy was sitting who seemed two or three years younger than himself and most of the others in the class. Albany Hancock offered a sideways smile, made room for the newcomer to insert his longer legs in the gap between bench and desk. Robert laid his lunch package carefully on the floor next to his feet, conscious that every move was being watched by forty pairs of eyes.

'Boys,' said Dr Bruce once his new recruit had settled and been given his slate, 'I want you to take special care this week to make Master Robert comfortable and help him find his way. Remember that the object of a liberal education is not merely to make a man of business, or to cultivate one's intellectual powers, but also to refine the moral sensibility, to become an honourable as well as a useful member of society. Kindness to our fellow man is at the heart of our moral code.'

Homily over, Dr Bruce turned his attention to mathematics, and the class spent the next hour wrestling with mensuration. Robert found it difficult to concentrate at first, still bemused by the mute hostility some of the boys had exhibited, but gradually he was drawn into the subject. Dr Bruce was a good teacher, with no artifice or pomposity. Robert was impressed too by the generally quiet industry of the pupils compared with what he had grown accustomed to at Mr Rutter's, and not least by the quickness of his neighbour Albany Hancock, who did not seem disadvantaged by his age. Robert noticed one odd aspect of his behaviour; every so often Hancock would dip his fingers into his coat pocket nearest Robert and bring out a crumb of cheese that he would transfer to his other hand and from there to the opposite pocket. The mystery was solved when the class broke up to take some air. While the other boys filed out of the classroom, Albany once again placed a hand into his pocket on the left side and brought out what Robert recognized as a dormouse. He fed it with a larger piece of cheese this time, stroked its nose and replaced it in his pocket before he turned to Robert and spoke for the first time.

'Is your donkey a jack or a jenny?'

'Oh, I haven't decided on a name yet.'

'I mean, is it male or female?'

'It's a him, I think. I'm not sure.'

'Let us go and find out.'

Albany led the way. He made no sign of acknowledgement to the other boys as he scurried outdoors like a small burrowing animal intent on its purpose. He sought out the donkey, confidently pronounced it male and even suggested a name for it, Dapple. 'After Sancho Panza's mule in *Don Quixote*. Have you read the story?'

'I haven't.' Making a mental note to do so. 'You heard of *Robinson Crusoe*?'

'The book with the cannibals. That's one of my favourites.'

Robert watched as Albany Hancock whispered in the donkey's ear with a tenderness that seemed almost familial. He felt they could be friends, despite the difference in years. 'Are you a boarder at this school?' he asked.

'Oh no, I live just a step away from here, in St Mary's Terrace. You can come and eat lunch in my garden if you'd like.'

Which Robert did at the end of the second period. In return for his invitation, Albany was allowed the pleasure of riding Robert's cuddy the short distance to St Mary's Terrace, where his adult sister Mary Jane gave Robert milk to drink with his rye bread and cheese.

'Would you like a bite o my gowk?' Robert was eating lunch on the grass in his new friend's garden.

'Sorry?' Albany, sifting through soil under the bushes, looked round to see Robert offering up his half-eaten apple. 'Oh, no thank you.'

'What are you searching for?'

'Insects. I keep a box for collecting the more interesting specimens.'

'Here, let me help.' Robert sprang to his feet and walked over. He was intrigued to discover a stone sundial at the edge of the lawn. The geometry of it fascinated him. He ran his fingers across the grooves of lines and numerals.

'How does this work?' How can you tell the time from it?'

Albany left his insect-hunting to explain. 'You watch where the shadow cast by the style falls onto these hour marks. The style is set at true north. Can you tell what time it is now?'

'I reckon it's just after one,' said Robert.

Albany screwed his eyes against the sunshine and looked up at him with a certain respect. 'Well done. It usually takes those new to it a little longer to interpret the time from the marks.'

Robert felt a mite guilty, knowing that he had been helped by hearing one o' clock chime from the nearby Haymarket, but he resolved to enjoy his friend's appreciation without demur.

'It's time to go back,' said Albany. 'If you wish, Dapple could stay here on the grass instead of having to be tied up at the school.'

'He'd like that. But I don't think I will call him Dapple - what did you say was the mule owner's name in the story?'

'Sancho Panza.'

'Then I'll call him Sancho; it suits him better.'

As they returned through the school gate, they were watched by Thomas Buddle and a close classmate, Richard Hodgson. 'Here's Stephenson with his donkey,' Buddle called out loud enough for all the boys to hear.

'I left him yonder,' Robert said, naively.

'Then who's that ass beside you?' Buddle gave a forced laugh and nudged Hodgson to join in. Robert's instinct was to bunch his knuckle. He stepped forward to champion his smaller friend, but Albany restrained him.

'Leave it be, Rob. He's only trying to provoke you.'

Buddle worked his way round the two boys, parroting into Albany's ear. '*Leave it be, leave it be*, says little mouse. Turn the other cheek.'

'And what a rosy cheek the donkey boy has,' Hodgson added. 'But did he wash behind his ears this morning? Take hold, Buddle, let's find out.'

Buddle made a sudden grab at Robert's shoulders to pin them back.

'Get off us!'

'Watch his back legs, Tom. The donkey boy has a kick.'

Robert struggled free as a hand bell rang at the doorway.

'Quick, run inside,' urged Albany. 'Tell Dr Bruce.'

'I'll run nowhere. Howay, you two. I'll face up to yez.'

'*Howay!*' Buddle mimicked.

'*I'll face up to yez!*' from Hodgson. 'Priceless.'

By now the rest of the school were filing indoors, leaving this group exposed to scrutiny. Robert hesitated. A fight on his first day, even for a just cause, would be bound to disappoint his father. He dropped his fists. This gave Hodgson his cue to step forward and point a finger belligerently. 'Next time, coal-dirt, you won't have the bell to save you.'

The temptation to swing at him was almost too strong, but Robert resisted. He turned instead to take Albany by the arm and steer him beyond the two older boys. Buddle's grin as they passed was carnivorous.

Back home, he left out of his first day account any report of unpleasantness between himself and Thomas Buddle. When he returned he found his father straddling a large boiler next to the wagon way behind the house, fixing a blast-pipe onto the travelling engine he called *Blücher*. George was convinced he could better Trevithick's version of the

70

locomotive. He had told everyone who cared to listen that this latest innovation would make his engine more efficient than the horses that were still preferred at Killingworth, but progress was far from smooth. His son's appearance at the track-side gave him some respite from an hour or two of frustration.

'Ho now, you're sharp back from town. Old Bob had that cuddy sized up right, eh?'

George was keen to hear the details of Dr Bruce's lessons, and showed even greater interest when Robert told him of the sundial in his friend's garden. 'By, what a singular feature that would make outside our cottage,' George said. 'There's hardly room among my vegetables, but I dare say we could build one vertical into the wall where the sun would fall on it. What say we mount it atop the lintel to finish off the improvements?'

Now that Robert was old enough to take an active part, the two of them liked nothing better than to pore over plans and drawings, coaxing ideas into life, first as mere schemes committed to paper, then realised, albeit with some false starts. Experimentation was George's way of making up for a certain lack of theoretical grounding, and while he was undeniably ingenious he would often go charging with great enthusiasm down the wrong road. Robert lost count of the times they had to start afresh on projects, though they usually learned something new even as they were following a mistaken track. George's way could become tedious however, and the more Robert attended school the more he was inclined to find out first what the books had to teach, to point the pair at least approximately in the right direction. For the contrivance of the sundial he got his father's agreement to consult Dr Bruce, who suggested they study Ferguson's *Astronomy*.

'Unfortunately, there is no copy in the school library,' Robert told his father. 'The master mentioned somewhere called the Lit and Phil.'

'Ay, Brandling spoke of it. I'll mind him of his promise to get you in.'

Brandling was as good as his word, and it was not long before Robert was trying a new route from school to stop off at the Assembly Rooms in Westgate. He was apprehensive the first time he pushed open the heavy door to the library and walked into the quiet there. He paused at the entrance, taking in the ornate ceiling above the book-lined shelves, and jumped as a voice barked at his ear.

'Now then, scamp. Don't think I haven't been watching you from the window, because I have.'

The gentleman had a florid complexion behind half-rimmed glasses - the kind of mutton-chopped face that could look cheery on feast days or ready to erupt with annoyance, as here. Robert took a placatory tone, a little hollow. 'Have you, sir?'

'And if you think I do not know who tied that ass to the palisade, you must take me for a fool.'

'Not at all, sir.'

'Have you any idea what manner of building this is, boy?'

'Yes, sir.' Robert answered as if he were being officially examined on the matter. 'The name of the whole building is the Assembly Rooms and this part is, I hope, the library of the Literary and Philosophical Society.'

'Then you should be aware it is no place for grubby boys and donkeys.'

'I'm not so very grubby, I don't believe.'

'Let me see your hands.'

Robert stretched out his palms for inspection, as he used to for his aunt when he was six. The man bent over them, gripping one leg of his spectacles. 'Hmm, by these you've not done much to earn your keep.'

'I'm still at school, sir. At the Percy Street Academy.'

This information diverted the librarian's attention from Robert's hands to his face. 'Bruce's school.... Really? He send you?'

'Well, it was more to do with Mr Brandling.'

'Brandling? Which Brandling? Not...?'

'He lives at Gosforth Hall, sir.'

'I know where he lives.' Guardedly, 'What's Brandling to you?'

'I believe he's enrolled me, sir. That is, I trust he has. As a reading member.'

'Well, bless my soul.'

'Are you Mr William Turner?'

'I am.' The librarian and secretary of the Lit and Phil straightened to assume professional dignity.

'I have a guinea for you.' Robert dropped his hands to root in his pockets.

Mr Turner, who had already tested a variety of attitudes with the newcomer, settled on teasing benevolence as *le mode juste*. 'Are you over twenty one?'

'No, sir, I am but twelve.'

'Then you pay just half a guinea. There is no better rate in the whole of Great Britain.' He moved across to his desk. 'What is your name?'

'Robert Stephenson.'

'Stephenson, of course. Your name is not yet dry on my list. Let me give you a copy of our rules.'

The librarian rummaged for the appropriate paper while Robert stood before him, making proper observation of the room for the first time, awed by ranks of shelves and cases. The smell of wood and leather was rich, seductive – he wanted to wrap himself in it. He watched dust swirling in the window light and took it as evidence of enchantment in the place.

'May I choose a book today, Mr Turner?'

'You may choose, my lad, from more than eight thousand. Not so many for children, but there are some Grimm's Fairy Tales, the Arabian Nights, Mr Defoe of course...'

'Do you have *Astronomy Explained upon Sir Isaac Newton's Principles* by Mr James Ferguson? Brewster's edition, if you keep it.'

Mr Turner could not conceal his surprise. 'We... do indeed.' He carried his sheet of rules to a table near the window. 'Sit here where the light is better, I will disinter it for you.'

Robert, encouraged by his obliging manner, dared to ask, 'Would it be possible to take the book home? Only for a few days. My father would like...'

'Well, that's not strictly...' the librarian waved a vague forefinger at the rules. 'Is your... You don't yourself reside in Gosforth Hall, I take it?'

'Very near, sir.'

'Well, in that case...' Scurrying away. 'I'll be a moment.'

As Robert waited at his window seat he noticed a lady enter the library who seemed as uncertain as he had when he came through the door. He did not know her immediately, but when her eyes met Robert's she gave a start of recognition, and hurried to him as if for rescue.

'It's Bobby... Robert, isn't it?'

'Hello,' trying to remember where he had seen her.

'Sorry, I'm a friend of your... aunt. We met once on our return from the Harvest Festival.'

'Miss Hindmarsh.' Robert beamed his sunniest to excuse his failing to recognize her at once. 'You let me ride in your carriage.'

'That's right.' Betty seemed buoyed up by his obvious pleasure in the memory, and shared it for a moment. She stopped herself remarking on how much he'd grown, not wishing to patronise, choosing instead to ask, 'Are you using the library for study?'

'I've been admitted as a reading member of the Society.'

'As I have, only recently. Mr Sands on the Bigg Market has been ill a long time, and his Circulating Library is to close. I am glad to see a familiar face - ladies have not long been allowed here, and how welcome I'm not sure.'

Certainly the librarian did not immediately acknowledge her presence when he came bustling back with the large volume of Ferguson. 'Here we are, Master Robert. It is quite a tome.' He chuckled. 'Will you manage it on your *steed*?'

'I'm sure I will.'

Mr Turner now deigned to address the female. 'Madam?'

'Miss.' Betty hesitated, put off by her own correction, then rushed her request. 'Hannah More?'

'Is that your name, Miss, or the author you are searching for?' Impossible to tell whether he was being deliberately obtuse.

Betty regained her composure with an effort. 'Oh, the author, yes. My name is Elizabeth Hindmarsh. I am newly registered as a reading member.'

'Hannah More, you say? Let me investigate...' and he disappeared between rows of shelves again, like a beaver inspecting his dam. Robert and Betty exchanged smiles, united in appreciating the slight absurdity of all this, and in their mutual newness. They both felt a little awkward with each other too, until Betty found something else to say.

'Does your aunt keep well? Please remind her that she has not yet taken up my invitation to call at Black Callerton.'

'Quite well, thank you,' said Robert. 'Perhaps you could call on her - she has her own room now. I'm sure she'd be pleased to see you.'

'Perhaps I should,' Betty agreed. 'Perhaps I will.'

Father and son spent the next few evenings at home making the necessary calculations and sketching out the design for the sundial, following Ferguson.

'So that's circle number five,' said George. 'Read the passage out to us again to check we have it right thus far.'

Robert read aloud while George reviewed his work, kneeling on the floor. '*The easiest and most expeditious way of drawing a Meridian Line is this: Make four or five concentric circles, about a quarter of an inch from one another, on a flat board about a foot in breadth; and let the outmost circle be but little less than the board will contain. Fix a pin perpendicularly in the centre...*'

'A pin.' George leaned back upon his knees and called so he could be heard in the kitchen, 'Nelly, do you have a hair-pin? Bring it quick.' Then to Robert: 'Pin, yes, what of the pin?'

'Fix a pin perpendicularly in the centre, and of such a length that its whole shadow may fall within the innermost circle for at least four hours in the middle of the day. The pin ought to be about an eighth part of an inch thick...'

Nelly, coming through with the pin, was the only one not fully attending to Robert's reading, so was the first to hear footsteps approaching the cottage in great haste. She was about to remark on it when the front door flew open and a workman burst in, not bothering to knock.

'Beg pardon, Mr Stephenson, there's fire reported in the deep main!'

Nelly snatched her apron to her mouth.

'Fire, how bad?' George was up and reaching for his coat even as he asked the question.

'Got a geet hold. There's men trapped in-bye.'

'McCree's on shift, aint he? What's his plan of action?'

'Mr McCree's nowhere to be seen, sir. That's why I come to you. I think he was below when the blash was heard.'

'You did right to come. Run back and muster all you can on bank. I'll be ahind you.'

Nelly's apron dropped from her face. 'Fire! Lord... Brother, take care. Robert, where do you think you're going?'

'I'll stay safe at the pithead, Aunt. They may need help with water or anything.'

George did not prevent Robert pulling on his boots alongside him; his mind was already turning on what might be done when he got there. Within moments they were out of the cottage and close on the heels of the miner sprinting back to the colliery. Nor were they the only three abroad. The news seemed to have spread almost as quick as the flames, to judge by the women and children teeming out of their homes in a state of panic. Some had even woken their babies, quickly wrapping a shawl around and hurrying, the infants mewing at their necks, to find out what they could. Old men, too broken by years of hard labour to manage the short walk to the colliery, came outdoors to lean against walls and listen for scraps of news. Explosion and fire were a terrifying reality for families hereabout, with more than twenty deaths in such accidents at the pit in recent memory. They felt the shadow, too, of the ninety men killed in that one horrifying blaze at Felling.

At the pithead all was chaos and uncertainty. The crowd there had the appearance of a rabble; women howling in anguish, men arguing. Robert felt his chest tighten with fearful excitement. George left his side and leapt up where he could be seen at the lip of the main shaft, gripping

75

a lighted torch in one hand and the rope that held the pit cage in the other.

'Hold! Hold! Everybody, fix your eyes on me.'

The noise persisted until he swung his torch for attention, quietened the crowd sufficiently for his orders to be heard. He commanded men by name as he picked them out from the faces looking up at him. 'Henderson and Smith, bring bricks and mortar. Wilson, fetch your tools from the shed. Evans, Garbut, your job is getting water.'

Once materials were assembled and laid in the corf ready for lowering, George addressed them again, 'Listen to me. I need half a dozen gooduns for this work. Who's man enough to go down with us?'

He had his enemies at the pit, more so since his elevation to engineer in charge, but there was no resisting him. Whether through genuine loyalty or grudging respect, the impulse to rescue family and friends, or sheer blind courage, George soon had his pick of volunteers. Robert watched him winched down with his team into the shaft. Smoke was already rising from the deep main; it was like being lowered into an active chimney. When Kit Heppel began marshalling a reserve force to go below, Robert presented himself on impulse. He stepped onto the corf, only for Kit to haul him off again.

'I never took you for such a fool, young Bobby.'

'I'm wanting to help.'

'Well, you'll be nowt but a hindrance down there, bonny lad. If you mun, go and get some water bottles filled for men coming out, and some cloths dampened ready. Hear me?'

'Yes, Kit.'

He turned away too late for Kit to miss the tears, and he felt his arm grabbed. 'Harkee, there'll be greetin enough without you startin.'

'Yes, Kit.'

The miner squeezed where he held. 'Be sure o this, lad – yourn can look after himself, and if he can't I'm there for him, ain't I? You've got my oath on that, aye?'

'Aye.'

With that Kit let the boy go, watched him away from the cage entrance before he joined his gang on the corf. Robert would not see any of the rescuers again for more than two hours.

While his son waited anxiously with the others on bank, George continued to direct operations below. He instructed his men to dip cloths into the water bucket and tie them round their faces to give some protection from the smoke and heat. Kit was one who seized a cloth and

76

tagged on at the end of the line. Crouched below the level of the smoke, George led them in. They half-crawled along the floor of the deep main until they found the gallery where the fumes seemed thickest. Peering through the reek, they could see an orange line of fire coursing along a fissure in the roof of the gallery towards the main tunnel. 'Sent from hell off the divil's finger,' Kit said as they watched. It could only be a matter of minutes before the fire completed its journey along the side passage to the main. George passed instructions up the line for his men to bring the materials they had brought down with them to the opening of the gallery.

'We mun work as fast as ever in our lives, lads. I need a wall built right here.'

A complaint went up. 'You mean to block this gallery?' What about the men in there, maister? They'll not get out.'

'Work, don't talk!' from George.

Kit set to with the rest of them, and for a while there was nothing more to be heard but the scraping of brick mortared onto brick, and a faint roar of fire from the blackness beyond. The mood was black too; an air of resentment against the order. George himself broke the silence, less abrupt this time, seeking words to explain what seemed a harsh decision.

'They're as like to be dead than alive already. If we don't choke the fire afore it reaches the end o the gullet it'll shoot straight up the main shaft and seal the fate of every man and boy under the ground yet. You're saving lives, marras, not destroying em.'

'You're right like, Geordie,' Kit said, 'but it's cold sweat work to seal up a living tomb.'

What the labourers feared most was hearing any cry or scrabbling noise from behind the wall as they constructed it, knowing they would be faced with the choice of tearing it down again to rescue one fugitive from the flames and risk the safety of all in the mine, or carrying on regardless. They did hear some disturbance, but it was from their side of the wall, coming from out-bye. George went to investigate, crawling back along the way towards the cage. At the bottom of the up shaft he found a rabble of hewers, alarmed by the smoke billowing through the alleys, fighting for a place on the corf and screaming to be hauled to safety. One in his haste barged over a trap boy not Robert's age, who was disappearing under a stampede of legs as George arrived.

'Stand aside. Let that laddie up. Give him some room, damn you.' George hauled at the culprit's shoulder. The man turned as if to plant a grimy fist in his face, but stopped when he saw who it was, and backed off. George knelt beside the young trapper. 'All right, bonnie lad. Lean agen me, I'll lift ye.'

'Thank you, Mr Stephenson.'

George peered through the grime. 'Is it John Tate?'

'Aye, sir.'

'Good lad. Our Bobby's waiting for you on bank with water. Daresay you're clammin?' The boy nodded. George picked him up easily from the roadway and lifted him into the cage, then wheeled round to face the mob. Those nearest to him, won over by his action, strained to resist those pressing from behind, trying to give the *maister* space to take charge.

'Listen!' he yelled, cutting through the confusion. 'The fire is under control. The only danger now is from yourselves. All of you, sit down right now where you are. Howay, every man jack of you, down on your arse!' Some obeyed him promptly, others tardily, grumbling, but within a minute every pitman there had found his own space on the tunnel road.

'Now then,' said George. 'Children under thirteen, come to me now. You'll be lifted first. For the rest, are there Christians amongst you? Well, remember the Samaritan. Look to your neighbours. Any that's suffering worst from the smoke or the heat, let them come next.'

'I've got Dan Watson here,' called one voice in the gloom. 'He's in a bad state. Canna walk on his own.'

'You and another help him through. Make way for these men, good lads.'

In the colliery yard Robert was kept busy with his water bottle, but each time he heard the creak of the winding rope he looked up to the pithead in anticipation of seeing his father among the next batch of tired survivors. Eventually he caught sight of Kit against the darkening sky. The boy ran to the foot of the ladder, expecting both men to appear there, but Kit was unaccompanied. Robert could see his shamed face even under the pit dirt.

'He sent me up, Rob, afore he'd come himself.' Kit spat black phlegm upon the ground. 'Aggh, he's a mule head, your dad, that's a fault in im. He wanted to check the wall we made was sound, and wouldn't have us in tow.'

The crowd on bank had thinned considerably. Kit and Robert kept their watch while men walked, limped or were carried homeward by workmates and family members. Others more seriously affected lay on the ground until medical help could reach them. As the night grew colder, the two waiting for George walked together in the yard to keep their blood flowing. There was still a small knot of people, mainly women, by the pithead steps, lingering to hear news from below. The man and the boy joined this group for a time, but Robert felt his anxiety redouble with theirs, and he had to break away, wait on his own by the wall of the toolshed. He ran forward as soon as he saw his father emerge at last, a weary figure under the winding-wheel.

'I feared you weren't coming back at all,' he said, as George descended. 'Are you the last out?'

George took Robert's hands in his, but did not embrace him as fully as he might. His eyes were on the woeful cluster beyond as he answered the question. 'Aye, son. Last of all that's coming out.'

Next morning George tramped back to the pit with a heavy heart to supervise the dismantling of the fire wall and the gruesome task of recovering any bodies that lay beyond. He told his family nothing about this when he came back, simply sat on the fireside stool looking into the embers after they'd had their tea, the work on the sundial neglected. Nicholas Wood, the colliery viewer, must have had some inkling of his low spirits for he came to visit, and and the two of them sat together at the hearth. Mr Wood patiently worked on George as though trying to coax a flame from smouldering ashes, and he had some success at last. Robert and his aunt learned from the men's sombre conversation that there had been five deaths in all - a toll far less than there might have been but for prompt intervention – but Robert knew enough about his father to be sure that those five were a starker fact than the lives he'd saved. His old adversary Dick McCree was among the dead.

'I'm truly sorry for the loss of him,' said Wood, 'but McCree of all people should have known not to use a candle by that seam.'

'It's a heavy price to pay for winning coal.'

'There's always been blood spilt on the black, Geordie. And there always will be - that's the risk of it.'

From his place at the table Robert studied his father. His eyes had never strayed from the fire, had seemed as opaque as ever Robert could remember, but as he watched, some light reflected there. His brain was at work again.

'Surely summat can be done to guard against the gas - tame it, trap it, neuter somehow the explosive divil in the stuff.'

'If you can find a way, George, the owners will reward you,' said Wood. 'There's two-thirds of the field can't be worked for fear o the firedamp. Suppose they could open up half...'

George stopped him with a look; almost spat. 'Fig for the owners. If there's one less widow in the village on account of anything I can engineer, that's reward enough.'

*

Filled with the sense of a new mission that rivalled even his locomotive project in importance, George set aside for the time being the plans he and Robert had made for a sundial, and their kitchen table became a work bench for the task of designing some form of lamp that could be used safely down the mine. Robert was delegated to begin the research. Many an evening after school Sancho might be found secured to the palisade outside the Assembly Rooms while Robert was inside, studying at his father's behest all that Mr Turner could help him find about gases, sparks and explosions. The son was less ardent in his passion for conceiving the perfect safety lamp, but he found plenty to interest him along the way. When he read in the *Edinburgh Encyclopaedia* of Benjamin Franklin's famous experiment with lightning, it set him off on a secret mission of his own - to see if he could replicate it.

Robert conspired with his friend John Tate, now fully recovered from his ordeal in the pit, and they prepared carefully for the day the weather would give them their opportunity. Together they built a serviceable kite. In a lean-to behind his home John hid the quarter-mile of copper wiring that Robert had bought with Albany Hancock one lunchtime at a brazier's shop in Newcastle. Robert took charge of the silk cord they needed for insulation, and procured, from a battered chest of knick-knacks among his grandfather's possessions, a key so large it might have once opened the door to a cathedral.

'There's thunder coming,' Auntie Nell warned one Saturday, hauling in the rug she had been beating out of doors. 'You can feel the change in the air.' Robert needed no further encouragement. He quickly climbed the ladder to his snug closet and took the silk cord and key from his box under the bed. He stuffed them inside his shirt and ran out to fetch John Tate, almost colliding with Mr Wood at the garden wicket.

'Sorry, sir,' he called over his shoulder. 'There's thunder coming.'

'Aye, very like.'

'And you should take a coat, if you're going out,' Nelly shouted after her nephew, who was already too far along the lane to mind. 'Oh, morning, Mr Wood.' She blushed slightly at his having heard her raise her voice. 'If you are looking for George, he's with our brother Jemmy yonder, working on the *Blücher*.'

80

When Wood scrambled down the slight slope to the wagon way he found George peering along the tracks, with neither the engine nor James in sight. George had a Graham chronograph in one hand, by which Wood divined that the trial he had come for was already in progress. As he reached George's shoulder he heard the *Blücher* for the first time, and was consequently surprised when she very soon appeared round the far curve of the wagon way.

'You were right, George. She does seem a tad quieter now.'

'That's the effect of turning in the blast pipe. What it does to the speed, but.' As the front of the locomotive reached the first of the marker poles George started the chronograph, then placed it behind his back, as if he were a child concealing a scrumped apple. They watched the iron monster's approach. Her chimney, like an elongated cannon firing at the heavens, belched out a dark mixture of steam and smoke. Her driver was entirely hidden behind the huge boiler and its metal forest of apparatus until the *Blücher* came alongside the watchers, when James gave them a brief and unsteady wave from his position on the footplate, his other hand gripped tight on the driver's bar. George, unable to make himself heard while the train was passing, tugged at Wood's arm and pointed out the new cylinder rods connecting to the wheels. The *Blücher* chugged by. When she reached the second marker pole, George applied himself once more to the chronograph, then set off briskly along the tracks after the slowing engine.

'Well?' asked Wood, impatiently, trying to keep pace with George as he walked.

George looked down at the timepiece, made a mental calculation, lifted the dial to exhibit proof and announced, 'Just short o nine miles an hour. Unladen, like, but she licks the horse-drawn chaldron at any event. When I turned the exhaust into the chimney it was in my mind to deaden the noise, and it does somewhat, but now the beast draws wonderful - and we'll make her quicker yet.'

'Is that the end of the expense? Ravensworth wants to know when we can expect a return.'

'You can tell his lordship the cost is all under foot now.'

'What does that mean?'

By way of reply, George pointed down to the wooden tramway. Every few yards the wood was splintered and broken from the heavy impact of the locomotive. 'The weight, see. That's largely what defeated Trevithick. I'm working with William Losh on the remedy.'

'Iron rails?'

'Cast iron. The whole wagon way ull need re-laying.'

Wood stopped and sighed. He raised his head to gaze out over the meadow where young Robert Stephenson could be seen carrying a kite clear of the wind-swept grass, a friend in tow with a burden on his shoulder. As he watched, Wood heard a deep rumbling from a distance, and he instinctively switched his attention back along the track, half-expecting to see *Blücher* falling apart.

'It's just a thunder brattle,' George laughed, noticing Wood's alarm.

The pair resumed their walk. 'We should build a big shed for this work,' said the viewer.

'A spot o rain's no bother,' said George, misunderstanding.

'No, I mean away from prying eyes. Here's an odd thing happened. You mind the fellow Dan, got smoke-sick off the firedamp blast?'

'Toxicated, aye, I mind him. Is the poor chap surviving?'

'Doing well, I've no doubt, since he got the best medical treatment money can buy.'

'A face-worker? How's he paying that sort o bill?'

'He's not. According to the crack, Sir James Lowther is.'

'Sir James... Who's he?'

'Owns all the mines round Whitehaven,' said Nicholas Wood. 'If you've not heard his name, you'll likely not know of his engineer, neither. Has some claim to be an inventor of sorts. Name of Carlisle Spedding.'

'Never heard of him.'

'You know him by the name of Dan.'

'Dan? No, I don't think...' George suddenly caught the drift and stopped, touching Wood's sleeve. 'You mean the same Dan?'

'I do. It seems Lowther had Spedding sent over here, guise of an ordinary pitman, to spy out what we're doing. Your reputation goes before thee, George.'

George laughed aloud. 'Perhaps we should tell our rivals all our secrets,' he said.

'Why so?'

'Let em have the expense of them.'

While George and his colleague talked together by the wagon way, Robert knelt with John Tate in the meadow, tying one end of the copper wire to the kite and the other to the key. As they worked the thunder rolled again above them.

'We mun hurry,' Robert said. 'If there is to be lightning, it will come soon.'

82

'What is the silk for?'

'To protect us from the electric, or we'll be struck dead.' He freed one end of the silk cord and threaded it through the handle of the key as he had with the cable, tying it securely. 'You take the kite,' he said, and the two boys jumped up and ran in opposite directions. John held up the muslin kite and Robert played out the line, first of copper then of silk. The wind obligingly whipped up, coursing along the tall grass and into the folds of the kite, almost lifting John up with his craft as he waited until the last moment to let go.

Robert watched his line quiver. It came at first like a snake slithering quickly towards him in the grass, then up and tugging to get away as he wrapped his hands tightly around the silk. He leaned back into the wind and craned his neck to see the kite lift impressively under the clouds. John came running back across the field, his eyes also on the kite. There was a flash in the distant sky and, a few seconds later, a roll of thunder like heavy cannon on the move. 'Did you see it?' Robert shouted in great excitement to his friend. 'Lightning's coming.'

He walked backwards through the grass, playing out more line to raise the kite higher, then had to loop his hands round the silk; it was a fight to keep hold. As he watched the sky, there was a moment's louring stillness, then a sigh of rain. The first drops fell onto his upturned face, his eyes, his mouth, and the lightning flashed again, closer this time. 'Come on,' he urged, under his breath. As if summoned, the storm crackled above. The line shuddered in his hands as the copper was struck, and a vivid orange spark leapt from the key.

'Hooray!' from both boys. 'God's finger!' Robert shouted.

Now he was sure his experiment had succeeded, he grew more confident with the kite, swooping it lower and higher again. In the next field from the meadow, some of Farmer Wigham's cows were on the move from the storm. Robert deliberately steered the kite to follow them. As the string dipped another flash of lightning struck the copper conductor and a spark spat from the key towards the tail of the hindmost cow, making it scamper and low with fright. The boys turned to each other, cackling, complicit. Robert blinked the rain away and scanned the field for another target.

'Your dad's horse,' urged John beside him. Robert wheeled around on the string to where Bobby was standing, morose in the wet meadow.

'Poor Bobby,' but the childish imp in him defied his better feeling. He swung the kite across towards the horse, and now caught a glimpse of his father leaping the fence away to his right. Shirt billowing;

83

weather aiming to beat him back. George was calling, but Robert could not hear him above the wind and the rain. He guessed, though, it would be a warning to leave the horse alone. Shame about his intentions overtook him. He manoeuvred the kite away from the animal just as another crack of lightning struck the wire and set off the most terrific bolt of electricity. Bobby whinnied and galloped off to find a safer part of the meadow. George was gaining on the boys. At last he was near enough for Robert to hear what he was calling.

'Let go of the string! Let it go now!'

The urgency in his tone alarmed and confused Robert. He started to haul in the kite, but stopped, realising; he dare not touch the copper wire in the lightning storm. He tried to rid himself of the silk cord, but he had wrapped it so tight around his wrists and hands he could not easily free it. The silk was wet with the rain now, making it more difficult to slip off. Only now he saw, as his father had already, the danger of the wet silk. He renewed his efforts to free himself, but panic merely worsened his plight. The silk scored a groove in his wrists. He turned to his father in appeal as thunder clapped over the colliery spoil heap. George ran towards him like a savage, drawing a knife from his belt. He grabbed the cord above the boy's wrists and slashed at it with his knife, freeing it in a moment. The kite lifted, trailing its line behind as George clung to Robert in the field. Together they witnessed a violent crack of lightning whip the copper cable into a tree, scarring a large branch with electric force. The key snagged among the smaller branches, and a great struggle ensued between wind and tree for possession of the kite. It ended with a mighty tug that snapped the cable, releasing the kite to follow the thunder storm over the black hill and away.

Wary of a skelping, John Tate slipped off home while there were no eyes on him, leaving the Stephensons in the meadow. They held onto each other, the boy's arms encircling his father's waist, legs caught between knees as if to prevent him being plucked from the earth by some elemental force. Robert clinging tight, felt another force; his father's fury within.

George's mood calmed with the going of the storm, and when he spoke again it was more in disappointment than in anger at his son.

'A little learning's a dangerous thing, they say. Did you not consider the wet?'

'I remember now, Franklin took shelter in a shed and flew his kite from there.'

'You could have been pole-axed for want of attention.' He held the boy at arm's length, pinioning him as he delivered his lecture. It ended

84

with, 'Learn from this, and be sure to prepare your experiments more carefully in future. And don't go scarin my horse or you'll feel the sting of my strap on your backside.'

Robert had an opportunity just a fortnight later, should he have wanted it, to cast up his father's words, after George caused an explosion that could have wrecked the cottage; but the boy managed to hold his tongue despite the embarrassment he felt as a consequence around his new associates at the Lit and Phil. It happened when they got to the practical stage of their investigations into the properties of firedamp, as George continued his search for a method of protecting the underground workers.

'We mun test it, but how to control the risk...' George was saying while they sat at home and contemplated a prototype lamp he had made, incorporating tiny holes in a shield around the wick. 'What's called for is some kind of receiver with a tube to introduce the gas by degrees to the flame.'

Robert spoke up, perhaps a trifle too readily. 'Oh, the Society has plenty of apparatus. Glass retorts and jars, all kinds of pipes.'

This information excited his father. 'Do you think you might borrow it?'

'Oh, well I'm not sure,' said Robert, the doubts creeping in, and with them the wish he had not opened his mouth. 'It's all kept in cases.'

'A deal of use such gear is, locked away in cases. Ask if you might lend it, and if they should kick up just remind em of the sum paid for your membership.'

That proved unnecessary as Robert found Mr Turner cheerfully cooperative over the matter, eager to support a scientific endeavour, and on Friday evening the boy was able to lay out half the utensils from the Lit and Phil's laboratory collection onto the Stephenson kitchen table, ready for employment in the trial of the prototype. His father and Mr Wood had brought a pair of pigs' bladders full of gas collected from the mine. Aunt Nelly took fright at these and retired hurriedly to her own room at the back of the cottage while the men were transferring the contents into a large collecting jar. 'You're a madman, Geordie Stephenson,' she said as she left. 'You'll have the roof blown off.'

George had devised a complex regulating system, involving tubes and water, by which the poisonous mixture could be introduced in safe measures to the lighted lamp. Nicholas Wood was controlling the tap. Robert's job was to check the velocity of the flow by means of a pendulum clock. George was watching the flame.

'If I see the flame go down this tube, I'll call for more water,' he told Wood. 'We must keep the current steady.'

Wood nodded his agreement, but he was far from clear in his own mind exactly what George had in his. He looked at young Robert, who seemed assured enough in his role, so Wood shrugged off his own uncertainty and bent to his task. They started the experiment, and for a few moments all went well as the lamp burned steadily and safely. Suddenly the flame dropped low in the tube.

'More water,' called George. Wood, taken by surprise, turned the cock the wrong way, accidentally shutting off the flow. The flame sank right down the tube. 'Ware gas!' yelled George, just before the flame touched off the explosive mixture. Glass burst in all directions. It showered the room and the backs of all three as they dived to the floor. In a moment George was up on his feet again to grab a tablecloth and smother the fire set off in the wake of the blast. Nelly came dashing in from the back of the house.

'God in heaven! Who's hurt?'

'Nobody, I believe,' said her brother. 'Everyone sound? Take care for broken glass.'

'What did I tell you? I said this would happen.'

'Get away, woman,' said George, as he helped Robert to his feet. 'The roof's still on, aint it?'

Robert sustained a bruise on an elbow from his dive under the table, but it was more his sensibility that suffered when he could take back only half the equipment to the Society library, and had to explain what had happened to the glassware. Mr Turner was with another member at the time and, having heard Robert's account, far from being angry, they considered it a good enough joke to require grabbing on to each other as they laughed aloud, eliciting tuts among several in the reading room. To Robert's emerging sensitivity there was some poking of fun in Mr Turner's response, but when he offered the money he'd been given to pay for the damage the librarian refused it, saying, 'No, put it away, Master Robert. Only be sure to ask your father to promise he will perform a practical demonstration for our members when his lamp is ready.'

'On condition he doesn't blow us all up!' said the other gentleman, stifling more laughter in his handkerchief.

The whole episode put Robert in a quandary of emotions that kept him awake that night. He was discomposed and vaguely resentful, but whether the fault was these men from the Lit and Phil or a father whose actions had made them both look foolish, he could not settle upon. Behind his hurt feelings, he nurtured a certain sense of pride that the Society had held out the offer of a public demonstration once the work was done, but worried that, should it ever be taken up, it might turn into another comic interlude at the Stephensons' expense. Brooding on these thoughts, he came to realise that his greatest concern was that he was having such concerns. He had never been troubled in this way before.

George continued his experimentation without further mishap at home. As was his usual practice with inventing, he built three versions of the lamp, each improving on the earlier one, until he was satisfied that he had solved the problem. Mr Wood maintained his interest at a safer distance. Nelly would stow domestic items away in cupboards as soon as anything suspiciously scientific appeared on the table. Robert continued apprentice and secretary to the endeavour.

By autumn they were ready for the ultimate test. George and Robert waited with some impatience at the cottage one November evening for the tinsmith to deliver a base with air-holes that would keep the lamp from extinguishing altogether in presence of the foul gases. When it arrived they completed the assembly, filled the lamp with oil and trimmed it ready for use. The new metal glinted in the candlelight. Erect on the board between them, the lamp looked like an award for its own invention. Not beautiful, nor particularly elegant; yet consummate.

'Look sharp, Bobby,' said his father after a moment of silence. 'Fetch Nichol and meet us at the pit head.'

Robert's excitement mingled with trepidation. For the first time, his father was to allow him to travel underground with the men to witness the trial of the lamp. Mr Wood's house lay about a mile away in Benton, and the boy hurried to make the ground as quickly as possible.

He hesitated at the outer wall of the churchyard. By day this was his normal shortcut, and it would save two or three minutes to take it now. He should have no need of a light, surely knowing the route through well enough; but his nervousness increased as he picked his way among the graves in the gathering darkness. He thought, as he was wont to when his brain was feverishly active as tonight, about his mother lying in the cold earth. Once, when he and Johnny Tate were still at Rutters' school, they had made themselves late searching in vain for her tombstone. Thinking about her now, far from offering distraction, made him more conscious than ever of mortality; and of trespassing on hallowed ground, walking on old bones, perhaps disturbing and tormenting souls...

All at once he stopped. Before and to the left of him there was a soft light about the level of the tombstones. He waited, heart pounding, for the light to move - perhaps some pedestrian on the opposite journey to himself - but it stayed steady, reflecting from a white marble slab, as if someone had stopped to read the inscription there in the remotest part of the graveyard.

The light was still, but surely something was moving near the ground below the slab. Robert peered, trying to part the darkness, and distinctly saw a pale arm reach across into the beam, and out again. The shadow of a head and shoulders, bowing over the stone. The boy started with fright, and fell backwards across a low grave rail. He scrambled up, started to run as fast as he could from the apparition. As he reached the churchyard wall he could hear a rhythmic noise behind, which he took for the husky panting of a hellhound at his heels. In panic he threw himself at the wall, skinned a wrist on the dry stone as he clambered over and tumbled into a pile of dead leaves on the other side.

He felt along the rough wall as he made the circuit of the churchyard, dipping low to hide himself from anyone or anything within. Stalking the boundary thus, his mind raced, interpreting what he had witnessed; and so became convinced that he had been given a premonition of his father's death. The notion gripped. It was all very well experimenting with pigs' bladders full of firedamp gas and laughing it off when one exploded; risking oneself in a poisoned mineshaft was of an altogether different magnitude. The lamp Robert had seen in the graveyard must represent his father's invention, and George was to perish testing it tonight. Robert had been sent from somewhere a vision of his dead father reading the inscription on his own tombstone in the light of his cursed lamp. Here was a warning.

The boy soon came upon a break in the wall where a fretworked gate led back into the churchyard. He stopped and fractionally raised his head to check that nothing was waiting to pounce as he passed the gate. Nothing untoward. Emboldened, he dared to sneak a look back across the graveyard. The ghostly light was still shining where it was before. From his new viewpoint he could see that it was indeed a lamp, though an ordinary one, resting on top of the marble tombstone. As he watched, to Robert's horror, a figure of just his father's build emerged from the sacred ground below, indeed from under the ground. The waff reached down to retrieve something from the yawning grave. It gleamed in the light of the lanthorn... and only then Robert recognized it as a spade. The grave-digger was working late in the lamplight, no doubt for a funeral on the morrow. Robert pressed his hands against the chill stones of the wall, then cooled his face with open palms, collecting his thoughts; reinterpreted the grating noise he had heard as the regular sound of the workman's digging. His presentiment proved false, the boy ran easier the rest of the way to Mr Wood's house.

An hour later the two of them, along with Moodie the under-viewer, were accompanying George with his lamp to the foulest of the underground galleries in Killingworth Pit. For Robert this was a journey almost as frightening as the one through the churchyard. The fact of deaths in this pit would keep entering his mind. Not that he now seriously expected to encounter ghosts in the darkness, more that he was afraid of breaking his neck in a fall or cracking his head against the roof; his father set such a pace that even the two experienced men were stumbling to keep up with him. Robert felt as his poor blind grandpa must in unfamiliar surroundings, needing someone to lead him by the hand. As that would never do in face of his father's boldness, he tried to concentrate on following the faint glimmer of the lamp in front, the occasional spark from the men's boots on the roadway, and the noise of their walking.

George was disappointed by the present accumulation of gas in the so-called poisonous gallery, though it could clearly be heard hissing through a blower above their heads, and he instructed Moodie to have some deal boards erected around the area of issue so that it might collect in sufficient quantity for the test. As they waited for the construction to be completed, they sat more or less silently in a rolley-way, their backs against the wall, the damp slowly seeping through their breeches. By pit standards this was a generous passage - high and wide enough to allow a pony through - but Robert felt closed in almost to the point of suffocation. Keeping up with the men had left him breathless, and here he could not find the air he needed to recover properly. He had a strong impression of the weight pressing down on the roof from above, tons of earth that could crush them all in a moment. He thought of the cowed trappers he had seen along the way - boys like John that he knew from the village, others younger and smaller than himself, crouched in the tiny space between the wall and the door they were charged to open and close for ventilation, fortunate if the movement of air did not extinguish the feeble candle they held between their knees - and for his own part he sensed how a soldier must feel who has heard the whistle of a musket-ball as it missed his temple. But for happenstance, Robert could so easily have been sitting like a wraith by one of those doors, or sifting stones from coal as his father had done when he was even younger than himself, much younger.

Robert's fears for the safety of the party heightened when Moodie came back to report that the work was done, and that the foul air had already built up so much in the enclosure almost to guarantee an explosion if a flame was brought to it. 'I trust my nose on this,' he said. 'It's my duty to warn you there's mortal danger if you make the attempt.'

'There'd be no point otherwise,' said George. 'We canna claim a lamp be safe in theory.'

He was not prepared to let Robert near the place, however, and after some discussion it was resolved that Wood and Moodie should stay with the boy at a distance while George made the first trial. Robert noted how his hand was squeezed as George left them; surmised that his father may not feel quite so confident as he made out to be. He watched the dim flame disappear into the recesses of the mine, and breathed but shallowly if at all while he faced the blackness and waited.

Deprived of objects to focus on, his eyes seemed sightless. He closed the lids slowly over and opened them again, finding no difference. He pressed his back against the damp wall, seeking reassurance in its definite solidity. He thought again of his former playmates, the child miners. It was not luck, after all, that had kept him out of this dank place, but his father's enterprise. And what if he was to perish now, testing his lamp? What would the future hold for Robert? The boy shivered, drawing his knees to his chin. It was all he could do, when anxiety took hold, to prevent himself leaning for comfort against the shoulder of Mr Wood next to him; but he did resist, with an effort to straighten up that brought his body unnaturally erect, and tense as a bow-string as he waited for the returning light.

When it came, it did not penetrate, but emerged like a ghost, emaciated. It was dimmer than the lamp in the graveyard, and less steady. Robert was pricked again by presentiment: here was death's tidings, brought painfully to him. Slowly a figure resolved itself behind the light, forming from shadows.

It was not death, or its herald, but his father. His corporeal self, alive and vital. When George got near enough to the group, Robert could make out a face more radiant than his invention.

'It works. It truly does.' He looked messianic, and chose words to match. 'Come, you can all be witness to it, and have no fear.'

They followed him obediently to the enclosed spot, where the rank air was now thick enough to be tasted. George turned to address his acolytes, stepped back to make the circle and illuminate their faces with his lamp. 'What was it you said, Moodie? *There's mortal danger here.* Look.' He raised the lamp to the fissure where the gas was escaping, to within a few inches of the blower. There was no explosion, and no flicker from the flame inside the glass.

'Nothing braver than this flame,' said George, as if he had been challenged on the question. 'It stands erect against its enemy, like David against Goliath, and says *Fie to you*.'

'*Fie to you. Fie to you*,' his son whispered like his echo off the walls.

Mr Turner pressed his claim on George to perform a demonstration of the new lamp at a meeting of the Literary and Philosophical Society. Robert travelled there with his father and Nicholas Wood in Mr Brandling's barouche. The cargo also included several gas-filled bladders for the purpose of the demonstration, creating a certain unspoken apprehension within the boy of a repeat of the incident at the cottage, though on a much grander scale. It was one thing to destroy the Society's laboratory instruments, another altogether to blow a hole in the Assembly Rooms' ornate ceiling.

Not having been tested before an educated public, when George heard that almost one hundred members had turned up and the meeting moved to the tea-room in search of more space, his characteristic confidence deserted him.

'Here, Nichol, you'd best take the speaking part. I'll handle the lamp at the practical and come to your aid if there's questions. You're better dealing with these type o gentry.'

'Well, if you're sure...' said Wood, hardly less nervous.

Robert stationed himself at the back of the room, partly hidden behind one of the fluted pillars. Nicholas Wood opened the proceedings. The boy's eyes would keep straying to his father, standing at the side and just within sight of the audience. This was not mere filial attention – half of the people in the room seemed distracted by George's antics. Whenever Mr Wood faltered in his explanation, which was often, his partner would gurn and grimace, sometimes rocking on his heels with impatience. Robert felt a light touch on his arm, and was surprised to find Elizabeth Hindmarsh standing close behind him, smiling. He had only seen one or two other ladies among the large audience.

'What are you doing at the back?' she whispered. 'Shouldn't you be with your father?'

'I feel more comfortable here. Tell you the truth...' he added, only half-joking, 'I'm afeard they might blow a hole in that magnificent ceiling. Do you want to risk a closer view? There's a few chairs still, near the front.'

'Oh, no, no. I'm better back here too.' She rose onto her toes. 'Why is your father not making the presentation himself?'

'I think his nerve failed him at the last. He won't long rein himself in, though. Mr Wood's making too many mistakes. See how agitated Dad's getting.'

At first George limited himself to interjections from the wings, but a specific error from Wood brought him from the shadows. 'No, that's not right, Nichol.' He ventured forward and addressed the audience directly. 'Why, gentlemen, there's more holes in that explanation than there is in my lamp.'

Encouraged by warm laughter, he continued. 'Sorry, Nichol. Yours is a canny speech in parts, but it's plain wrong to say the metal's shielding the flame from the gas. Gents, forgive the roughness of my ways, for I'm nowt but a practical man. Nichol, why don't we show exactly how the lamp works by means of a demonstration? Would you bring the bladders from the poke? See, we've brung some samples o the foul air collected today from near an unworked seam at Killingworth. This is the most dangerous and explosive gas you will find anywhere in England...'

There was a thrill of expectation in the room. Robert felt the delicate touch of Betty's fingers on his shoulder as she craned forward to witness this crucial stage of the demonstration. He was glad of it. He turned his face to hers, whispered from the corner of his mouth, 'I only wish Dad hadn't placed his lamp so *very* directly under that great glass chandelier,' and was rewarded with a sparkle of amusement in her eyes; affection, too. He felt his heart grow.

George primed the oil in his lamp while his partner waited to cut the lace and free the gas. Nervous instinct took the boy nearer to the pillar, hugging it; his cheekbone rolled across its ridges. 'Release!' called George dramatically, enjoying his role as showman now. Robert closed his eyes as Wood's knife cut through the lace. All went silent, then, an explosion, not of gas but of spontaneous applause from the audience, heralding the success of the demonstration. One or two even cheered. Robert opened his eyes to see his father beaming with triumph, Wood supernumerary beside him until George seemed to recognize him belatedly with a tug on the arm, whereupon his colleague stepped forward to share a little of the general approbation, making a brief formal bow in gratitude.

At the end of the meeting, taking tea, George was surrounded by members eager to offer their individual congratulations, or enquire about some point of detail. He was in full flow now, chatting informally and knowledgeably, though, for the first time, Robert became conscious of how coarse his father's Northumbrian tones seemed in contrast to the more modulated delivery of the questioners he was dealing with. The younger Stephenson could not help but wonder whether that was how he himself sounded to his schoolmates at Percy Street, some of whose fathers were among the gathering.

Robert looked around for Miss Hindmarsh, but she must have departed promptly. Others seemed in no hurry to go. More than half an hour after the talk, Mr Brandling had to break through quite a crowd to collect his passenger and tell him, 'George, Dr Burnet has just been telling me of a committee convened by The Royal Society that might have an interest in this matter.'

'In my lamp?'

'I would say so. Their subject is the prevention of explosions in mines. They have Sir Humphry Davy looking into the science of it.'

'He can look into the science to his heart's content. If they want the answer, tell em to come to Geordie Stephenson.'

'Perhaps we should send you down to London.'

'Why shouldn't they come up and see me?' said George, puffed up by the success of the evening. 'I'm as busy as them, I'll warrant. Besides, how many pits is there in London? They mun come to Killingworth - I've plenty for such as them to wonder at.'

*

No word came from The Royal Society or its committee of coal owners, though the Geordie lamp went into production and came into general use locally, not long after a pit boy holding a low candle had been killed by an explosion in the very gallery where the lamp had been tested. George had, as he'd told Charles Brandling, little time for securing national attention for his device. He was occupied by the work on his engines, shared a patent for cast iron rails with William Losh and, in his leisure hours, returned to the making of the sundial. He and Robert carefully chose the stone, hewed, carved and polished it themselves and, when their sundial was finished, cemented it above their front door as an interesting architectural feature. Robert was watching his father chisel the date in the stone for posterity one fine afternoon in August as Kit Heppel walked home from the fore-shift.

'How, Geordie. Another new scheme?'

'One we've come back to, Kit. It was left off a while.'

'What is it, like?'

'It's a sundial,' said Robert. 'You can tell the time by it.'

'Oh, I've seen sundials,' Kit said, feeling his whiskers, 'but never an uppy-downy one like that. An not one set in a building neither.'

'Which has a new name the boy's come up with.'

Robert rehearsed it. 'Dial Cottage.'

'Very good,' said Kit. 'There's a mania for naming things these days, eh? Like your lamp - you'll uv heard what the lads call it, the Geordie Lamp. What it is to be famous. Still no word from those chaps down London?'

'About the lamp?' George climbed off the ladder. 'Why, no. What does that signify? It's doing the job it was meant to, and the pits round here are safer for it.'

'Aye, sterling job. This new sundial o yours, though, George,' said Kit. 'I've got one quarrel with it.'

'Oh, what is it?'

'When my shift's done, and I pass by here, I'll be able to tell exactly how many hours of sunshine I missed down than stinkin hole.'

George laughed, his large hand offered to his friend in acknowledgement of the comment. 'I'm truly sorry for that, Kit, I am.'

It was Robert who first learned that his father had a rival for the title, inventor of the miner's safety lamp. He was bringing an armful of books back to the Lit and Phil library when Mr Turner caught sight of him from his desk and called out in some excitement, 'Remarkable thing, Master Robert. Sir Humphry Davy has a lamp the very twin of your pater's.'

'Excuse me?'

'I saw it with my own eyes, last night. And the great man himself. Do you know one of our members, the Reverend John Hodgson?'

'His son goes to my school.'

'A man very well connected with the scientific establishment. Not only personally acquainted with Sir Humphry, but able to persuade him, at no expense to the Society, to demonstrate his new lamp to certain favoured individuals among us. I wonder your father was not invited... Oh, but of course he is not himself a member.'

'You say Mr... Sir... Davy's lamp was the same?'

'Sir Humphry's, yes, to all practical purposes. Some minor differences in appearance as far as I recall your father's version. Essentially the same in principle and design. Sir Humphry was very impressive. Look, I have his name recorded in his own hand in our visitors' book.'

Robert did not stay to marvel at the precious autograph; returned instead to Sancho and as quickly as possible home to give his father the news. George was momentarily nonplussed, but comforted himself with the knowledge that he was at least three months ahead of the most vaunted scientist of his day. 'He should have come and see us,' he said, 'stead of wasting his time down south. He's like the cow's tail.'

George's sanguinity over the matter lasted only until Charles Brandling arrived at Dial Cottage to pass on what he'd been told, that the country's colliery owners had awarded Davy the sum of two thousand pounds *for his invention of the safety lamp.*

'Invention!' George roared out the word like a furnace opening. 'Imitation, more like. Nichol Wood warned me about spies. Robert, you tell Squire Brandling how long ago I made the first of my lamps.'

'You do not need to convince me, George. But, now I think of it, a full statement of the facts would not go amiss. I could use it to present your case in the appropriate quarters, ensure you get your proper reward.'

'Due credit means more than reward to me, Mr Brandling. I've had nowt in the way of education, but in the workings of things, in all matters mechanical, I'll bow to no man, and I don't care how many letters he might have after his name, or titles in front of it.'

'I agree with you heartily, George. I'll do my utmost to ensure you get the acknowledgment you deserve. Should you but furnish me with the facts I will go into battle on your behalf.'

Putting pen to paper was not one of George's undoubted strengths, but with the help of his son a draft was written over a couple of evenings. George's manner of authorship was to pace about the room, both hands in play giving even more physical emphasis to the words that poured out of him while Robert's pen flew between inkwell and sheet, the writer frowning with concentration as he attempted to channel the torrent into orderly paraphrase. For Nelly it involved much dodging out of her brother's way as she tried to go about her usual household business or occasionally rescue an ornament from wayward limbs. When the report was completed to their satisfaction, father and son dressed in their Sunday best and set off to deliver it personally to Mr Brandling.

This was the first time Robert had actually entered the main building of Gosforth Hall, having only visited the grounds (and, of course, the stables) previously. If he had been bemused as a small boy on seeing Elizabeth Hindmarsh's front door answered by a servant, his awe reached a higher plane as a thirteen-year-old when the heavy portal at Gosforth Hall swung open to reveal a footman in full livery and powdered wig waiting attendance on them. They were shown into the library - another revelation for Robert - where Mr Brandling took the document from George and read it carefully while the Stephensons, resisting all invitations to make themselves comfortable, stood side by side in silence on the hearth rug, the backs of their legs gradually roasting from the generous heat of the fire.

'No, George, this will not do, you know,' Mr Brandling said at last.

'It's all true, sir,' George started to protest.

'That may be, but it's badly written.'

George glanced at Robert, who blushed his culpability as scribe. Perhaps Mr Brandling saw this, for he followed up with, 'Oh, not poorly set down, you know, but lacking some force in the argument. Leave it with me; let's see if I cannot work it up a little. That's what it needs, working up, you see.'

Charles Brandling not only worked up Robert's notes into a document to influence the coal owners; he also used them as a basis for a long letter that he submitted to some of the newspapers. When Albany Hancock told his friend he had seen George's name in the *Newcastle Courant*, mentioned alongside Sir Humphry Davy's, Robert felt a flush of pride on behalf of his father. The first hint that this publicity might not lead to universal approbation - on the contrary, would escalate into an almighty row - came from Richard Hodgson in the courtyard outside school. Instead of addressing Robert directly, Hodgson called out, 'Hey, young Hancock, you know plenty of long words, don't you? Can you tell me what a plagiarist is?'

'A plagiarist? That's a sort of imitator. Someone who copies another's ideas and takes credit for them.'

'I thought it must be something of the kind from what my father was saying this morning.'

Thomas Buddle joined in, with mock innocence. 'Oh, who was he talking about, Dick?'

'Now then, what was the name? Not a memorable one, certainly. Damned if I can bring it to mind. Some oaf who has been setting himself up against one of Father's friends, Sir Humphry Davy. You'll have heard of *him*, Hancock, being of a scientific bent yourself.'

'He's a chemist,' said Albany.

'A very great and famous one. Can you imagine: this low fellow - name starts with S if I'm not mistaken - this ignoramus, has gotten hold of a plan for one of Sir Humphry's inventions, cobbled up a copy, and claimed it for his own.'

'The very sauce!' Buddle chimed along.

For the second time in his school career, Robert was hugely tempted to throw himself upon Thomas Buddle, and for the second time (with even greater difficulty) he resisted the temptation, knowing that was precisely the response they were hoping to provoke, so that they might pin the label of ill-bred primitive on him with just cause. Instead he aimed to win the argument with all the eloquence he could muster.

'I am aware that you speak of my father, Hodgson, and let me tell you this. First, this ignoramus as you call him has made Killingworth the model for all collieries around. Including Wallsend, Master Buddle, which I understand to be your uncle's domain. What's more, I have been witness to my father's experiments these many months and can give my bible oath that his wonderful lamp was made without the benefit or knowledge of Sir Humphry's... theorising. Indeed, while Davy still had his nose in his books, Stephenson had the answer in his hand.'

'I know why your pater does not lose himself in books,' said Hodgson, 'for I've heard that he struggles to read and write at all. Doesn't he have to get Squire Brandling to fire his arrows for him, or quills, I should say?'

'The Stephensons can fight their own battles.' Robert's anger began to get the better of him. 'Aye, and win em too.'

'Come away, Rob,' said Albany, touching his arm. 'Let the evidence speak for itself.'

'Do you trust the pen to be mightier than the sword, Hancock?' from Hodgson.

'Yes, I do.'

'What about you, donkey boy?'

Robert could not answer without acknowledging the appellation, so he just glared.

'Struck dumb, like your mangy creature? Well, let me advise thee, my father is even now setting down the true facts for a riposte in the papers. Truth will out, depend on it.'

'I do,' Robert said at last.

The Reverend Hodgson did take the fight to the *Newcastle Courant* and laid a few low blows, saying of George's experiments on hydrogen gas, *How came it he never found out any other of its properties than that of its power of exploding, before he was told of Sir H.D.'s discoveries?* Buddle's uncle John also appeared in print, extolling the qualities of the Davy lamp, and hotly denying a rumour that he was responsible for conveying Stephenson's secrets to the Royal Society notable. The weight of local opinion was, however, on George's side. He and Robert often amused themselves, reading aloud satirical pieces penned by advocates who seemed to emerge from the ether to join in the spat, calling themselves such names as Aladdin, A Friend, or Fair Play. Robert saw how his father (so prism-like in his character) at once enjoyed this attention and waxed increasingly angry with his detractors. George was thirsty for some more formal recognition of his work, if only to silence the critics. When Mr Brandling told him he had news from the body that had rewarded Davy, George was eager to learn what they'd had to say, and crushed when he heard it.

'One hundred pound? For a... what did they call it?'

'A good effort.'

'A good effort. What am I, one of their charity school boys turned out surprising well? Here's a pat on the head, they say, now off you trot, back to your dark little corner. In other words, *Stephenson, hadaway to hell.*'

'I do feel I've let you down, George. I could have represented you better...'

'Whish, never worry about that, Squire, you couldn't make a better on it. They'll allus see the sow's ear.'

'But I do worry, George,' insisted Brandling, 'and I have an idea that I have discussed with Lord Strathmore and others. We northerners must stick together against the London Whigs. I propose to place an advertisement to commence a public subscription and announce a tribunal that will examine the matter from top to bottom. Dates, details, witnesses. We will put Sir Humphry and his party in their place once and for all.'

George was immensely flattered by what he called his *highfalutin* support and, as the subscription became generally known, he was especially delighted to see one name appear among others on the burgeoning list. Farmer Thomas Hindmarsh. He showed the paper to his sister.

'May be he's changed his old opinion of me, Nell.'

'May be it's time you called upon his daughter once again,' Nell returned. 'High time.'

*

Some months later Elizabeth Hindmarsh was arranging a fresh vase of flowers for the table when Kate knocked and lingered in the doorway, looking uncertainly at a card pinched between her thumb and forefinger.

'What is it, Kate?'

The servant girl remained hesitant, unused to the convention. 'There's a man... gentleman - I'm not sure - enquiring after you, Miss.'

A sharper observer than Kate may have noticed the slight tremor at the wrist as Betty's hand reached out for the card, which was cream, with one corner turned down. The name printed in large italics was *Mr. Stephenson* - no first name or initial. At the bottom right, in lieu of a club, was printed in smaller type *The Literary and Philosophical Society, Newcastle upon Tyne*. It made her smile, not for its forgivable pretension but for its reminder of the happy outcome to the controversy over the lamp that she had been following so avidly in the papers. Just a fortnight before, she had read in the *Courant* that both George Stephenson and Sir Humphry Davy had been elected honorary members at the conclusion of the great debate hosted by the Society. The card must be new.

'Did Mr Stephenson leave his card, or...?'

'He's still at the front door, Miss. He said he'd wait, case you should be at home. Well, what he said was, he'd chance it.'

This expression (so George-like) made Betty smile again. She spoke, blithely at first, 'Would you please ask the gentleman to come in?' then, 'No, wait a moment, I'm...' She gazed without focus around the room, then steadied herself, smoothed the front of her skirt, and nodded at Kate. 'I'm ready.'

The visiting card had in fact been Robert's idea. For three Sundays running he had watched his father saddle up and ride off in the direction of Black Callerton, and seen him ride back an hour or two later, looking disconsolate. Through his Aunt Nell, Robert had discovered the planned purpose of the visits, and finally George confessed to both of them that he spent most of his time over there in the shadow of trees at some distance from the house, hoping to catch sight of Betty on a walk, or coming alone from church - waiting for some circumstance that might allow him to manufacture a chance meeting. Robert was surprised that his father, not so many years off forty, confident in his work and his relations with the best of men, could in this affair of the heart be acting with as little maturity as any of Dr Bruce's students. George's suffering wrapped in his son. Affectionate memories of his own early encounters with Miss Hindmarsh determined Robert to help. Through his friendship with the Hancocks and others, he had learned some habits of the middling classes, and had observed how the calling card was becoming these days the commonly accepted social passport; hence his suggestion.

'Have you no shoes for me, George?' Betty teased her visitor gently, once he was seated and the servant girl had left the room. Her allusion to old times was meant to put him at his ease, but she had unwittingly increased his awkwardness. Because their courtship had been summarily ended by Mr Hindmarsh all those years ago, George had been unable to deliver the last new shoes he had made for her, and for a nervous moment he wondered if she was obliquely upbraiding him for this. Her demeanour seemed to suggest otherwise, and he relaxed slightly.

'Oh, I still have your size. I could work you up a pair, no bother.'

'It was just said for sport. I know you have many more important things to do these days than making shoes, as comfy as they were.'

'More important, may be. I can't think of a more welcome task.'

Betty blushed slightly, and it seemed that George did too, for he took the end of his cravat and dabbed at his face with it, though it was January. They sat silent for a minute or so, a little in their own thoughts, a little in each other's.

It was Betty who resumed. 'I've been reading about you in the papers. You are famous now.'

'Aye, in my own back yard. We'll have to bray louder for London to hear.'

'The big meeting seemed to go very well. About the lamp, I mean.'

'Aye. Losh played the swell as barrister. Everybody was examined and cross-examined. The committee was satisfied I could have learned nothing from Davy. He may have come upon the principle scientific-like, but they concluded I was first to apply it in construction.'

'Well done. And how has the subscription gone?'

'That's partly why I came. I wanted to thank your dad for his handsome pledge.'

'Oh, it was but twenty pounds. It would have been more, but now the war is over...'

'It was more than generous. Everyone's been more than generous. Liz, they've... I'm to get a thousand pound all told.'

'Goodness.'

'And a memento of some sort.'

'Your reputation is made by this.'

'I believe it is. There's to be a presentation, a dinner at the Assembly Rooms. That's...' He leaned forward in his chair towards her. 'That's the other reason I'm here.'

'Yes?'

'As guest of honour, I'm... And they've asked if I'd like to bring a companion. Well, of course I could take one of my brothers, but... it's... The way it's been arranged is that after the dinner there's to be a ball.'

'How lovely.'

100

'Yes. Course, I could ask my sister to accompany me, but she's not... And as a matter of fact she's started walking out with someone.'

'Nell is? Oh that's delightful!' exclaimed Elizabeth, genuinely thrilled. 'Someone I know?'

'Name of Liddle. Stephen Liddle. They met at chapel, I think. I've yet to... So, anyway, I wondered, was wonderin... if your father allows it... whether you'd care to come with me.'

Betty's left hand closed over her right in her lap, to prevent it flying to her heart, where the words struck. She took another moment to compose herself before she spoke softly. 'George, I am thirty-five years old. I have waited more than ten years for you to return to me. Do you think I would let my father come between us now?'

Though Robert was considered too young to be present at his father's testimonial evening, George had a great deal to thank him for in preparing for the twin ordeals that awaited him; Robert had written the bulk of the short acceptance speech he was to make at the dinner, and he had procured a copy of the brand-new edition of Thomas Wilson's *Complete System of English Country Dancing* by which George was able to con the steps of the group dances he would need to know if he were not to embarrass himself in front of Betty and the assembled company at the ball. Fortunately the manual was especially written for *those who possess no knowledge whatsoever of country-dancing* as even Nell was woefully short of experience. She did, however, prove a willing practice partner for George, who cleared a space in the front room and walked her through the steps he had memorised from the plans and diagrams in the book. Robert doubled as dance master and prompt from a chair pushed up against the wall. He acted encourager-in-chief too as the couple twirled and stumbled.

'Damned if I'll ever get the hang o these steps.'

'Certainly you will. Don't go at it in such a rush. Be all grace and smoothness. Grace and smoothness...'

The interior of Newcastle's Assembly Rooms was generally reckoned to be more commodious than any in the kingdom other than the House of Assembly at Bath, which was just as well because over four hundred guests crowded into the low-ceilinged Supper Rooms on the ground floor for the dinner that preceded the presentation. George had Miss Elizabeth Hindmarsh, simply but elegantly dressed, to his left and his patron Charles Brandling at his right hand side. When the meal was over it was Brandling who stood up to make the testimonial oration. He warmly welcomed the guests, and went on to make specific mention of several by name as he recounted the events that led up to this celebration.

At the climax of his speech Brandling placed one hand on the shoulder of 'our honoured guest', and begged his audience to 'remember the humble and laborious station in which he was born and lived, the scanty means and opportunities he has had for pursuing the researches of science.' He briefly bent down below the table and brought into view a splendidly ostentatious silver tankard which, as he pointed out, had been engraved to mark the occasion and, more particularly, Mr Stephenson's historic and significant achievement.

'A great deal of controversy and, I'm sorry to say, animosity, has prevailed upon this subject of the safety lamp. This, I trust, will subside, after the example of moderation that has been set by Mr Stephenson and his friends here assembled. Let us hope that all *personalities*...' - an ironic cheer from the guests - '...that, as I say, all personalities will cease to be remembered. As to the claim of that individual, I am confident that every doubt must have been removed by the perusal of the evidence recently laid before the public.'

Brandling reached into his pocket to retrieve the promissory note that had been drawn up for George, placing it ceremonially in the well of the tankard which he moved to his left, saying, 'Mr Stephenson, I beg you to accept this token of our esteem. We wish you long health to enjoy it, and to enable you to employ those talents with which Providence has blessed you for the benefit of your fellow creatures.'

George stood up to great applause and opened his mouth to respond, but was made to wait for several minutes while the accolade ran its course. He told the family at breakfast next morning how he felt as if a candle had been brought to his face, and as he looked out from the top table it seemed that each face he saw glowed too, more from a shared sense of pride than from the temperature of the room. Charles Brandling was right; this was a victory for every northerner as well as himself - and, when George did finally get to speak, that was his theme. He could not match his host for formal eloquence or humour, but he was sincere in his thanks for the support he had received, and all in all showed more humility than he sometimes did in company, though there was a flash or two of the old conceit.

'For when I consider the manner that I have been brought up and lived,' he said, echoing his patron, 'and when I consider the high station of Sir Humphry Davy... his high character that he holds among society and his influence on scientific men and, and.... scientific bodies...' He paused, looking a little lost for words; retreated to Robert's notes to conclude, 'I shall ever reflect with pride and gratitude that my labours have been honoured with the app... approbation of such a distinguished meeting; and you may rest assured that my time, and any talent I possess, shall hereafter be employed in such a manner as not to give you, gentlemen, any cause to regret the... the... countenance and support which you have so generously afforded me.'

George sat down with relief. Everyone rose to applaud the man more than the speech, leaving him uncertain whether to stand up again so they could see him properly, or stay seated to receive their obeisance. Finally, with Betty's hand on his arm, he settled back in his chair, and experienced for a glorious few moments the sensation of an Egyptian pharaoh saluted by palm-bearers, or that's how he reported it to his son, adding, 'Of course yon pharaoh commanded such respect only by birth. How much greater is the glory to be found in respect genuinely achieved, worked for by hand and brain. That's allus to be our road, Bobby. That's our difference.'

When George took Elizabeth's hand to guide her up the stairway to the great ballroom, he was so light-headed he felt they were floating, though in plain fact his partner several times had to rescue the hem of her tulle gown from his wayward feet, reaching down to pluck the material discreetly out of his path. He had never been in the ballroom before, and he was struck by the contrast with the room they had just left, for here the ceiling was high enough easily to accommodate seven large and brilliant glass chandeliers illuminating the waiting space.

As the pair entered at the head of the company, music broke out from the gallery immediately above the doors. A man with long bony wrists and an extravagantly waxed moustache rushed from the opposite side of the room hissing, 'Promenade, promenade,' through a fevered grin as he signalled the direction of travel with a silver-topped cane. They turned right at his bidding. Elizabeth helped George keep reasonable time with the band as they led the circuit of the room.

'Just a little slower, George,' she whispered.

When almost all the guests were in, the musicians struck up a grand march. All the partners responded in formation, weaving the patterns of the polonaise around the dance floor. George smiled into his companion's eyes, and inwardly blessed Robert, Nell and the resourceful Thomas Wilson.

After the first set, George had little opportunity to test his memory of Wilson's dance figures, for Betty's card was filled courtesy of a procession of gentlemen while George was almost constantly engaged by his own male admirers drawing him into the saloon room under

103

Downman's painting of Sir John Falstaff to regale him with their personal congratulations and generous advice on how to make best use of his testimonial sum. The couple did, however, come together again to enjoy the gaiety of the scotch reel among a group of eight and, towards the end of the evening, the intimacy of the new waltz from Vienna.

After the ball, every street around Westgate seemed to be lined with vehicles waiting to take their owners home. There being no hackney carriages operating in Newcastle, Squire Brandling had once again allowed George the use of his brougham, complete with coachman, while he insisted on riding himself home in his phaeton, despite being a little in his cups by this time. George, who had not touched a drop all night, sat rather self-consciously with Betty behind the driver, saying little on the way to Black Callerton.

The coachman attended at the farmhouse gate while George lit the way to Betty's front door. The couple faced each other there in the glow of the lamp, still quiet. Elizabeth's hands trembled slightly.

'You're shivering,' said George. 'I mun let you go in.'

'No. No, I'm not cold.'

Her gaze was yielding, inviting him to say more, and he smiled back, then looked past her shoulder into the darkness. 'Mind when we used to meet in your orchard?'

'I do. I seem to see you under the trees still, when I walk there, where the house can't see.'

'Is that so?'

'It is. It has always been so.'

Elizabeth could not stop herself trembling again. George set down the lamp on the path so he could take both her hands in his, though doing so was far from settling for either of them. He gave up waiting for calm to return.

'I know what you said about being your own woman now, but I don't want to cause any rift between thee and thy father. Do you think he would object anymore, if I was to walk out with you sometimes?'

Betty squeezed his hands. 'Of course he would not object. He is very proud of you. He claims acquaintance every time you're spoken of. And you are spoken of a great deal. I mean, by everyone.' She smiled. 'Sometimes I am quite jealous not to have you to myself these days. I mean, my thoughts of you.'

'Were you jealous tonight?'

'No, no. I was proud, delighted for you. You have become a great man, George. I knew you would.'

He breathed deeply of the cold air; it invigorated him, fuelled his intent. 'Liz...' he started to say, paused until he drew her closer to him, one hand like a giant's still enveloping both of hers, the other, delicate, near her cheek. His eyes glittered. 'Liz, the lamp was nothing - a useful diversion, is all. But there are great things... Steam... the locomotive. I have so much to show you. There are great things to do. Things to astonish all England.'

Her eyes shone to match his. She lifted her face to his touch on her cheek, and he watched every movement of her lips as she replied, 'I cannot wait. I cannot wait, my love.'

VII

*Louder and louder yet, it shrieks and cries as it comes tearing on resistless to the goal;
and now its way, still like the way of Death, is strewn with ashes thickly. Everything
around is blackened. There are dark pools of water, muddy lanes, and miserable
habitations far below. There are jagged walls and falling houses close at hand, and
through the battered roofs and broken windows wretched rooms are seen, where want
and fever hide themselves in many wretched shapes, while smoke and crowded gables,
and distorted chimneys, and deformity of brick and mortar penning up deformity of
mind and body, choke the murky distance. As Mr Dombey looks out of his carriage
window, it is never in his thoughts that the monster who has brought him there has let
the light of day in on these things: not made or caused them. It was the journey's fitting
end, and might have been the end of everything; it was so ruinous and dreary.*

Robert had already put aside the volume when Margaret, his housekeeper,
knocked to tell him that Edward Pease had arrived as appointed. Though
it was in his opinion better written than the American adventure, he was
sensitive to the prod of the author's forefinger in these diversions on the
railway revolution. Mr Dickens had been perfectly affable, if a little self-
important, when they first met at the Athenaeum Club, but his satire
either betrayed his true feelings or his instinct for the public sentiment;
whichever, the effect was to deepen Robert's melancholy rather than lift it
as he had hoped it would when he settled down with the new novel.

He had no expectation that his visitor would raise his spirits;
nevertheless, Robert greeted him warmly, for the memory of better times,
and (surprised to find himself in need of it) moral reassurance. He could
imagine those of the Catholic faith having similar affinity with their father
confessor.

The old man was, as usual, direct. 'I find thee little altered. Losing
sleep still?'

'I am no stranger to wakefulness but, yes, I have been spending
more hours than I'd care to account for, staring at the ceiling.'

The Quaker's eyes fell upon the half-empty cigar box next to
Dombey and Son at his host's elbow. Robert silently acknowledged his over-
indulgence, inwardly cursed his failure to move either box or book from
sight, and braced himself for chastisement. It did not come, and they
moved on to other subjects, ineluctably to recollection.

'Thy father has been much in my mind, too, since his passing. I have been thinking about our first meeting, how he appeared on my doorstep quite unexpected.'

'I remember him saying that he and Nicholas walked twelve mile in the dark from Stockton to Darlington on purpose to see you,' Robert said, 'but why he went to Stockton I can't recall, unless he thought to pace out the proposed line there and then.'

'I believe it was their original intent to call on our solicitor Raisbeck and discover more about the company's plans to construct the public railway, or tram road as we first conceived it. Finding Raisbeck was not at home, thy father persuaded Wood to join him in seeking me out as chief projector. They came to beard the lion in his den.'

'*Carpe diem.* It could have been his motto in life.'

'Indeed. I liked that about George, and his bluntness, which offended only the supercilious. Why, on that first meeting he told me we were wrong to think of employing horses as our tractive power, that his engines at Killingworth were worth fifty horses.'

'He lost no time in telling you how to run your business. That's like him, yes. Was...' Robert corrected himself.

' I could easily forgive his presumption, for he had such an honest and sensible appearance, and such a passion that we talked for hours. They had planned to return to Newcastle by nip, but missed the last coach and faced another long walk, to Durham; but they had succeeded in their object of persuading me to visit Killingworth - and so our association began.'

'And a very profitable one, as it turned out'

The door opened and the housemaid Susan brought in tea. Conversation stopped until the ceremonials were completed. In the presence of his visitor, Robert felt some embarrassment about the crest that decorated the crockery. His late wife Frances, following some fancy of her own, had traced his family by a very indirect route to some Scottish branch of the Stephensons that boasted a coat of arms. Robert had reluctantly indulged her whim to adopt it, though he had always considered it foolish, and now especially so. If Edward Pease noticed the affectation he did not comment on it, returned instead, as soon as the servant left, to Robert's last remark.

'Profitable, yes, eventually. I make no apology for that. There is no sin in making money, unless it become an end in itself. Much good can spring from it - social good, I mean - and I believe the Pease family has helped to render man happier and better through our work. But money made for base enjoyment, or money made by exploiting others, as slave masters do, is a form of wickedness, anathema to our creed.'

'What is your opinion of buying and selling in the public stocks?' Robert's mind had been running on such matters since he heard about the investigation into the affairs of George Hudson.

'There is a vast deal of difference between investment and speculation,' the old man replied. 'Investment to find better security or to aid a worthy business can do much; but I have no time for those who make a practice of selling, week by week, upon speculation only - I consider that to be gaming in another form, with all its attendant ills. Consider the Railway Mania and the untold damage that has done, not just to the gulls who allowed themselves to be sucked in, but to the real victims of the fever, the many cases of innocent families who have suffered great loss and hardship. Meanwhile the unscrupulous and corrupt line their pockets.'

'I suppose you put George Hudson among those devils. Have you heard that he is subject to some amateur exposure, and like to have to answer for it?'

'Scandal is no meet subject for discourse,' said Pease, reproving. 'It is no accident, though, that I never had business relations with Hudson. Conversely, he has often looked up from one of his grand schemes to find a Pease in opposition. Quakers do not always deplore a fight.'

'You must deplore my own position, then, as I have often been in his camp.' A short pause, then, guiltily, 'As was my father, betimes.'

Edward Pease raised his right hand slightly from the arm-rest of his chair, then set it down as he considered his answer. 'Unavoidable,' he said at last. 'Having built so much of England's railways, you must either travel in the carriage of the Railway King or be crushed by his wheels. I do not blame thee for it - the Stephensons have ever acted with principle.' He leaned forward. 'Years ago, thy father recommended wrought iron rails for the Stockton and Darlington, though he and Losh owned the patent for the cast iron type. He could have put five hundred pounds in his pocket, for my board were set on laying cast iron, but he spoke from his experience and advised them not to lay a single one.'

'He was right. Cast iron may be cheaper, but you would soon lose any saving with the expense of repairs.'

'Indeed. And that was the position he took, not where his own advantage lay. He never altered in all the years I knew him - one more reason why I say he deserves more respect than the state has seen fit to award him.'

'Our solace is that he helped create his own and greatest monument in the railway,' said Robert, confident that at least his guest would concur in that. After all, it was partly Edward's bequeathing too, and partly his own; but the old man's response discomfited him.

'Perhaps it is my age, Robert, that my mind seems lost in doubt as to the real benefits for humanity. Certainly, there is the diminished use of horses, and the lessened cruelty to them. What else? Ease, safety, speed, a lessening in expense is obtained - but at what cost? What effects on the other side of the scale? It used to be a saying with me, Let the country make the railroads and the railroads will make the country. But when I look around at what we have made... Why, sometimes my mind misgives me.'

The pair continued to talk and reminisce for a while longer, but their conversation became perfunctory, punctuated by those silences that are characteristic of Quaker introspection, and hardly conducive to company. Robert was not sorry when his visitor finally stood up to go. He was already thinking of the substance that might give him relief when Edward Pease turned at the doorway, transfixed him with solemn eyes under his wide-brimmed hat.

'For all his qualities, I fear thy father died an unbeliever.' Robert remained silent. The old man took a step back into the room, placed a hand on Robert's sleeve. 'Be temperate,' he said. 'Upon my soul, be on the watch.'

Robert did not retire to his study as he had intended on his guest's departure. Instead he called for his hat and coat and, for the first time in a week, ventured out on a walk. He hurried by St George's Burial Ground and crossed the road, following the railings of Hyde Park to its newest entrance at Victoria Gate.

There was the usual collection of late summer hawkers and vendors around the gate: the potmen holding their jugs of porter and stout; the shoe-black; the fruit merchant; the flower girl with her tray, calling out, 'All a-growin, all a-blowin' and, 'Flowers for your lady-love, sir?' as Robert passed. He ignored her, but tossed thruppence into the shawl spread at the bare feet of a young girl who danced a hornpipe unaccompanied. She gave him an alluring smile, then broke off her dance to stoop for the coin before some rascal could snatch it away.

He slowed his pace as he crossed the meadow, with Kensington Gardens to his right. When he first came to London, nearly thirty years ago, these open spaces had been dotted with grazing cows, kept to supply the capital with fresh milk. Now the early morning freight brought churns aplenty, another of the hundred and more transformations wrought by the railways. How could Edward Pease fail to give full credit to such improvements?

He made his way to the Serpentine, claimed a viewpoint on the bridge overlooking the new boathouse. Most of the brightly painted craft were tethered to the bank, and the Free Watermen, standing disconsolately in pairs at the lakeside, were more numerous than potential customers. Small wonder, Robert thought, catching the stench from the stagnant water as he leaned over the parapet. He felt in his inside pocket for a cigar, and stood smoking it to mask the smell while he gazed into the dangerous filth below. He reflected on those who had chosen to put an end to their lives in the lake – the poet Shelley's wife, for one. He could not prevent himself thinking that the introduction of this bridge by his old rival John Rennie must have made the Serpentine an even more popular and practical spot for suicides.

In need of fresher air, he crossed with his cigar to the southern bank, and took the footpath that divided the lake from Rotten Row. At his shoulder, affluent young citizens paraded their horses and the latest fashions to each other at a trot and canter along the strip, which was freer of coaches than it used to be. To his left, at the south east corner of the lake, he observed how the hovel that had gradually grown from the apple stall located there seemed to be spreading into a cottage now, establishing itself by degrees like a maturing tree.

As he approached Hyde Park Corner, Robert stopped to look at the huge bronze of Achilles, and to read the inscription on its granite base:

To Arthur Duke of Wellington
and his brave companions in arms
this statue of Achilles
cast from cannon taken in the victories
of Salamanca, Vittoria, Toulouse, and Waterloo
is inscribed
by their country women
Placed on this spot
on the XVIII day of June MDCCCXXII
by command of
His Majesty George III.

The muscular hero had a fig leaf sculpted over his genitalia, though this had failed to protect him from the controversy that had arisen from placing London's first public nude statue in the park, one so large that it proved too high for the entrance gates and required a hole to be knocked into the adjoining wall. Achilles stood with his shield raised, as if to ward off attack, or perhaps to point the way to the home of his progenitor, next to the park gates.

Robert continued his walk in that direction, and as he left the park he paused for a minute behind the knot of spectators that always seemed to be there gawking at Apsley House. It was not a building he particularly liked, mainly because of the iron shutters that the Duke had erected at every window, disfiguring the otherwise graceful frontage. The shutters had gone up during the tumults that broke out on account of Wellington's opposition to the Reform Bill, and he had kept them there ever since, despite his recent return to favour - a record of the people's ingratitude, he said.

While Robert watched, the sun broke from behind a cloud and cast the shadow of the Duke's equestrian statue full upon Apsley House. He looked over his shoulder to take in the original - Wellington astride Copenhagen on top of the victory arch - and squinted as he did so, partly against the glare of the sun, partly to reduce the assault on his sensibility by a second colossus.

Robert resumed his walk along Knightsbridge only as far as another imposing residence, one of two Italianate buildings either side of Albert Gate. That on the other side of the gateway remained empty, as it had since Cubitt built it speculatively a decade ago. It was said at the time that neither property would ever be taken, they were so inordinately large - Malta and Gibraltar, one newspaper wit dubbed them - but Number One Albert Gate, the focus of Robert's attention, had found a buyer for the enormous sum of fifteen thousand pounds. He had spent a further fifteen thousand, so it was said, on furnishing and decorating the mansion to suit his wife's expensive if vulgar tastes. The buyer's name, George Hudson.

Robert knew he would need no calling card here; he would be immediately recognized and welcomed in. He deliberated about it. Perhaps Hudson should be given the chance to put his side of the story. But Robert was already beginning to admit the truth to himself - that the embittered gentleman he'd met on the train from Chesterfield was merely corroborating evidence that Robert had previously chosen to ignore. Why, had this very house not been purchased partly by donations originally inspired by Hudson's suggestion that George Stephenson deserved a testimonial? A testimonial which had subsequently and mysteriously metamorphosed into a subscription on behalf of Hudson himself.

Robert turned on his heel and retraced his steps to Hyde Park Corner. It was his intention to return home by way of Park Lane. When he neared the gates of Apsley House, however, he found his route blocked, for the onlookers there had swelled considerably. He skirted round the back of the crowd, and as he did so detected a commotion amongst them. Faces shone excitement and 'The Duke! The Duke!' was passed like an incantation from lip to lip.

Estimating the entrance to Park Lane to be immediately opposite his present position, Robert shouldered his way through, and found himself at the front of a line of spectators on the south side of the road. He was about to step across the gap when someone shouted, 'You'll frighten the horses, fool,' and he was pulled back by the arm. Robert followed the gaze of the crowd, lighting on two riders approaching from the right. With his groom a respectful pace or two behind, the Duke of Wellington, in a plain blue frock-coat with white waistcoat and trousers, was impassively riding a chestnut hunter, seeming to look neither to the left nor right; yet, where hats were raised as he passed, he acknowledged them with a touch of two fingers to his own hat in a patriarchal form of salute.

Whether the quality of Robert's clothing set him apart from *hoi polloi* or whether the Duke happened to chance among the sea of faces upon one he distinctly recognized, when he came abreast of Robert, Wellington turned his head and stared directly down at him, even drawing bridle slightly. Robert raised a hand, was about to offer a greeting; but in that instant the Duke's expression turned cold, his eyes hooded over and he reverted to his former position, looking straight ahead, chin set firm, and passed on. Robert had been effectively cut where he stood.

Some spectators abandoned their position at the roadside to follow the horses; others went about whatever business they were engaged in before the Duke's appearance on the scene: Robert remained where he was for at least a minute as he turned over in his mind what the chilling exchange might have signified. Not reaching any conclusion that satisfied him, he started to walk the long straight of Park Lane towards Gloucester Square. His grim mood redoubled with every step.

VIII

It was Aunt Nelly who told Robert that Newburn Church, where they stood with the rest of the wedding party, was also the scene of his father's first marriage. Perhaps George had genuinely forgotten; he'd mentioned Fanny so rarely in all these years that the youth sometimes wondered if he had put her out of his mind entirely. For Robert, in the freshness of his aunt's telling, it seemed momentarily unnatural to be signing witness to the union of George Stephenson with Elizabeth Hindmarsh in a register that carried on an earlier page the mark of the young woman who had borne him. It was indeed her *mark* (a surreptitious search revealed) and her maiden name was written in George's hand. Betty needed no such assistance with her signature. Her new husband completed his with a flourish, not the smudge of his earlier effort.

'I wish your grandpa and grandma had lived to see this day,' Aunt Nelly said, 'to see our Geordie yoked again at last.' Robert nodded; thought how the old folk would, like his aunt, have commented on the contrast between the two weddings in point of their ceremonial trappings - not least the string quartet that had been engaged to play on this occasion as the church did not boast an organ, and the fine carriages drawn up outside the church to convey the married couple and their guests to a wedding breakfast at Black Callerton Farm. Yet so much remained simple and homely. At the church door, Betty surprised Nelly by gently lobbing the bride's bouquet in her direction. Her sister-in-law almost stumbled in catching it, and was evidently grateful to be caught in turn by Stephen Liddle who drew her into his chest as he steadied her. Nelly blushed for that and for the meaning of the bouquet.

After the breakfast - which included the finest selection of cold game outside a royal feast; good wines; and, instead of the traditional Bride's Pie, a dark, rich fruitcake with ornate white frostings of scrolls and leaves - Robert took little persuasion to play the flute piece he had composed especially to mark the occasion. Winning praise for it, he and his stepmother next performed a duet on piano and flute, to polite applause. The guests were much less restrained when someone offered a snatch of an old north country tune. This had others joining in the chorus, and prompted a sing-song that soon had half the gathering serving up well-loved songs and ballads. George gave his favourite *John Anderson my jo*, cannily censoring the earthier verses for the sake of the company. His voice, burred and breathy, had Robert imagining the wind brushing over gorse.

John Anderson, my jo, John,
We clamb the hill thegither;
And mony a cantie day, John,
We've had wi ane anither:
Now we maun totter down, John,
And hand in hand we'll go,
And sleep thegither at the foot,
John Anderson, my jo.

Afterwards George cajoled most of the male guests into joining him in the field next to the orchard for games of putting the stone and throwing the hammer. They presented a strange sight in their wedding clothes, with more than one risking a row with his spouse for the strain they put on seams and the mud they spattered onto clean collars. Robert hung back at first but, anxious to prove himself, in due time stepped forward for the hammer. He was almost as tall as his father now, if puny by comparison. George naturally took it on himself to improve his son's technique.

'Here, the knack of it is to release at just the right moment. Like this, see.' George nudged him aside to demonstrate, reached between his legs to grasp the hammer by the handle. He set himself and swung the heft forward, stretching his arms past the horizontal before casting it high into the air as the onlookers whooped and cheered his effort. One of the young farm boys set off in pursuit, and soon brought the hammer back for Robert to try his strength.

'I'll be lucky to make half the distance,' he admitted as he moved into position.

His father proffered more advice, to his general embarrassment in front of the company. 'Not so wide in the footing. Now, anchor down and swing.'

Robert gripped the shaft hard and swung through his legs, trying for the easy motion his father showed, and the long release. As his hands came up he let go, just a moment too early. His head jerked sideways in a flinch as the hammer spun out of control, and the heel of the handle struck his cheekbone hard. Robert and hammer fell heavily, just inches apart in the clover. He lay stunned, inert. George was first among the men who rushed to his aid; picked him up bodily and carried him into the house, refusing all offers of help.

114

Recovering on the sofa inside, the patient seemed to be surrounded by women, fussed over to such an extent by Aunt Nell and Betty that his father's concern turned a tinge of green.

'Don't moither him so. He's not a bairn.'

This was true, for now Robert was apprentice to Nicholas Wood at Killingworth, and on his way to becoming an engineer. Despite his fainting and the drama that ensued, he suffered nothing more than a bruise from his accident with the hammer, and the day after next was back at Wood's side at the colliery. He was more comfortable on bank than he was underground, for the dust affected his lungs, and he had never really shaken off his childhood fear of the pit, though he was careful not to let his preference show.

Fortunately for Robert, the area where most engineering attention was needed was the growing fleet of working locomotives at the pit - not just *Blücher* now but *My Lord* and *Wellington* in operation at Killingworth, and other engines on order for the Duke of Portland's wagon way in Scotland and the new line his father was helping to build a few miles away at Hetton Colliery. Indeed, with George often away pursuing his interests in Hetton or with Mr Losh at his Newcastle ironworks, Robert had little option than to take on far more responsibility for men and machines at Killingworth than most apprentices his age.

These oily days in masculine company were balanced by the evenings and rest days Robert spent with the women in his life, notably his dear stepmother Elizabeth, whom he had to thank for cultivating his finer tastes, especially for music and literature. The adventurous Lord Byron became a hero to him.

And I have loved thee, Ocean! and my joy
Of youthful sports was on thy breast to be
Borne like thy bubbles, onward: from a boy
I wantoned with thy breakers – they to me
Were a delight; and if the freshening sea
Made them a terror – 'twas a pleasing fear,
For I was as it were a child of thee,
And trusted to thy billows far and near,
And laid my hand upon thy mane – as I do here.

Betty encouraged him to read widely, to develop his flute-playing by joining the church band at Long Benton, and she even convinced her husband that Robert needed a holiday; thus he found himself, at the end of a long and dusty coach journey, in the nation's capital for the first time, incinerating loneliness with adolescent excitement at the sights and

115

sounds of London, struck by the artificial brilliance of the main streets, the surge of people - so many of whom seemed, like him, to be new arrivals converging as if called to assemble there by some higher power - and by the incessant roar of the city.

'Have you ever seen St Paul's, Mama?' he asked at a family supper the night he returned.

'I have never been to London,' said Betty. 'You have the advantage of me there.'

'Nor me,' said George, to Robert's surprise.

'Oh, it's wonderful. There's the great dome, which outside is best seen from the Thames, and inside is quite magnificent. And it has a curious Whispering Gallery.'

'What is that?'

'It runs right round the interior of the dome. If you should whisper against its wall at any point, your whisper can be heard on the opposite side by a person pressing her ear against the wall.'

'*Her* ear?' Betty repeated with a smile.

'Oh,' Robert had the grace to colour a little, caught out by his own words (his private thoughts). 'It happened that a... young lady was listening the one time I tried it, that was all. She came round to tell me so.'

'Very forward, was it not?' teased Betty. 'What was her name?'

'Oh, that she didn't tell me.'

'And what did you tell her? I mean, what did you whisper?'

'Oh... I forget.' He hesitated, then spoke again quickly, to change the subject, 'The odd thing... The odd thing is that if you speak in a normal voice there is no effect.'

'That *is* curious,' said George. 'What other wonders did you see in London?'

'Mmm, I toured the new waterworks - which was instructive. And Somerset House, where the Royal Society is. Hyde Park...'

'No rides anywhere? Remember Trevithick's *Catch-Me-Who-Can*?'

'Not a ride, but a wonderful exhibition of ancient Egypt, built at Piccadilly.'

'Oh, that must be Mr Belzoni's tomb. I have read about it,' Betty said with interest. 'Did you see the Sphinx?'

'A model of it, yes. With a lion's body and a man's face. And other Egyptians with heads like foxes and apes. Women too, carrying pitchers. All set in a pyramid, which is the ancients' tomb. I liked it very much, but I heard some complain of the smell, and two very fine ladies in

116

front would keep calling out to each other in very loud voices to say how tiresome and unfashionable it was.'

'Why did they bother going, then?' said George, making Betty laugh.

That night in bed she turned on her pillow to face her husband. 'Can you hear me if I whisper?'

'Aye. We mun be in St Paul's.'

'I have been thinking about Robert, how much he loves to learn. Do you think perhaps you should send him to the university?'

'Which university?'

'Why, Oxford or Cambridge. You have enough put by to pay for it now.'

'What will it profit him? Bruce give him all the book-learning he'll likely need, and he's learning now, as I did, by practical application. Besides, I need him here, and so does Wood. No, Liz, he mun work as I have worked, an learn as I have learned. He needs to stick to his last.'

'He *does* stick to his last,' said Betty, with a tinge of frustration.

'I unt saying different. He's a good lad, Rob, an happy at his work.'

Perhaps George was not quite so able to read his son as he believed. Perhaps his wife knew more, if anyone did. In the next bedroom Robert, stimulated by his trip to the metropolis, had wider horizons in his mental view. If he had visions and ambitions, then these were not solely brought on by the excitement of London; his dream, when it came, was a recurring one from his childhood, where he rode the steamboat across the Great Lakes of America.

The next morning brought George's new acquaintance Edward Pease on his promised visit to see the steam engines work at Killingworth. No special ceremony was laid on to greet him; indeed, George was already underground with Robert fitting a rope haulage engine when Pease was being directed to the house that had the sundial in front. It was left to Betty to pass the time of day with the visitor while they waited for her husband to return, a somewhat awkward task as she knew nothing of industry or business matters, and the Quaker's strict practices had left him entirely ignorant of the arts, proscribing Betty's preferred topics of conversation. She found herself chattering to him about Robert instead, praising his quick intelligence, until she remembered how much store the Friends place on modesty, whereupon she excused herself from the cottage temporarily, saying, 'I think I hear George on the track', and

117

waited anxiously for several minutes at the back of the cottage until she really did hear *Blücher* coming, and ran in again with some relief to inform Mr Pease.

If the great man was disconcerted at George's sooty appearance, and more than a little alarmed at being asked to mount the footplate of the belching *Blücher* alongside George and his brother James, he was partly won over by the thrilling power of steam. James had harnessed the engine to a full load of wagons which they pulled to the Tyne staiths at a steady five miles per hour while his brother extolled *Blücher's* capabilities, making himself hoarse as he declaimed to Pease over her full-throated roar. There was no room for another but George wanted Robert near, so he walked briskly after them along the old wagon way, and kept pace pretty well.

When they reached the staiths, James jumped down and went in search of help to unload the coals they brought. Edward Pease said to George, 'May we walk along the river path a little? My brain still rattles from the journey. I need to recover some tranquillity before I talk to thee of business.'

Robert was there to help Mr Pease down from the footplate, and they respected their visitor's request for quiet as the three of them walked by the Tyne, watching the keelmen at work. Significantly, the conversation resumed on the troublesome subject of noise. 'Yon engine is very powerful. I suppose that accounts for the great din it makes.'

'It is noisy, aye,' George agreed, 'an geet powerful, though we can mek it more so. Rob here would not be able to keep up if we opened her out. But have you stopped to consider what drives the engine?'

'Well, thee and thy brother drive the engine, but of course I understand the answer must be steam.'

'What do you say to the light of the sun?'

The quality of the question invited pause for thought, as it was designed to do. Robert had to admire the subtlety of his father's stratagem, quite unlike his normal directness. Edward Pease was wont to look heavenward, and he did so now involuntarily. 'The light of the sun? How can that be?'

'It is nowt else,' said George, 'but light bottled up in the earth for tens of thousands of years; light, absorbed by plants and vegetables, that's necessary for the condensation of carbon during the process of their growth. And now...' He pointed to where *Blücher* was still steaming by the staiths, 'after being buried long ages in fields of coal, you see how the light is liberated, made to work in that locomotive for... for great human

118

purposes.' George's bottom lip swelled with his own loquacity; his eyes glittered.

'Well,' said Pease, taken aback. His religious sentiment was touched. 'The idea is... almost pantheistic. But evocative, George, for all that. Yes, most striking.'

George instructed his son to ride with James for the return journey while he talked further with Mr Pease by the river. Robert would have liked to be there to help conclude the business, but he recognized this as a shrewd move too, for *Blücher* was much less impressive in contrary motion, even when pushing empty tubs, than pulling full ones. Edward Pease had seen the best of her, though they were continually making improvements.

Robert and the under-viewer Moodie were engaged at their usual lunch of herring and a penny roll over a small glass of beer at the Three Tuns when George came to join them.

'Where is Mr Pease?' from Robert.

'Oh, you won't catch him in here. He's even now on his way back to Darlington.'

'Unimpressed?'

'How could he fail to be impressed? Pease is all but won, Rob. He still has his board to convince about using steam in preference to horses, but we are already one step along the way - he has asked me to conduct a new survey of the line for examination by Parliament.'

'Can I help?' Robert stood up in his eagerness. As much as the excitement of the project, he was spurred by the thought of working in open countryside as a change from the close and unhealthy conditions of the pit.

'Well, Pease has put up John Dixon, but darsay I could use an extra pair o hands for the work. We'll mek a start once the corn is gathered in.'

*

Surveying the Stockton-Darlington line, Robert seemed to be standing at the cusp between his childhood past and whatever life held in store for him as a full-fledged adult. Following his father across the gleaned fields, trying to keep up with him as George vaulted over hedges in his top-boots and leapt across water-filled ditches without pause, he was taken back to their rambling walks when they would seek out birds' nests and pan the streams for sticklebacks. Topsy-turvy, it was the apprentice who

119

did the serious work of the survey, ensuring the accuracy of the measurements and making the appropriate calculations, assisted by the reliable Dixon, while his father paced restlessly, impulsive, always anxious to be moving on to the next field. Often George would spot what he considered to be a useful viewing-point, when he would stride ahead of the others, keen as ever to be the pathfinder, the true pioneer. Sometimes, playing out the chain measure, Robert felt again like the child holding the kite string while his father now acted the kite, skittish, tugging on the wind.

Their meals of bread, butter, milk and potatoes were generally taken with their backs against hedgerows, though George did not scruple, when the weather was unkind, to knock on the door of a cottage or farmhouse in search of better shelter and, as often as not, some homely fare. He had a natural way with working people that helped them open their hearts to him along with their doors. As a result the surveyors found themselves generously treated.

Except, that is, by the landowners. Edward Pease had warned George of the fierce resistance, which had started before the company had made their first application to Parliament for the construction of the line. Lord Darlington had organised massive opposition for the sake of his fox covers. A second survey had rerouted the line, only to raise the hackles of Lord Barrington, who had to be bought off. The Stephensons' was the third survey, and still the objectors came, like a wasp's nest disturbed.

One late afternoon George had hauled himself onto the third branch of a tree to check the contours while the other two recorded their latest measurements below him. From this vantage point he saw a pair of horsemen approach at speed, following the faint track that helped define the edge of the field the surveyors were in. George dropped down to the lowest branch; sat easy in its fork to wait their arrival. At the last fifty yard stretch one rider struck out in advance of the other and yelled, as he pulled up at the tree, 'How dare you trespass on my lordship's land!'

'And a good afternoon to you,' replied George, cheerfully. 'You've got a fine-tempered horse there. I know plenty would uv pitched their riders arse over tip, wi such a roaring in their ear.'

Robert and John exchanged glances. John winked slyly, and they carried on with their measuring.

'Don't you cheek me, tyke,' said the man on the horse to George. 'And get down from that tree before you speak again.'

'First I'll know who your lordship is.'

'Lord Boyne.'

120

'Why, the very gent that gave us permission to be here. Mr Edward Pease has his letter to the effect.'

'Not for here he don't.' This from the second rider as he pulled up. He was stouter than the first, and gave the appearance of having worked harder to make the ground, though his horse had the mien of a purebred. 'This is not the line that Overton proposed.'

'Why, no. Our job is to improve on Overton's route. That's why we're here.'

'This is good arable land. You cannot drive a line through it.'

George glanced to the north; his eyes traced the route he knew Overton's survey had recommended. There was no discernible difference in quality between the two territories in question. 'I'm sure it ull make no odds to Lord Boyne.'

'I am sure it will,' said the stout rider.

'And what makes you so certain?'

'Because I am he.' Lord Boyne straightened in his saddle. 'Besides, this line runs far too close to my own house.'

George pulled himself up by the branch above, and climbed a little higher in the tree to look around more thoroughly. He could not see a building in any direction. He dropped back to the lower branch. 'Where is it?'

'You may not be able to see my property from here, but I am certain the noise will carry. Tell Pease that if he wishes to change his plans, I will require further compensation.'

'And get down from there, or we'll press for damages too,' his steward put in, to have the last word at the miscreant before they left. George jumped from the tree unexpectedly from his standing position, landing in front of the man's mount and causing it to shy away in some alarm, the rider fighting to hold it. George made an exaggerated bow, in the manner of a circus performer, at the horsemen's departing backs.

'Wipe my arse with your avarice,' he muttered as he straightened up.

At the end of the day the three surveyors visited the home of Edward Pease to report progress and tell him about their encounter with Lord Boyne. Entering the parlour, they came upon two of his daughters practising embroidery. 'Are you in need of a teacher of the art?' George asked them. 'I learned embroidery long ago as a brakesman at Killingworth, mekking the miners' button-holes by the engine fire at night.'

The girls shook their heads, hid their faces beneath their bonnets as they bent again to their work, though not before one of them glanced past George at Robert, and smiled shyly. Robert smiled back, turned bashful himself in the act, and had to divert his attention to inanimate objects around the room.

Pease was unsurprised by the news of Boyne's intransigence. 'I have come to expect it. Partly it is motivated by greed, but also I think their lordships find their *noblesse* under threat. They are wedded to the old order and will not be divorced from it without a fight.'

'We're engineers, not reformists,' said George.

'Or, as they see it, dangerous modernists, besieging their lands, disturbing centuries of tradition. It is no accident that the Lord Chancellor sits upon a woolsack.'

George was all derision. 'Why, he ought rather sit upon a bag o coals, though it might not prove so comfortable a seat.'

Throughout this exchange Robert was studying a copy of the railway prospectus on the chiffonier. He pointed at the engraving on the cover. 'Is that a Bewick?'

'It is,' said Pease.

'I thought I recognized the style. I have his *History of British Birds.*'

George strolled over to inspect the cover. Under the motto PERICULUM PRIVATUM UTILITAS PUBLICA was a pastoral scene, albeit with the sketched image of a colliery unassuming in the distance. In the foreground was a horse pulling four coal wagons, or rather standing sedately in front of them as if to reassure the viewer that it would not make the least disturbance to its surroundings. George continued sardonic. 'And I see you are still wedded to horses, Edward.'

'Thou knows thy *Blücher* has persuaded me, but we must tread carefully against so much opposition. Never fear. The new Bill allows for any proper moveable engine or locomotive, and for the conveyance of passengers as well as goods.'

'Passengers?' from Robert, surprised. For all the talk of a public railroad, he had not envisaged it might actually be used to transport human cargo.

'Why, aye,' said his father. 'We're about to give the stage a run for its money. And we'll win handily. If we're appointed, that is,' he added, fishing.

'The opportunity is thine to grasp,' said Edward Pease.

Only a week later the survey was complete. Robert personally attended to the preparation of the document, and it was with a certain pride that he handed the final draft to his father, for it was his first professional undertaking. George flicked through the pages cursorily, handed them back, said in his blunt manner, 'There's summat missing.'

Robert was crestfallen. He felt as he had at thirteen when Mr Brandling criticised his notes on the subject of the safety lamp. 'What's missing?'

'Here, on the front.' His father jabbed a forefinger at the title page. 'It needs to say, *Robert Stephenson, Engineer*, as bold as you like. It's your work; claim it.'

George's unwonted generosity on the matter of authorship had an unlooked for consequence, or at least unlooked for by all but the shrewd engineer, who may have already anticipated that the designated surveyor would be called for examination by the parliamentary committee appointed to look into the Stockton and Darlington scheme. Thus it was that Robert returned to London, not this time to visit St Paul's or Belzoni's exhibition, but to argue the case for the railway. His stepmother saw to it that he had modestly appropriate new clothes for the occasion, and despite his youth he looked quite the part. That did not stop some of the Members trying to trip him up at every turn.

'I note how your survey shears four miles off that presented by Overton. Have the towns of Stockton and Darlington moved closer together?'

'No, sir. We have prepared a more direct route, partly by using four inclined planes to surmount the hill ridges flanking the River Gaunless. We have also straightened the approach to Stockton where the gradients are easier, and at the other end produced a shorter branch line to Darlington.'

'How do you intend to cross the Skerne?'

'By means of a stone bridge.'

'And Myers Swamp?'

'A combination of drainage and ballast.'

'Something puzzles me. You envisage traffic flowing from both ends, but have only a single line to cope. What the deuce will they do when they meet head on?'

Robert had not been looking forward to the question, as he privately found this a weakness in the proposed operation, but he assumed an easy confidence in his reply that helped carry it off. 'We have four passing loops at every mile. More than enough to obviate any problem.'

His ordeal at Westminster over for the day, Robert had further business on behalf of the Pease family at the City of London, where he was introduced to Mr John Sanderson, a gentleman in his forties who made a good living in the arrangement of capital investments. At the end of their pleasant meeting, Mr Sanderson surprised Robert by asking, 'Do you have any plans for your evening in town?'

'Not particularly, sir. I thought I might stroll around to take in some of the sights I had not time to visit before.'

'Have you ever been to Vauxhall Gardens?'

'No.'

'Some clients of mine, the London Wine Company, have recently purchased the attraction and have kindly provided me with some complimentary tickets. I intend taking my family tonight, and wondered if you would care to join us.'

A couple of hours later Robert walked from his lodgings to knock at an unfamiliar door in Broad Street. There Mr Sanderson introduced him not only to his wife but to their daughter Frances, known as Fanny, whom Robert guessed to be about the same age as himself. Though no-one would have described the girl as a particular beauty, she was subtly attractive, her complexion smooth, her figure neat; and Robert immediately detected something within – a sort of contained vivacity that surfaced every now and again, here at her lips, there in the stretch of her slender fingers, or that he glimpsed like a secret in the depths of her dark, blue eyes which fascinated and disturbed him at once. He searched for a conversation topic as they sat together in the carriage on their way to Vauxhall Gardens.

'Fanny, that was my mother's name.'

'*Was?* She...?'

'Died when I was but three. I have a most loving stepmother now. Elizabeth. I am just learning to call her *mama*, for my father and she have been married only a year or two.' He paused, then added, for something else to say, 'Though they were sweethearts in their youth.'

'How romantic,' said Fanny.

'Yes, I suppose it is.' He caught Mrs Sanderson smiling at them, turned to look out of the window in confusion, then it occurred to him she might think that rude. 'Oh, is this Westminster Bridge?' he asked, to excuse his looking away, though the question was redundant as the Houses of Parliament were in clear view.

'Indeed it is,' said Mr Sanderson. To his wife, 'I think I mentioned that Robert was addressing a committee of Members earlier today.' Mrs

124

Sanderson nodded and smiled again at their guest, who felt even more of a fool to be heard asking naive questions of a location he'd only just visited.

The Bridge Street entrance to Vauxhall Gardens was thronged with arrivals. Robert heard several complain at the turnstile about a rise in the entrance charge to four shillings and sixpence, and was glad that Mr Sanderson had his tickets for free. Turning right from the gate, he could immediately appreciate the attraction of the place. Stretched out in front of the group was a colonnade of trees, forming one side of a great quadrangle that shimmered with what must have been thousands of variegated lamps hung among the branches. Most visitors were walking sedately along the main paths of the grove, or making their way to one of the many boxes set out under the trees for supper parties, but Robert noticed how several of the younger and more boisterous sort preferred to flirt and chase each other down the dark walks that led away at intervals from the regular, covered paths. He wondered what was there out of the reach of the lights.

Mr Sanderson took his party to the Prince's Pavilion, where they attended in politeness to musicians giving a selection from Handel before strolling across to see the statue of the composer at the riverside entrance to the Gardens. He sat in the guise of Orpheus playing or rather leaning against a lyre, and Robert was surprised at how casual he looked - his legs crossed, wearing a loose open gown and slippers, one of which was lying below Handel's foot as if to place him in a state of drowsiness. Despite its marble nobility there was something almost louche about the figure, suggestive of a quality that lay beneath the grandeur of this pleasure garden.

'Let us go and find something to eat,' said Mr Sanderson. 'Helen, would you take my arm? Mr Stephenson, if you would not mind...'

Robert, after some slight awkwardness, partnered with Fanny and followed her parents to the food tables, where he was shocked by the high prices - half a crown for a plate of lettuce with a sliver of ham so thin you could see through it; and a slice of bread that cost the equivalent of a full loaf anywhere outside these exclusive environs.

Afterwards they looked into the Rotunda - once famous, Robert was informed, for spectacular displays of horsemanship but now converted to a Pavilion of Concord that displayed allegorical devices representing the four corners of the globe - then they made their way to the open theatre that lay north of the quadrangle to capture a seat and await the entertainment. Robert sat counting spectators by block before

125

turning to Fanny to exclaim, 'There must be upwards of three thousand people at this arena alone.'

'Is that what you have been doing, sitting so quietly?' said Fanny. 'It's very clever of you to work it out,' leaving Robert to wonder whether she was paying him a compliment or subtly admonishing him for failing to pay her proper attention.

The performance was generally disappointing, being of the circus type but without animals other than prancing show horses, and featuring too much juggling and rope dancing for Robert's liking. He was, however, intrigued by the appearance of the copper-coloured Bellinck Family from 'Indian America'. This was a tightrope act whose star performer Juan - complete with Red Indian head dress - performed a series of daring stunts on the rope, including somersaults and dives through hoops of fire that were lit by mouth from a fire-eating child billed as *Young Bellinck the Infernal Devil.*

At the end of the performance a bell rang out. This was clearly some kind of signal as the vast majority of the audience on hearing it deserted their places to join others running along the sequestered path that ran beyond the theatre. The Sandersons were pulled along in their wake, trying to preserve some dignity but anxious not to be left behind. Fanny skipped ahead of her parents. Robert tried not to abandon his role as escort, stretching to keep in fingertip contact with her elbow as if they were two children playing tag.

At the end of an arched passageway they came across a fence with people crushed expectantly three or four deep along its length. A dark wood lay beyond the open field bordered by the fence. Robert had just discerned a large curtain erected in front of the wood when the curtain rose on an illuminated scene of London Bridge, with water apparently flowing under it. He made to point this out to Fanny...

'It's the Cascade!' she exclaimed, and brushed the back of Robert's hand accidentally with her breast as she stretched up on her toes. It was the merest touch, but it electrified him. He stared ahead, not daring to look at her.

An old woman sat spinning at the foot of the bridge. The audience gasped at some movement above; the mail and a heavy coach passing over the bridge into town, followed by what seemed to be a bull driving an ass in front of it. The effect was achieved, Robert observed once he'd recovered focus, through a combination of paintwork and mechanism, and managed to be at once awe-inspiring and tawdry.

After some minutes the curtain dropped slowly down on the scene. The moment it reached the ground there came a flash and

126

explosion above the heads of the crowd. Robert felt himself gripped at the arm, and he turned to see Fanny, pressed alongside him, eyes alive with fear and excitement, searching the sky. A strand of hair had escaped from her bonnet; it trailed across her cheek. He felt his scalp tighten and he returned the pressure with what he hoped would be interpreted as reassurance as they awaited developments.

He saw that the explosion had come from a tower standing about sixty feet from the ground, to the right of the Cascade. As he watched, the outline of the tower was picked out in sparks spitting from fireworks. Three rockets were launched from the upper door of the tower, bringing more delighted gasps from the crowd. Soon the whole sky was lit up with comets and flying bugs, while Catherine wheels spun, or sometimes failed to spin, in a dazzle of colours from spars nailed to the tower. Occasionally Robert sneaked a sideways glance at Fanny as she scanned the scene, her profile lit by the brightness of the display. He hoped that her father was not near enough to see how she maintained her hold on their guest's arm, and hoped too that she would not relinquish it.

'The climax,' he told his mama a few days later, 'came when a man called Mr Blackmore climbed a rope to the tower, surrounded by flames of fire, to rescue Madame Saqui. She had flames of all colours around her on the platform, and when they descended together on some sort of slack cable, it seemed to be shot through with fire.'

'Extraordinary. How did Miss Sanderson enjoy the spectacle?'

'Oh, very much. But her favourite place is the Covent Garden theatre. I've promised to take her next chance I get to return to London.'

'Well, let's hope you have another opportunity before long,' Betty said, raising her voice a little to include her husband in the conversation, but his attention was presently engaged on carving the roast.

*

Robert's next destination was not to be London, but Liverpool. A business associate and strong champion of George's work, William James, had found ears ready to listen to his advocacy in a city where the canal owners had been abusing their monopoly of commercial transport for long enough. James gained financial backing for a bold proposal to build a railway between Liverpool and Manchester, and a commission to conduct a survey for a possible route. Of course he wanted George to partner him in this hugely ambitious venture, but support from that quarter was not as whole-hearted as James would have expected. It may have been reluctance on George's part to act foster parent to another's offspring – whatever the reason, he declared himself too busy with the details of the Stockton and Darlington construction to attend personally to the new scheme. He dispatched his son in the first instance to act as his deputy.

Having learned much from assisting with one survey, Robert was looking forward to this one, not least because he would not have the impetuosity of his father to deal with; but he encountered something much worse. The resistance of the canal owners was far better organised than that of the Durham county gentry. Everywhere the survey team tried to go they met a mob paid to confront them with violent protest, and they often had to retreat from field gates under threat from guns and pitchforks, or actual assault from a hail of stones and bricks thrown by local women and children recruited for the purpose by the opposition.

'They would immolate me if they could, but we must fight fire with fire,' said William James, characteristically ebullient, the night before they were due to enter St Helens. Robert accompanied him on a tour of the public houses, bent on engaging bodyguards for the morrow. Their successful recruitment included one huge navvy who was to be entrusted with the chief object of the protestors' hostility, the theodolite. This giant, Ethan, had already been approached by the other side, but was happy to switch allegiance for an extra shilling.

The James party, their numbers swollen by half a dozen mercenaries, marched next morning in fair fettle down the ignominious-sounding Thieves Lane by Sutton Workhouse, where they intended to start the next stage of their survey. Ethan brought up the rear, carrying the theodolite stand in the manner of Little John holding his staff, ready for a challenge. They were not impeded in their morning's work until they neared the entrance to Sutton Manor Colliery. There, perched like carrion birds on the gates above the wrought iron motto *Ex Terra Lucem*, a dozen grim colliers watched the approach of the survey group. One or two of them held staves made from pick handles. In front of the gates a small crowd of both sexes gathered, dominated by a pugnacious-looking couple: the man a match for Ethan in size; his wife (she must be) not much shorter, with powerful arms bare to the elbow and red raw, as if she had just that moment pulled them from a hot wash tub. Her voice was no less coarse. 'Garn, away yersens!'

Mr James stepped forward, plump palms open, placatory. 'Madam, we mean no harm at all. We are only here to survey the land.'

'Ur, for stinking railway. Thull ha birds dropping out sky, poisoned, an cows confusin to gi milk. Thull mek our babbies badly.'

128

'Ay,' agreed her husband, 'an homes set ablaze from sparks. Or explosioned up when boilers burst off of thi damned engines.'

'Trust me, you have been peddled falsehoods,' said Mr James. 'What you've heard is nothing but stuff and nonsense.'

'Dun thou stuff an nonsense me, lardarse,' said the big fellow, confronting James. His fists were clenched but still at his hips when Ethan pushed forward from the back, handed his theodolite to a startled Robert, shouldered aside his employer, and punched the Sutton man full in the face. The miner staggered back astonished, dabbed at his nose, examined his fingers for blood, then with a cry of rage grabbed at Ethan on both sides of his head, fixed him by the ears and tried to swing him round. His wife, meanwhile, belaboured the navvy's legs as if she were kicking at a pit prop to cause a fall. Ethan set himself square. The result was a sort of violent stalemate while both sides looked on transfixed.

This tableau lasted a few seconds until a weasel-faced youth clinging to the gate shouted, 'Get the devil's instrument.' He pointed directly at the theodolite stand, presently held by Robert, who felt the blood drain from him. Weasel's comrades swarmed over the gate. Their yells shocked Robert out of his immobility, set his heart racing, and as they charged forward he backed away through his own group, still clutching the stand. Most of the group backed away with him, but one of his chain-men faced the attackers, swinging a length of chain like a mace to ward them off. This halted the charge but briefly. Four or five of the colliers rushed forward in a pack. Two of them dived below the swinging chain to grab the defender and hoist him off his legs. They trussed him up, protesting, with his own chain.

'Drop im down pit shaft,' Weasel shouted from his position on the gate. His friends responded with a cheer, bearing their victim in the direction of the colliery and chanting *Drop! Drop! Drop! Drop! Drop!* In desperation Robert rushed forward, beating at the men's backs with his stand. One or two of them relinquished their hold on his colleague to ward off the blows. Those with pick-handles turned on Robert. His fleeting courage deserted; all he could do was to raise the stand above his head for some protection. This made the men hesitate, expecting Robert to strike, and in that moment Ethan finally wrestled himself free. He launched himself among the crowd, swinging his fists wildly. Those carrying the chain-man dumped him unceremoniously on the ground; those with weapons wheeled away from Robert to face their new assailant. Emboldened by Ethan's energies, the rest of William James's paid crew belatedly joined the fray, and before long the ground in front of the gates was a mess of bodies, some sprawling injured there, others in a

129

tangled knot of clinches and hand-to-hand fighting. Robert landed one more blow with the theodolite, breaking it in the process, before he was pulled away by James.

'Time for retreat, Robbie. We'll live to fight another day.'

Soon the whole survey party were retracing the tracks of their morning's work with a great deal more haste than they came, and within minutes were rushing up Thieves Lane towards their saloon bar rendezvous to regroup and nurse their wounds.

Following that incident, James embarked on a new strategy of surveying by moonlight, or very early in the morning when the wilder tendency among the saboteurs were safely sleeping off their previous night's over-indulgence. Nevertheless, the team continued to face regular aggravation in varying degrees, at least until they got to the area of Chat Moss, which was generally regarded by the locals as impassable terrain. It was confidently predicted that any locomotive engine attempting that part of the journey would be swallowed up and lost in the mud. William James came near to demonstrating the proof during the survey when he slipped in to the depth of his ample chest. He saved himself only by a monumental effort, grabbing a clump of reeds and heaving his lower body back onto secure ground.

'Don't alarm yourself; unplugged!' he called out cheerfully while Robert was still trying to pick a way across the marsh to help him.

Despite the obvious challenges of the project, Robert gained considerable satisfaction from the work in Liverpool and developed a respect for the far-sighted and over-worked James, which he communicated in letters home. He did not mention that his mentor also introduced him to the habit of smoking, which they indulged in each other's company of an evening at whatever inn that put them up. Even if he'd known about it, that was not the reason George took a dislike to William James; at least Robert became convinced there was another reason - that his very praise for the man was enough to damn James in the eyes of his father. The greatest fault in George, Robert was beginning to perceive, was his consistent failure to acknowledge merit in others. His son's case aside, it was as if George felt himself diminished by another earning good opinion or success in what he thought of as his exclusive areas of expertise. Was it a kind of jealousy, egotism, possessiveness...? Robert couldn't quite name it, but he felt its consequences. Just when it seemed that his professional association with James would become a more settled thing, his father suddenly acquiesced in part to Betty's views on the subject of a college education for Robert, and found eighty pounds for a term of tuition at the University of Edinburgh. James was left to shift for himself in Liverpool, and Robert was on his way to Scotland.

*

Somewhat bemused at this turn in his career but determined to make the most of it, Robert established himself at Drummond Street in the vicinity of the hotchpotch of buildings that comprised the university, and made diligent attendance at weekly lectures in Natural Philosophy, Chemistry, and Natural History. He was in class when, on an early occasion, he almost clashed heads with a bespectacled young man taking an unusually close if short-sighted interest in Robert's notes.

'Have you missed something in the lecture?'

'Zorry, baint maining to be no rubber noze,' said the student. His warm sibilant burr marked him out as a Devonian more faithful to his native dialect than Robert had latterly become to the Northumbrian. 'It's juz... Be that writing you can read?'

Something about the way he asked the question produced an immediate surge of affection in Robert, as well as a chuckle. 'It's shorthand. I studied it so I can take the lecture down *verbatim* and transcribe it in longhand later for my father.'

His neighbour cocked an ear to Mr Jameson at the front of the hall. 'Mmm. Zeems I made you miss that lars gob o wizdom.'

'Don't worry. One thing I've learned very quickly is that natural historians spend a great deal of time enquiring whether Adam was a black man or a white man. Now I really cannot see what better we should be if we could ever determine this one way or the other.'

'Ar, an I thought it were juz me. Uz ull be pals, zurely.'

At the White Hart Inn later, Robert's new friend introduced himself as George Parker Bidder from Moretonhampstead. 'Zixteen letters - yerd tell that be the longest place-name of one word in all England, only I couldn't zwear to it, cuz I baint been far.'

'How did you come to be here? Sent by your father?'

Bidder treated that as a good joke, rocking back on his stool and running his fingers through his untidy thatch of hair as he giggled over the notion. 'Way arf it. Rescued from him, more like. By Zir Henry Jardine, bless his zoul. No, if Dad had his way he'd be making a kickshaw of uz again.'

'Kickshaw?'

131

'Zibiting. Exhibiting, I mean.' Bidder leaned forward and confided to Robert, more in embarrassment than pride, 'I were the *Extraordinary Calculating Boy*. Dad made more money from that than he ever done from mazonry.'

'How did that work?'

'Like this. Give me a hard sum, multiplication.'

'Mmm, multiply eighty-nine by seventy-three.'

'Six thousand, four hundred and ninety-seven,' said Bidder instantly. 'Too easy. Try over with three figures, no, four by four.'

'Well...' Robert hesitated. Each time he conjured a sum in his head he dismissed it as surely too hard - he scrupled to make a fool of his new friend - but on the other hand he did not want to patronise. 'Oh, three thousand, four hundred and eighty-seven by three thousand, two hundred and seventy-three,' he said at last.

His heart sank when Bidder seemed to stare at him blankly - it *was* too hard - but in less than five seconds: 'Eleven million, four hundred and twelve thousand, nine hundred and fifty-one.'

'I don't believe it,' said Robert, astonished.

'Ar, iz right. Call for paper, if you like, work it out.'

'No, I don't... I mean, it's incredible. You must have had a wonderful arithmetic teacher.'

'My firz and only instructor in figures was my big brother, who's a working mason hizzelf. He helped me count up to ten, then coaxed me to one hundred and stopped. I amused myzel repeating the numbers over, until I zaw the pattern in em. Three times ten is thirty. Four times ten is forty, and so on. I didn't know one writ or printed figure from another, nor such a word as *multiply*, but I uzed to set out peas or marbles in rows, until I obtained my own treazure in a small bag of shot. I'd lay em out in squares, zay eight balls by eight, and took in how they amounted to sixty-four. Once I got the pattern of it I zaw how I could make leaps, see - that was the start of it all. I found I could make all the relations and acquaintances of my friends the numbers.'

'And your father made money out of exhibiting your talent.'

'Did it mezel first arv, as a nipper. See, I uzed to blow the bellaziz for an old blacksmith opposite. One day zomebody by chance mentioned a sum - may be nine times nine - and I chirped up, "Eighty-one!", which surprised em a little bit, but when they aimed to fickle me on two places of figures and three places, and had to fetch chalk to check the answers, thaz how I came to be the *calculating boy*, with halfpennies flowing into my pocket till my fame grew and Dad took a notion to let em flow into hiz.'

'He made you into a freak show?'

'Ar, but I maynt complain, cuz there I was seen by Zir John Herschel, who took an interest in getting me to school when he yerd me do twelve figures by twelve, then Zir Henry when Dad tried to put uz back in the booth.'

'You can do mental arithmetic to twelve digits?'

'Ar, mind only by great and distressing effort. I work from left to right, not right to left as taught in schools. Funny thing, I can't memorize a piece o verze or proze to save my life. Not the pattern in it, see. That shorthand o yourn, though, I might be able to pick up. Did you zay you learned it for your father's sake?'

'Yes, so he might benefit from my lectures second hand.'

'Your dad's quite different from mine, then.'

Robert thought a great deal about this statement afterwards. Of course it was true that George would never dream of exploiting his son, and that he always had his improvement at heart, but it was not without self-interest, and always on his own terms. At this stage in his life Robert was beginning to feel the marks of the bonds on him. He began to question, too, his father's assumption that the Stephensons had a special quality that somehow set them apart from the rest of humanity. The more Robert became acquainted with the world, the more he recognized that character and talent were not confined to the environs of Dial Cottage, and that George was not the only one to overcome disadvantage on the road to success, though one would think so to hear him tell it. Why, here was another George who had been the victim of poverty and, more than that, neglect, yet had husbanded the genius in himself. The Extraordinary Calculating Boy. How many more with such abilities might be found all over the country, not to mention the rest of the world, of which the Stephensons knew nothing? Whatever qualities Robert had inherited from his father, his boundless self-confidence was not one of them. At present, the son's sense of inadequacy was profound.

Bidder and he maintained their friendship. They joined the Wernerian Society and the Royal Society, made explorations of the various hostelries around Edinburgh, and took in the occasional performance at the Theatre Royal. Females they watched from a little distance but with much fascination, discussing ploys of engagement but never quite executing them, not wishing a love interest to interfere with their general enjoyment. Besides, Robert already had a place within for Miss Fanny Sanderson, which he told Bidder along with many other confidences when Scotch malts loosened his tongue. Not that he really needed alcohol to relax with Bidder. It was a liberating experience for Robert simply to

133

have a companion near his own age, something he had not enjoyed with any regularity since he had played in the fields as a boy. Their friendship lifted his spirits.

He was generally disappointed by the standard of the formal lectures at the university, though he continued sedulous and even won a minor mathematics prize. At home, George boasted about this achievement, but what meant more to his son was the opportunity Professor Jameson afforded some of his students to go on geological field trips. Robert and Bidder derived enormous pleasure from their excursion through the Great Glen along the line of Telford's newly-completed Caledonian Canal as far north as Inverness, traversing the shadow of Ben Nevis on the way.

*

Fifteen years before, George's time in Scotland had been terminated by a family crisis; now Robert was called back to the North East to help his father solve a problem of his own making. George's insistence that the Stockton-Darlington railway line should be laid largely with malleable iron created a rift with William Losh, his co-patentee of the cast iron rail. Losh could not forgive his partner working against their interest in this way; he refused to have anything more to do with George, which meant that the locomotives proposed for the new railway would have to be made elsewhere. But where? Who else had experience with these strange new beasts of industry? The only solution, George suggested to the Peases, was to start a manufacturing firm of their own in Newcastle; furthermore, he had the ideal candidate for managing director.

'It is to be called Robert Stephenson and Company,' he announced, the day after Robert was summoned from Edinburgh. They were standing with Edward Pease outside the premises in Forth Street, looking up at the sign above the door which already had Robert's name on it. George extended his arm; pulled his son into him. 'What do you think of that?'

What did he think of that? Robert was nineteen years old, had a smattering of experience and little in the way of qualifications. He had begun to think of himself as a student again, and here he was being asked to take on a senior post, a heavy responsibility. His father (harsh critic of others) seemed entirely confident that Robert could do the job; was clearly excited at the prospect. How confident did Robert feel? How excited? He followed his father's gaze above the door, saw his name depicted as a fact, tried to imagine what was imagined for him, felt a stirring of the pride he had experienced when he saw his own name attached to his first survey report, alloyed with trepidation about the responsibility the name implied, and a residue of irritation that George had not thought it mattered to discuss the idea with him first. Was this where he saw his future? Such a conflict of emotions made him falter in his response.

'I am... not sure.'

'What do you mean?'

Finding it impossible to be frank, Robert fell back on excuse. 'I have no money of my own to put into the venture.'

'Nowt to fret about. I've invested eight hundred pound of the money I made off my lamp. That's the Stephenson contribution.'

'It's not the same.'

'I understand thy concern, Robert,' said Edward Pease. 'I am prepared to lend thee five hundred pounds - lend it, mind - to make thy investment, and I am sure it will enjoy a good return, having done some good in the meantime.'

'Thank you, sir. That's very generous.'

'And the salary, Edward,' urged George. 'Tell him.'

'We will pay thee two hundred pounds a year to be managing partner.'

Why, after more inward debate, Robert made himself subject to mammon and to the will of his father, he did not fully comprehend himself except that, while the sense of love and duty to his parents were strong, he had another object at heart which surely influenced his decision. Fanny Sanderson had never been far from his thoughts since his visit to London, but the more he dwelt upon the evening they had spent together at Vauxhall Gardens the more his anxious imagination exaggerated the picture he had of himself as a gauche and ill-fit youth whose appearance must have been risible among the blades of the London fashion scene. It fuelled his resolution that, when they met again, Fanny would be impressed to behold a man of much more substance and *élan*. A generous salary would be a useful expedient.

Choice made, the utilitarian business of building steam engines must be commenced. George himself took the lead on the plans for *Locomotion* and *Hope*. Robert directed operations at the works, employed the men (including Uncles James and John and Aunt Nelly's betrothed, Stephen Liddle), and dealt with contracts, orders and accounts. From the start the young man was determined that Robert Stephenson and Company would be no mere local concern. As well as the continued interest in the Liverpool-Manchester project through William James, he sought contracts for stationary engines as far away as Bristol, Cornwall and Ireland. Everywhere, behind the resistance of the old order, he found industry expectant. So much depended on the success of the Stockton and Darlington.

George's ambitions rested on the possibilities of the project. Though the first Stockton engines were designed for the heavy task of hauling coal wagons at low speeds, he also ordered the building of a coach that he called the *Experiment*. It still looked very much like a stage coach, and was built to be drawn by horses rather than steam traction, but this, as far as he knew, would be the world's first railway carriage for passengers.

Once the construction of the line was well advanced, George led Robert and John Dixon along a stretch they had surveyed, walking for mile upon mile within the gauge of the iron rails that lay shining in the sun. An hour after noon he took them to the Fighting Cocks inn and, unusually for him, called for a bottle of red wine with their meal. When the wine was poured, George raised his glass by way of a toast.

'Now lads. I will tell yous that I think you'll live to see the day, though I may not live so long, when railways will come to supersede almost all other methods of conveyance in this country.' He lowered his glass, continued his speech leaning earnestly across the table. 'When mail coaches ull go by railway, and railroads ull become the great highway, ay, for the king and all his subjects. The time is coming when it will be cheaper for a working man to travel on a railway than to walk on foot.' He paused, letting the memory of his long walk to Montrose lap in. The two serious young men waited on him quietly. 'Oh, I know there's great difficulties to be encountered - but what I've said mun come to pass, sure as you live. I only wish I may live to see the day, though I can scarcely hope...'

He sipped at his wine. Guessing this was the end of the toast, they drank theirs too. 'To the railways,' John said softly. Robert set down his glass after one draught and reached to his inside pocket. He was drawing out a cigar when he became conscious of his father's silent disapproval, and put it back.

'Ay, ten years my experiment has been successful at Killingworth,' George continued, 'and I'm still waiting for my locomotives to be adopted generally.' He straightened up. 'Here's to the railway, as you say, Mr Dixon. Here's to the Stockton and Darlington.' George drained his glass and Robert observed a slight moistness in his eye as he turned to

136

look out of the window at the works beyond, though whether from sentiment or the pungency of the wine he was unable to tell.

*

Robert's own sentimental attachment to his home region was loosened significantly when the family at last left Dial Cottage and set up home in Eldon Place to be near the works in Newcastle. The city that once seemed so large and imposing he now considered parochial, having visited London, Edinburgh and Dublin. Places he had not been to yet called him like sirens. Many of his fellow students were just then embarking upon the Grand Tour, and Robert thirsted still for overseas travel. He could not contain his excitement when one of the firm's partners, the banker Thomas Richardson, revealed his connections with South America through an international mining company. First there was the prospect of selling steam engines for the continent, then Richardson spoke about a plan that had Robert recalling his grandfather's old tales of treasure hidden in enchanted caves.

'You have heard of Eldorado, I suppose?' Richardson began as they sat one day in Robert's office above the workshop.

'I have - the mythical city of gold.'

'Mythical, yes, but the legend sent many prospectors to Colombia, and the result was gold and silver mines that did indeed provide riches for some, until the years of revolution forced their abandonment.'

'I believe my father's friend, Richard Trevithick, went out there some years ago.'

'And doubtless made himself rich as Croesus. The point is this, my friend...' Richardson broke off for a brisk rub with his pocket handkerchief at a spot of grime that had somehow transferred itself from the works below to Robert's desk and thence to his visitor's hand. 'Now that the political situation in the country seems to have settled, the Colombian Mining Association proposes to re-open certain gold and silver mines in the country. And they need an able and enterprising engineer to help them succeed.'

'Have you mentioned this to my father?'

'Of course. His answer was that there is more than enough to do here. Nevertheless the mining company have asked me to approach you directly. They would like you to go and talk to them in London, with a view to travelling abroad on their behalf.'

Robert made no immediate reply, astonished by this unexpected invitation, and already in rehearsal for the turmoil he would create by

137

accepting it. 'I would be pleased to explore the opportunity,' he said at last, 'but I will not go behind my father's back. I will discuss it with him first.'

When Robert tentatively raised the subject at home, however, his father had another surprise. 'I canna possibly spare you, son, specially now I'm to tek over the survey in Liverpool.'

This was disconcerting news. 'What has happened to William James?'

'Dropped, it seems, by the Railway Committee. I hear the man is near ruined from taking on too much, and can't cope. Bankruptcy and the bum bailiffs next for him, more than likely. That'll serve im - if he hadn't spent so much time bustling about the country talking up other people's ideas like they were his own, mebbes he wouldn't ha got imself in such a mess.'

'I'm not sure that's fair. He has been one of our most vociferous supporters.'

Robert's piqued tone caused his stepmother to glance up from her embroidery, but failed to deflect his father from his criticism. 'Oh, he's made noise enough, I gi you that; but all to his own ends.'

'Much good it did him, then.' Robert's irritation took him to the front door and out before he could give full vent; rarely had he been so much in need of a short walk and a long cigar.

This anger with his father festered. By the time Robert returned to London to ease more parliamentary scrutiny of the company's plans for the Stockton and Darlington, he had determined to meet with the principals of the Colombian Mining Association, with or without parental approval. He also took advantage of his latest stay in the capital to pursue other designs he had in mind. Not long after booking into his room at the Imperial Hotel in Covent Garden, he walked to Regent Street for a fitting appointment with the tailor Joseph Crookes, where he ordered an entire new wardrobe in the latest fashion for collection the next day, and from there to the establishment of Perigal and Dutterraw in New Bond Street to pick up an elegant gold watch and chain to adorn his new fine-patterned waistcoat. This time he would be better turned out for the evening Fanny had agreed to spend with him.

His day at Westminster was dominated by the issue of the fees to be charged by the new railway for hauling coal. Mr John Lambton MP may have earned the sobriquet Radical Jack for his politics, but he was as staunch as any Tory when it came to protecting his own trade in coal exported by sea from Sunderland. He was adamant that the upstart railway company should be limited to charging just one halfpenny per mile for each ton of coal hauled to Stockton for the purpose of shipment. Robert could see that this low rate was uneconomic to the point of being potentially ruinous (Lambton was certainly looking forward to such an outcome) but what if, instead, it succeeded in diverting coal in such great quantities that an economy of scale resulted? Then Radical Jack would be hoist by his own petard. Robert, having begun the session in argumentative mode, ended it reflective, raising no more objection to the Lambton clause.

Thursday, which he planned to end with Miss Sanderson on his arm, was the day of his meeting with Mr Powles, the Chairman of the Colombian Mining Association in Leadenhall Street. The friendliness and hospitality extended to him by Powles came as a pleasant contrast to the hostility of Lambton and his associates.

'You come highly recommended by Mr Richardson, Robert. We see you as key to our success in Mariquita.'

'Mariquita?'

'It is a little more than one hundred miles from Bogota. There we have already leased four silver mines from the Colombian government. This is just the start - we believe the prospects are excellent, and we anticipate no difficulty in raising one million pounds in capital.'

'What sort of difficulty might I anticipate? I mean, in reopening these works. And what of the climate?'

Powles was frank but reassuring. 'You will find the climate healthy and agreeable. The biggest challenge is not the mines, but the terrain. Your first project will be to survey then make new road and rail routes between the workings and the ports. Machinery is even now on its way.'

'And labour?'

'Local labour is almost impossible to find, and I have to tell you the natives are indolent. But do not worry, you are to have the best of British workmen at your command. A small party of miners will accompany you on your voyage, and the main body will join you once you are ready to commence in earnest. We are recruiting mainly from Cornwall - good, stout navvies.'

Before two hours were up, the pair had adjourned to the Ship and Turtle, having shaken hands on a provisional agreement whereby Robert would become agent to the company for a period of three years at a salary of five hundreds pounds per annum plus expenses. In his mind (pricked by conscience) he had already resolved to commute a proportion of that money to his company in Newcastle; this would be one plank in the argument he had constructed to persuade his partners - essentially, his father - to let him go. He was not so assured of their consent as he had exhibited at the meeting, nor was his self-confidence about the task in prospect so high, though he flattered himself that his outward appearance was all untroubled urbanity.

Returned to his hotel after his long lunch with Mr Powles, Robert consulted The Mirror of Fashion in the *Morning Chronicle* to determine where in the West End he should take Fanny. His stepmother had suggested they should not miss the opportunity to see Mr Kean's reprise of Shylock at the Theatre Royal in Drury Lane, but Robert's eye was caught by the promise of a public demonstration of laughing gas, *the wonders of which*, said the advertisement, *were first experienced by Sir Humphry Davy*. Some combination of curiosity about the phenomenon and its association with this name from his past had Robert escorting Fanny that evening, not to Drury Lane, but to the Adelphi Theatre at the other end of the Strand.

If Fanny was slightly disappointed at Robert's choice of entertainment she tried hard not to show it, though, when her head fell somewhat towards his shoulder during Mr Henry's introductory lecture on the discovery and properties of nitrous oxide, it was not entirely by her own volition. Things soon became livelier. The practical part of the demonstration was prefaced by the slotting of a strong railing into specially prepared anchor points at the front of the stage and the placing of twelve strong men at the back - necessary safety precautions, according to the master of ceremonies, for what was to come. His announcement seemed to alarm and titillate the large audience in equal measure.

Stage hands brought on half a dozen chairs, ordinary high-backed chairs except for the addition of a distended bag hanging at the back of each, from which emerged a length of tubing with a mask on the end, that was hung onto a stand attached to the chair-back.

'Our preparations are almost complete,' said Mr Henry, 'but for one vital ingredient: our volunteers.' He allowed the buzz of anticipation to reach all parts of the theatre before he assumed full command again, arms outstretched. 'Upon success often follows imitation, and it pains me to report that there are certain imitators - I will not call them rivals - quacks, rather, with no pretensions to chemistry - who have attempted deliberately to introduce salaciousness into their vulgar displays by inviting young ladies publicly to inhale of the gas. Such behaviour is beyond the bounds. My sole intention is to blend and so enhance instruction with amusement without the slightest risk of indecency;

therefore I invite only the first class of gentlemen to offer themselves for the purposes of this short demonstration. Do I have volunteers?'

There was collective hesitation, caused by understandable fear of the unknown or perhaps by male members of the audience (Robert included) inwardly assessing whether they were eligible on the terms outlined. Mr Henry aborted the pregnant pause, drew laughter by announcing, 'I may have to volunteer myself,' after which one young man raised his hand in the stalls and was motioned forward, followed by a few others scattered in various parts of the theatre. Robert was intensely eager to know the effects of the gas, and may well have risen from his seat had Fanny not chosen just that moment to lay her gloved hand on his where it lay on the armrest. He glanced at her to check whether she was consciously restraining him, but her attention was directed to the front, her eyes glowing. Robert thought of their night at the fireworks and fell in love with her a second time.

When Mr Henry had his full complement of volunteers he led them to the chairs and helped one by one to hold the masks to their own faces, then reached behind and turned a valve to release the mixture of gases from the bag. Once he had each man breathing deeply from his mask, Mr Henry stepped aside and turning to the audience said, 'As a means of revealing true character, laughing gas has proved more accurate than phrenology. Let us discover what characters we have on stage with us this evening.'

The first to react was a small, portly man, probably in his thirties, who simply let his mask slip onto the floor as he flung his arms open, slipped down to rest his neck on the edge of the chair and sank into a mirthful sleep, his stomach rising and falling in rhythm except where it rippled in concert with the sleeper's occasional snorts and sniggers. Mr Henry stepped behind his chair to turn off the gas, and as he did so the man on the next chair flung his arm across his sleeping neighbour in exhilarated and affectionate abandon. Both slumped to the floor like lovers, to peals of laughter from the audience. Mr Henry nodded once to the strong men stationed at the back of the stage. A posse formed to pick the men up and replace them on their chairs, where they sat and mooned at each other like love-struck drunks.

At the other end of the row was a hirsute gent, around forty-five, in a suit of light mourning. After several deep draughts of the gas he stood in front of his chair and, with one hand posed dramatically at his heart and the other sweeping the air, treated the audience to a mournful solo from some Italian opera in a baritone that had more pathos than tunefulness.

'Hey, Signor Benelli,' one wag shouted from the circle, 'you're supposed to be on at the King's!'

Before 'Signor Benelli' had finished his song the young man who had been first to volunteer stood up on his chair and declaimed in a manner that suggested a political harangue, though it was difficult to hear through the cod Italian of the baritone he was competing with. Robert certainly heard mention of the Corn Laws and Peterloo before two of Mr Henry's assistants stepped forward, lifted the man from his chair and carried him off the stage and out of the theatre. The youth courageously kept up his speech even after he had been bundled through the doors at the back. His persistence made Robert wonder whether he had sniffed of the gas at all; it seemed rather an attempt to convey his message to a captive audience, though he had not chosen his moment well.

Robert was not convinced either about the gentleman who paraded from one wing of the stage to the other in military manner, saluting Mr Henry as he passed, or the man who staggered to the front of the apron and, leaning over the rail, begged a pretty young lady in the front row to come up and dance with him, which she refused. If they had not escaped from Bedlam, surely some of these performers were secretly paid by the management to make a show. Yet when the effects of the nitrous oxide had worn off and Mr Henry reviewed the antics of the participants most of them seemed genuinely ashamed, even horrified, to hear what they had done under the influence.

After the show, which also featured a balloon ascent to the roof of the theatre and concluded with a magic lantern phantasmagoria, the couple travelled by hackney carriage to the Albion Tavern in Aldersgate Street, recommended by Mr Sanderson as a respectable place to eat and not far from home for Fanny. Robert wanted to tell her about his probable secondment to South America (was there something in him ready to be persuaded not to go?) but the chance did not arise. He was partly subdued by the constant presence of a waiter behind each of their chairs; made aware too, by a supercilious look that passed between the waiters, that he had committed a *faux pas* by asking for small beer instead of white wine with his fish course. Fanny took her conversational cue from Robert, the consequence being that they ate a much quieter dinner than was comfortable for either of them.

Robert had embarked on his evening with Fanny in a mood of excitement and expectation. By midnight, when he had returned her safe to the bosom of her family and was travelling by carriage back to his hotel, his head was spinning in a conflict of thoughts and emotions involving work, ambition, family, love and, as so often with this complex young man, private investigations into his own self-worth. Alighting at the steps of the Imperial Hotel, he was too unsettled to go in immediately, but set off on a directionless walk through the streets of central London, seeking comfort in his cigar.

He wanted adventure and new experience. He wanted the reassurance of his family and his home life. He respected and admired his father for his past achievements, his embracing of opportunities, his courage, his pioneering spirit. He wanted to earn respect on his own behalf. He was still angry with his father for his dismissive attitude to William James and others whom Robert admired, for his arrogance, for his assumption of control over his son's life. Robert longed for independence, to step out of his father's shadow. He was in love. He was too young to be tied down. He was too old to be told what to do. He was not ready to be weighed down by responsibility for other people. He was weary. He was fearful of the future. He was excited by it. He had too much to do, and so much more he wanted to do.

Occupied by these contrary thoughts, Robert paid little heed to where he was going or the lateness of the hour. There were few people about. He was vaguely conscious, now and again, of distant revels behind closed doors - sly taverns reluctant to give up their customers to the night. Occasionally a carriage rattled by; a couple walking, whispering confidentially, passed on the opposite side; the odd shadow moved down a lane; a bundle shifted in a doorway. More deserted streets. Then a voice, close enough to startle; female, languid.

'Looking for company, dear?'

'Excuse me?'

She stood in the entrance to an alleyway not four feet from him, but he had not noticed her until she spoke, and only now, when she edged into the light from the street lamp, could he make her out. She was perhaps sixteen or seventeen, with a face not unpretty but pallid in the lamplight in stark contrast to her lips, crudely painted as if a child had been at work. As she stepped forward she withdrew her frayed shawl, displayed what seemed to be no more than a shift beneath, gaping untidily to reveal an expanse of naked chest.

'I'm your poppet. You can have me for half a crown.'

She moved towards him, stretched out her hand to touch his sleeve. He recoiled like one stung; felt a jarring all through his body. 'Oh, no, really, I... No, thank you.'

'There he goes with his eye out!' she spat after him as he hurried away, suddenly alive to his surroundings. He could hear his own footsteps, feared they were sending a signal to every vagabond and rogue

143

hiding up the dark alleys, inviting them to come and rob. He became aware that he might be venturing deeper, courting trouble away from the safety of his hotel. He stopped, vacillated about retracing his steps; worried the whore should misinterpret his coming back. Instead he carried on to the next street and turned right, intending to turn again when he came to any road that was broader and better-lit than this one.

Walking calmed him sufficiently to allow admittance of a certain deliciousness about the sense of danger in these London streets. He was more alert than he had been for the last hour. His anxious engrossment had gone. He was even able to entertain the memory of his encounter with the girl as an interesting experience. He had never been accosted in that way before and, though he would surely never entertain the advances of a common street harlot, he recognized what had happened as significant in his passage to maturity.

Approaching the light of another gas lamp, his heart lurched when he saw a figure loitering beneath it. He stopped, at a distance safe enough for flight, to consider his position. Dare he carry on, or must he turn about? He peered through the darkness. The shape was definitely male, with a top hat and possibly an opera cloak or some sort of riding cape. As he watched, a burst of flame illuminated the man's face while he lit a cheroot; finer features than Robert would expect in a ruffian and what looked like a decent white collar underneath. He decided to walk on.

Closer inspection confirmed this was a man of some breeding, if a shade rakish. He acknowledged Robert's approach, and said jauntily, 'Seeking out Mr Chung?'

'I'm sorry?'

'Headed there myself. Frederick Travis. Join you?'

'I... I don't know Mr Chung.'

'Oh, you should.' Travis blew a smoke ring and smirked. 'You should.' He left the pool of yellow light and inclined his head, inviting company as he sauntered along the street. Robert fell into step. The path sloped slightly as they neared the river.

'I presume Mr Chung is a foreign gentleman?'

'Foreign, yes. Chinese or some other slant-eyed strain. Gentleman? No, you wouldn't call Chung a gentleman, but he's sound, and serves very good black.'

'Black?'

'Opium.'

'Ah.' Robert tried to act blasé but his scalp tingled with a fresh charge of nervous excitement. Opium. Here was an opportunity for discreet experimentation. Physicians prescribed it routinely - it could no more do injury than laughing gas.

Travis turned off the street through a narrow arch and, after only a moment's hesitation, Robert followed him into near-darkness. 'Take care with these steps,' Travis warned, which was as well because they were very uneven and treacherous. At the bottom of the steps a single guttering candle, jammed into a crevice, dimly revealed a doorway screened only by thick matting, which was kept there by heavy stones laid across the low roof. Travis pushed through, calling, 'Customers, Chung.' Robert ducked under the rug after him, and had his nostrils assaulted by a powerful sweet and sickly smell. It was as if some sort of sugary mixture had been burnt on the stove. This idea was reinforced by the fug of smoke or fumes within, through which a stunted figure was emerging - not Mr Chung as this was a female, a child not more than ten years old, who carried a candle to guide them into the room, relieving each man first of a shilling.

When Robert's eyes adjusted to the interior he saw that an assortment of low divans and mattresses littered the floor, with the spaces between them covered in faded oriental rugs. A heavily bearded sailor was lying on a mattress next to the wall, apparently asleep, with what looked like a wooden flute fallen across his chest. At first Robert thought the sleeper was the only occupant, then he noticed another man reclining in a hammock slung under the blackened ceiling in the far corner. The girl moved to a mean fireplace on the other side of the room and knelt to resume the task that had been interrupted by the arrival of the latest visitors, stirring a pot that simmered on the hot coals. Robert was wondering where Mr Chung could be, when he appeared suddenly before them, presumably from some recess at the back, bowing his head towards his finger-tips in the servile manner that orientals often adopted in the presence of white men. He was every inch (though not many of these) the archetypal Chinese peasant, from his soft skull cap to his straw shoes.

'New man for you here, Chung,' said Travis. 'Give him your best pipe.'

The Chinaman nodded vigorously and scurried back to his alcove to search among his smoking tools for his finest offering, though Robert was very doubtful of what he was finally given: a long yellow bamboo that did indeed look like a flute except for the cup of dark baked clay that fitted into a spigot hole at the end. It was ancient, stained with the draw and spittle of many years' smoking. Travis laughed at Robert's involuntary grimace. 'Believe me, friend, there's more satisfaction to be had in a ripe,

145

well-saturated instrument, seasoned over the years by the best opium, than any virgin pipe, however elegantly carved.'

Chung, meanwhile, had taken possession of two little gallipots, filled by the servant girl from the sediment at the bottom of her cooking pot. This stuff, which looked like thin treacle, was the source of the burnt sugar smell, mixed with the aroma of laudanum. Chung used an iron bodkin, dipping the tip of it into the gallipot then holding it to the flame of an oil lamp until it almost hardened. He repeated the process several times until he had gathered a globule about the size of lead shot, which he dropped into the bowl of Robert's pipe. Travis demonstrated how to light the pipe from the lamp flame, and the young man was ready for his initiation into opium-smoking.

He perched on one of the low divans, too restrained to lie down, so that his knees stuck out awkwardly either side of the long pipe. There was no mouthpiece; the stem was sheared off, leaving a hole to suck at, which Robert did tentatively at first, then harder so the black smoke rose too quick up the stem, making him cough horribly.

'Don't waste it,' said Travis, who was stretched out on a mattress next to his feet with his own pipe.

Robert tried to be more economical with his breathing, sucking then expelling the smoke gently through his nostrils. The pipe gurgled. Robert could feel the veins in his forehead thickening, his face taking on a warm glow. Gradually the sensation of warmth entered, lulling his brain into a reverie that had no images but pleasant patterns swirling around. He felt at one with this sensation, and remote from it, a spectator and a participant. By intervals the patterns quickened in a way that captivated. He began to discern shapes he could only describe as exotic; shapes with no edges, undulations merely. He was drawn into a weightless journey that ended when the patterns opened into a place of perfect serenity. Robert let the pipe fall and relaxed full length on the couch, giving himself up to the tranquillity that under laid exquisite sleep.

Robert returned to Newcastle (on the eve of his Aunt Nelly's wedding to Stephen Liddle) a different person, a man of experience, and with a fixed purpose. George noticed at once merely the superficial change, and he did not like it.

'Is that what they've learned you down London? To wear fancy waistcoats and chains and fang-dangs?'

He planted himself foursquare so that they stood face to face, and he reached out to hook Robert's new watch from his pocket. He inspected the piece with some contempt as it dangled on the end of its

146

gold chain, then allowed it to fall loose. Robert retrieved his watch and returned it to his pocket, saying nothing, determined not to be cowed.

'If you'll tek my advice, which I darsay you won't, you'll not adorn yersel wi trinkets like those. I never did, and if I had I should not have been the man I am.'

George waited a moment for a reply; receiving none, he walked away. Robert glanced at his mama, cocooned in the fireside seat. She looked across at George, then at Robert, seemed about to intervene, but desisted.

Betty bided her time. She saw the change in Robert more clearly than her husband had; looked beneath the surface. She refrained from investigation until she could spend a little time alone with him. Meanwhile there was Nelly's wedding to attend to. It was a quieter affair in some ways than her own, though the congregation was larger and the service, at St John's in Westgate Road, more demonstrably religious. Less worldly, perhaps, certainly less animated without George at the very centre of it. The family celebrations ended with high tea at Eldon Place. After the newly-weds had departed, Betty asked Robert if he would care to take her for a short constitutional while the light was still good. They walked across Barras Bridge and up Lovaine Row to take in the view across Pandon Dean to the River Tyne.

'It's pleasant here, though the town is reaching out to it even now,' said Betty. 'Nothing compared to London, I'm sure.'

'It's very different; different qualities.'

'And now we are to have a house in Liverpool. Everything is moving so fast these days. But you are like your father - you welcome change, you embrace it.'

'Not if it is only on his terms, then I don't.'

'Robert.' She paused, regarded him in profile, his jaw set. 'You are not so fond of your father as you were.'

'Of course I'm fond of him, Mama. I love him, as I always have. But he maddens me more than he did. I know not where the fault lies.'

'Don't talk of fault. You must both learn to accommodate one another.'

'Do you know about South America?'

'He told me.'

'He had it from Mr Richardson about my offer before I was ready to tell him, and now he's dead set against it.'

Betty's emotion rose with the anxiety of her position as go-between. She touched his wrist, and for all her assumed placidity he could feel the faint tremble at her finger-ends. 'He is not being wilful for the sake of it,' she said. 'It's just that... He feels he needs you here when there is work to do on both sides of the country, and, more importantly...'

'What's more important to him than that?'

'He'd miss you so much... We both would.'

'He didn't think so much about that when *he* went away.'

'When he went away...?' She made it a question, but she knew before he confirmed it.

'To Scotland, I mean. When I was little.'

'Oh, Robert, that was a long time ago. When needs must...'

They fell silent, pretending interest in the view. Robert felt tears coming, and for distraction concentrated on counting the windows of Mr Armstrong's house by Magdalen Field. Betty dabbed discreetly at the corner of her eye with her handkerchief. Composing herself she asked quietly, 'Isn't there someone in London who would miss you too?'

Robert hesitated enough to concern her before he replied. 'Perhaps.' Then, 'Yes. Yes, I think Miss Sanderson would miss me.'

'Have you told her about your decision?'

'Not yet, no. I intend to soon. Mama, I think Fanny will understand that this is something I need to do. I think she will wait for me.'

'And you'd like her to?'

'To wait for me? Yes, of course.' He turned to his stepmother. 'I should tell you - she has no fortune to speak of.'

Betty's tone was as near as it ever came to reproving. 'When have such things ever been a consideration for us? No, there is only one question you must answer, and that you must answer for yourself.'

'If you mean, do I love her... I have already answered it for myself, and I will make my answer to you. Yes, Mama, yes I do.'

Betty's eyes followed the course of the distant river. 'I found it hard, waiting for your father all those years. Of course, I did not have around me the society bustle I suppose there is in the capital. Whether that makes it easier, or no...'

'Mama, she'll wait for me, I'm sure she will, because... She does not know how unworthy I am of her.'

'That is not true - do not say so.'

'I believe it is. But I am sure of her love, and her qualities. Of her patience. And when I come back I will marry her.'

'You will?'

'I promise.'

'Make that promise to she who must hear it. All the promise *I* want is that you should keep yourself safe, and return to us whole and

148

healthy. But I am glad you have found your heart. It assures me that you will return when you have done the work you have to do, and secure your happiness here. That is a settling notion.'

She was, though, far from settled to see the tension still at Robert's jaw, and how difficult he was finding it to look at her with his former openness. She divined there was something more than he was willing to tell her. She still did not really understand how he could be so ready to leave behind someone he loved. Nor did she herself want him to go, not by any means. She supported his position in spite of her own feelings. Later that night she spoke to George alone. 'You know Robert is determined to go.'

'An I am determined he mun stay. It's not but five minutes sin he took up his post - he'd be failing in his duty to abandon it now. I've told you, he mun stick to his last.'

'He accepted the position out of love and respect for you, against his better judgment. South America is a great opportunity for him. Would you stand in his way?'

From anyone else, George would have taken this as an accusation and would have contested it hotly. Betty always made him think more calmly. While he remained quiet, she advanced Robert's cause. 'Haven't you told me many times of the dream you had to sail America? You never went, and I am glad of it, for had you done so I would have been waiting for you until I was an old woman, perhaps for ever. But isn't there still something in you that wonders what it would have been like?'

'Times I think about it, aye.'

'It's rising in Robert now, and it needs release, like the steam in one of your engines. And it's only for a short while, really. He has told me that he wants to return soon and marry Miss Sanderson. We won't be losing him for ever.'

He reached for her hand; spoke quietly, almost pleadingly. 'What if we were to lose him though, Betty? I mean, if summat were to happen at sea, say? He's the one child I have left to me.'

'And is the son not to be allowed to take the risks his father did, and does yet, in pursuit of his dreams? Is he always to be in thrall to your peace of mind?'

'Nay, but... Of course not.'

George made no specific promise to his wife, but the next day he made application to Timothy Hackworth at Wylam, requesting his services as a deputy to oversee the Stockton and Darlington work while Robert was away. Betty, moved by reading news of Lord Byron's death in Greece,

149

scoured Newcastle for a leather-bound collection of his poetry as a parting gift to her stepson. Not long after, Robert was back in London, making detailed preparations for his departure.

As if sent to dampen the young man's ardour, rain visited on the city almost every day he was there. It drenched him as he moved between his lodgings in Finsbury Place and Professor Phillips' rooms for tuition in mineralogical chemistry; from Spanish lessons at the Mechanics Institution to meetings with the company's agents where he sought in vain for clarity on the contract. It dripped from the brim of his hat as he waited admittance to the Sandersons' home in Broad Street for the confession of his plans to a dark-eyed, tearful Fanny. It beat for hours against his bedroom window while his thoughts kept him awake inside. It sluiced the noisome channels of London's darkest alleys. It soaked the dirty rug hanging at a secluded doorway, and transferred some of its wetness to Robert's shoulder when he pushed through, the night he returned solitary to try again the heady mixture in Mr Chung's best pipe.

The sun reappeared on the early June morning that saw Robert and his expedition companions start out on the journey to Liverpool, where they were to set sail in the *Sir William Congreve*. Their coach was further weighed down by more than a ton of baggage and equipment they were taking with them. Before they even reached the outskirts of London, Robert was in a sweat of fear that the coach would topple over, crushing all inside with their own luggage. The springs had lost all elasticity. By Birmingham at least one of them had broken altogether, so that the body of the coach rested on the framework and the passengers suffered jolts from every pothole, large and small, and every rock of the hundreds that littered the road. The overwrought travellers were still thirty miles from Liverpool when a large crack opened in the roof of their compartment. For the remainder of the journey Robert kept his eyes on the split and his hand on the window ledge, poised to hurl himself out should the top tear asunder and the freight crash in on the human cargo.

George travelled less eventfully to Liverpool from Newcastle a few days later, to start work on the new survey and to see off his son. They were both invited to a dinner hosted by Joseph Sandars, Chairman of the Railway Committee. George was unusually quiet in the company, but he listened carefully to Robert discussing mineralogy with one of the other guests, Doctor Trail, and felt pride for his son's obvious erudition. Sandars, sitting next to George, sought to bring him into the conversation.

'When do you intend to start the survey, Mr Stephenson?'

150

'Oh, the morn, directly after Robert's ship sails. You'll not find us behindhand.'

'Of course, I did not mean to imply otherwise.'

'Aye, I was thinking just now, it's turtle soup and champagne the night; may be bread and milk or owt else I can catch in some poor man's cottage the morrow.'

Robert may have been the only one to note the glimmer of defiance in George's eyes as he spoke, the look that seemed to say, you gentlemen are all very well with your fine tastes and manners, but you don't know what real work is, what it takes to keep you secure in your wealth and station; you don't see how my rough hands are more skilled than your fair ones, and my mind quicker than yours, however eloquent you might be. Robert had read such looks in that face often. Since George's outburst over his *fang-dangs* he felt included in them. The son's senses were sharp, but perhaps he failed to make the distinction between sense and his own sensitivity; failed to read in the nods and smiles his father made, as he listened to him talk with others round the table, not only how he would miss the intelligent help his son provided, but how sorely he would miss his simply being there. Robert thought he knew his father better than the man knew himself. But perhaps he misunderstood more than he knew, on the eve of their three year separation.

IX

George came to Robert in a dream. Or rather they were together in the dream. Robert was driving his father's hearse when George lifted the coffin lid, demanding to know why it could not go faster. He climbed out to sit beside his son and expound his ideas for driving corpses to meet their maker with the urgency of steam.

'An while we're about it let's build a tunnel an tek the sinners straight to hell.'

No sooner had he said it than the ground opened before them and the hearse, now hissing steam, fell into a tunnel with a gradient indistinguishable from a fall. The lidless coffin slid forward and came to rest between their feet. Robert glanced down to see the face of George Hudson grinning up at him. 'I am only a tool in the hands of a genius,' Hudson said implacably from inside the box. A warning yell - *Ware, forward!* Robert looked out to see hell's firebox flung open, expanding to swallow the hearse.

He woke up bathed in sweat, his face burning, as if indeed he'd had a close encounter with the scorching flames. He lay, wondering if he was really ill, whether he should call the doctor. In fact his health had not been good since before his father's death, and had been further disturbed by an accident eight days after it at Conway Station. The train he sat in had just switched lines when a passing express caught its protruding angle and knocked it off the rail, shaking the passengers inside. Mercifully there was no serious harm done, but the incident had left Robert with a sore back, and added to his sense of general debilitation. Neither opium nor calomel seemed to provide him much relief these days, though he continued with both regularly.

His father's opinion of doctors had been but marginally higher than his view of men of religion. They each may have their place, but George preferred to find succour in nature rather than relying on professional ministrations, and on the whole nature had not let him down. He did after all survive nearly three years following his near-fatal attack of pleurisy, without medication, just plenty of exercise and mental activity. Robert determined to follow his example and stir himself to work.

He travelled to his office at 24 Great George Street in company with his business manager, Fanny's brother John. On the way John handed him the morning's domestic mail. Among the remnants of condolence was a penny post letter from the widow Stephenson, returning to the subject of her annuity. She made reference to the size of the inheritance - about which she could know nothing - implying that she was being badly treated. Robert tutted with annoyance, folded the letter roughly and stuffed it into an inside pocket. 'Mad for money. Why has the world gone mad for money, John?'

Sanderson smiled and looked out from the cab at the shops of Mayfair. 'I suppose, because there is so much now to purchase. It's partly your fault, Robert. You helped crank it up, don't you know. Expectation mounts proportionate to the railway's reach and quickness. Now we're all in a fever of wanting.'

Robert found something to cheer him at the office, for Bidder had returned from Wales with good news on the progress of the bridges.

'All eight pontoons iz in place for the second Conway tube. Erz ready for floating any time near high flood.'

'Excellent. What is the word from the north, the High Level?'

'Thars clozing of the arches now. Meantime the timber bridge is standing in good stead. Mr Udzon will be pleased - that northern line's as dear to his heart as yourn I'd zay. Or his wallet anyways.'

'Hudson? Have you heard from him?'

'No. Unuzual quiet lately.'

'Keeping his head down, I shouldn't wonder,' said Robert. 'He has some trouble brewing, apparently.'

'That he's well uzed to. He'll just plarnt his fat arze on it.'

'Perhaps not this time. And to tell you the truth, GP, I'm worried about my association with the man. I can see my reputation breaking under me like an egg shell.'

'You baint got no worries, Chief. Everybody knows you're straight as a die.' Bidder chuckled at a memory. 'You mind the larst Mania, various parties delivering cheques yere, not one less than a thouzand pound, and no word on why they were zent. What did we do? Fired em straight back with a note to the effect of we baint a power to be bought and sold. Nay, Rob, darn you fear for your reputation.'

'Nevertheless, I was aware of Hudson's, and worked with him regardless. That's a fault, I believe, and I may pay for it.'

No more was said on the subject, and work continued in the office until early evening, when Bidder left and Sanderson stayed to help his brother-in-law finish off his correspondence. Only when he was getting his coat did Robert remember the letter from Mrs Stephenson.

'What should I do with this?' he said, handing it to his colleague. Sanderson looked over the note briefly, and shrugged.

'Your dad's will is clear enough. Refer her to your solicitor, I'd say.'

'You are right, as ever. I'm not being heartless, am I, or bitter?'

'Of course not.'

Robert read the letter once more, smoothing the folds with his hand, then scrutinised the signature, as though trying to detect a forgery. Sanderson worked away quietly on the opposite side of the desk.

'Did I ever tell you...?' Robert said. 'Did I ever mention that Fanny wanted me to marry again?'

Sanderson looked up. 'No. No, I don't believe you did.'

'She begged me to, almost to her last breath. Because she had not brought me children, she said. We both so wanted... And she knew how much my father would have doted on a grandchild. A boy especially.'

'Is this by way of telling me you have someone in mind?'

'No, not at all. That is my point. I... How could I replace her?' He sank into silence. Sanderson watched him, tried to think of something comforting to say. He understood that Robert's grief for George had unearthed earlier sorrows. He remained quiet, his own thoughts on his late sister, and it was Robert who spoke again.

'John, do you suppose it possible that my father married this woman because he thought she could bear him a child?'

Sanderson was shocked by this notion. 'At his age? Do you really think so?'

'Ellen Gregory... Stephenson is, I would think, still capable. She is five years younger than I am. And why wouldn't he want that? Otherwise the direct line ends with me.'

John Sanderson studied his employer across the desk. There was a fever of anxiety in Robert, at odds with his usual calm, professional disposition. Sanderson sought to release the strain. 'It has been a long day. Shall we go home and see what Miss Tomlinson has planned for dinner?'

'You do that, brother. I'll stay out a while. Perhaps I am in need of society, having been so reclusive lately. I may take a stroll to the Athenaeum, spend an hour or so. Please tell Margaret I will dine away from home, but I will not be late.'

All the staff had gone by the time Robert left the office, so his reply to the widow was carried with him across St James's Park in the evening fog and deposited in the mail box at the Athenaeum. 'Quiet tonight?' he remarked to the hall porter.

154

'Everybody's up in the drawing room, sir. Mr Dickens is in, so naturally there's quite a crowd around him. He's had some recent sadness too, sir, like yourself.'

'His sister, yes. I read of her passing in the *Times*.'

'Mr Dickens is only just got back to town.'

'I see.' Robert walked to the foot of the stairs, and hesitated, as though faced with a mountain climb at the end of a tiring journey. He could think of several reasons why a meeting with the author was unlikely to lift his spirits presently, and the prospect of mutual mourning was another one. He returned to the porter. 'I think I will dine down here.'

'Very good, Mr Stephenson. Someone will be with you directly, sir.'

Robert sat alone in the coffee room, eating the best dinner London could offer for three shillings and sixpence, listening to the muffled sounds of conversation from the floor above. Not being entirely averse to company, he kept the door to the hallway open, but other than the servants no-one came or went for the duration. He was sipping at a glass of port to round off his meal, privately bemoaning the club's no smoking rule, when there was movement on the staircase. The familiar figure of Charles Dickens came into view, followed down the stairs by several members eager to continue attendance on the great man. They held back respectfully as Dickens paused in the lobby to let the hall porter retrieve his hat and cane. While he waited he looked around with the practised eye of an observer, and his gaze fell upon Robert at table in the coffee room. He spoke over his shoulder to no-one in particular, 'Excuse me, gentlemen,' by way of dismissing his entourage, and stepped into the coffee room, assuming as he did so the comportment of one entering a sick-room, gently closing the door behind him.

'My condolences on your recent bereavement, Mr Stephenson.'

Robert rose from his seat. 'And mine on yours, Mr Dickens. I know your sister was very dear to you.'

'Ay, ay, she was.' He seemed to lose his poise momentarily, and Robert, fearing he might actually fall, leaned over the table to pull out the facing chair. The author nodded his gratitude, and sat down with unwonted heaviness opposite the engineer.

'United in our sorrows. I... I must say I am very glad to see you here, Robert. I feel for your loss, very much, yes.' His voice softened, inviting closeness. 'Yes, not least because I have had reason lately to reflect upon my relations with my own... Your father was a paragon, sir. You have never met John Dickens, I suppose? No, no... good. Very...

155

different.' He tailed off, apparently abstracted. Robert noticed some moistness about the eyes. Sentiment was not confined to the pages of his novels, it seemed.

'Forgive me,' Dickens said, with a vague wave of apology towards his companion, 'I have been travelling a great deal recently... touring with my theatre company, one thing and another. Fatigue and grief make poor partners. Though I have to say,' he added after a moment's reflection, 'journeying by railway is much less wearisome than the stagecoach, however less romantic. No doubt Mr Pickwick would have enjoyed the novelty.' He must have caught Robert's sardonic look, for he smiled thinly in return, and said, 'Ah, you have read *Dombey*. Please do not misinterpret my metaphor. Or rather, please appreciate that you and your father have created a symbol more potent than a writer's mere imagination can conjure, and I felt impelled to use it. The railway epitomises our age and hurtles us through it with such speed I can barely contain my pen long enough to describe it. That has been my object only, not to denigrate the immense contribution the Stephensons have made. Far from it, believe me.'

'I found the story very powerful. My congratulations. I wept for Paul, and I fell in love with Florence, of course. She rescues our sympathy for her father.'

'Thank you,' said Dickens, revived by Robert's praise. 'I'm glad you liked my dear Florence. Her virtue is so... Dombey is not a bad man at heart, rather one disappointed in his expectations. I do have designs on creating a truly evil man of capital. *Entre nous* I even have a practicable model. Someone you... Well, I say too much.'

Robert felt the imprint of the chair on his back. 'Not Hudson?'

'I would deny it in a court of law.' Dickens tapped a finger at the side of his nose in a deliberate way, as Fagin might, then leaned towards Robert, pressing one hand on the table for emphasis. 'Within these walls, I confess I find a burning disgust arising in my mind against the Giant Humbug. Like a dog who can't endure a particular note played on a piano, I feel disposed to throw up my head and howl whenever I hear the name of Hudson. The man's a monster.'

This outburst revived in Robert a forgotten memory of the last conversation he had held with George Hudson, at his Newby Park residence in the summer. Hudson, in typical cocksure pose, his white waistcoat puffed out, was boasting of his acquaintance with the great and the good.

'They're all running ti me now, for one favour or another. Why, just last week I had our celebrated Mr Dickens begging to get his amateur players tugged around Scotland for free. Fellow didn't have the nerve to approach us direct - asked by way of Peter Cunningham - but he got his come-uppance from me, all the same.'

In the Athenaeum coffee room Robert leaned back in his chair and nodded sagely, a sign that his club companion may have taken for approval of his tirade against Hudson. It was, rather, the unconscious outward acknowledgement of Robert's private recognition that Dickens's *burning disgust* was not so acrid as to prevent him from seeking advantage, however trivial, from the corrupt rascal he professed to despise. What was the word Dickens had borrowed from one of his own characters, Mr Scrooge, to describe George Hudson? Humbug. That was it. Humbug. There was a lot of it about.

X

When Robert set his long legs astride his new mule, ironically named Hurry, to begin the twelve hundred mile trek from Caracas to Bogota, he could not help reflecting on his first donkey ride from Killingworth to start school in Newcastle, just ten years previously. There he wore home-made clothes of serviceable corduroy and boots better suited for pit work as he rode alone and uncertain into the bustle of town. Here he was at the head of a small band of travellers, self-consciously armed against the possibility of brigands abroad in the wild terrain, his white cotton suit covered by a blue and crimson poncho that he had been assured would double as a blanket when he slept in the net hammock he carried in his pack, and a wide-brimmed hat made of plaited grass to protect him from the fierceness of the South American sun. He felt something of the trepidation he remembered from his boyhood journey but would admit that only to himself where others depended on him.

His health had not been good since leaving England. Though more or less recovered physically from an illness on board, he was not in full vigour. His confidence, too, had suffered some erosion from the problems he had encountered already, and the seeming impossibility of making any economic return on the first schemes the company had asked him to assess - a breakwater and a pier at La Guayra harbour and a railway to unite the port with Caracas. It was becoming clear to Robert that the principals of the Colombian Mining Association had no real notion of the difficulties presented by this mountainous region, nor of how any construction could be expected to withstand the earthquakes that were a common occurrence in this part of the world. He was, however, excited by the stories he had heard of the mineral wealth still to be exploited, and had brought along with him a guide who claimed he could take him to sites that offered the richest prospects.

The progress of the party was even slower than Robert had anticipated, with precipitous climbs that gave him grave concern for the men and their animals on many occasions. 'I fear any moment that this mule's poor legs will snap under me,' he confessed to Walker the interpreter as they made yet another perilous descent.

'I fear more for my own bones,' said Walker. 'My brute almost tipped me off the cliff back there.'

Their guide Pablo had a disconcerting habit of striking out in front of the main party and disappearing for hours, sometimes even days, leaving Robert to lead his group largely by guesswork, by the few clues that the land supplied to the whereabouts of a trail, and by the rare appearance of a tiny settlement. Several times when Pablo re-emerged from one direction he would persuade them by vigorous gestures to change course and follow quite another, answering any doubts by eager nods and the repetition of the phrase, '*Mucho tesoro*, this way *mucho tesoro*.'

After several fruitless weeks of this, when one of Pablo's absences had stretched to five days, Robert determined to be rid of him. The guide returned, however, more enthusiastic than ever, and more specific. '*Mercurio*. Quicksilver. *Sesenta millas*. Follow, follow.' With no alternative strategy, Robert had little choice but to follow, privately resolving to suspend the rogue by his feet from a tree if after sixty miles he still had nothing to reveal.

Amazingly on this occasion Pablo seemed to prove himself. After nearly three days of following, the group was brought to a huge rock with a fissure large enough to secrete a man inside. Around the foot of the rock, as if it had seeped through the fissure, was clear evidence of what must have been a significant deposit of quicksilver, now dried out. There were no mine workings in the vicinity, so Robert reasoned that the source of the quicksilver must still remain untouched. He was delighted, and rewarded Pablo, whose new-found reputation was enhanced by his being able to lead the group to a nearby village where they could buy some supplies and even enjoy the dubious delights of a primitive drinking-den.

While his companions gladly slaked their thirst, Robert set about looking for some figure of authority in the village. He was anxious to establish a claim on behalf of his company to the mining rights in the area. No-one locally owned up to any degree of official responsibility, but Robert was directed to the home of someone described as a former governor of the district. The man, Eduardo, pleased to have this precious chance to practise his English, welcomed the young engineer warmly. Robert endured his well-meaning courtesies for half an hour before he could turn Eduardo's thoughts to the business he came on.

'Are the mining rights still available in this area?'

'Oh, *amigo*, our mines were - how you say - long time worked down.'

'Worked out? So there are no current rights?'

'No rights, eh, no mines.'

'Excellent. Perhaps you could tell me to whom I should speak. My company wishes to secure the licence for a new winning here.'

'Winning?'

'A new mine.'

'Oh. What? Coal? Copper? Not gold?'

'Quicksilver.'

'Ah, yes, quicksilver here one time, sure.'

'And will be again. I believe we have found a new source.'

Eduardo looked thoughtful. '*Mercurio*,' he muttered to himself, then aloud, 'Where this is found?'

Robert hesitated to divulge the information, but quickly realised he would need to if he had any hope of cooperation from Eduardo. Besides, this old man was unlikely to rush off and establish a mining concern in competition. He described the location as carefully as he could, including the detail of the fissure in the rock. Eduardo listened closely. As the description continued, a broad grin spread across his face. Before Robert had finished he was laughing openly, gripping his guest by the arm to steady himself.

'Please, *amigo*, do not open mine for sake of your found. Rock is only rock.' He gave himself the chance to calm down before he continued. '*Mercurio* is not come from rock. Not from that ground but from, er, *carro del buey* what is... cart of bull. Cart from many years is carrying, er, quicksilver, and is spill there at the rock, all spill. What you see is... er?'

'Traces,' said Robert, comprehending; deflated.

'Trace, yes. For years yet. The mine... two, three leagues away, worked out now. Sorry, *Señor* Stephenson, that is all *tesoro* you will find here.'

'That rascal...'

'Ah, well, but... Please, hear my advise, *respetuoso*. You Englishmen come with your men, your maps, your money. You ask where be gold, silver. Who hears is what you say, rascals, *bandidos*. For your money they tell you what you like to. You come to find fortune. They here to find fortune of you. You must take a care for such men, is like watch out for poison snake. That is my advise, *amigo*.'

Later that evening the scrawny Pablo was drooping drunk at the tavern when he felt a rough tap on his shoulder. Turning round to swear at the pest that bothered him, he came face to face with his immediate destiny.

'You, go now!' ordered Robert. 'I never want to see you again.'

'No, *Señor*, I find *tesoro* for you. Quicksilver.'

'There is no treasure here.'

'Yes, here, other place I take. Find in ground gold, brass, what is call, pinchbeck, steel, liquor, tobacco...'

160

Pablo continued to protest thus even when Robert lifted him unceremoniously from his stool and carried him over to the doorway. His foolish promises gave way to drunken moans that could be heard from the other side of the door long after the toecap on his ex-employer's Spanish leather boot had assisted his passage across the threshold.

*

Robert had plenty of time on that arduous journey across the mountains to think about home and people he was missing. It was not until much later, when letters found him many months after they were written, that he fully appreciated how much he was being missed in turn, especially once those he left behind realised how long he was to be away.

There was no-one in England, on 25th April 1825, missing Robert as much as his father: more than Edward Pease, whose concerns about the company's management and for the timely completion of the Stockton and Darlington line were growing daily; more than Elizabeth Stephenson, now resident in Liverpool, waiting eagerly for the next letter from her stepson; more, even, than Fanny Sanderson, living on dreams of the marriage Robert had promised would follow his return. 25th April was the date George was due to give evidence to the parliamentary committee examining the proposals for the Liverpool and Manchester Railway, and he sorely wished his son could be by his side.

In the months leading up to his appearance before the Members, George had never been so pulled about by business - his presence needed here, his advice sought there, interest in his locomotive ideas from everywhere - and he was acutely conscious (though he would never admit it to anyone) that he had lost his grasp on the finer details of the Liverpool-Manchester survey. Aware, too, that mistakes had been made by the young assistants he had allowed to finish the job. He knew there were significant errors because William Cubitt, brought in by the committee to check the measurements, had privately told him so as a courtesy from one engineer to another.

Courtesy seemed, on the face of it, to be the prevailing mode in the chamber. Even Edward Alderson, lead counsel for the opponents of the Bill, was cross-examining with apparent politeness and good humour; but Henry Brougham, retained for the railway side, warned their chief witness to be on his guard.

'Remember, George, that behind Alderson is every canal owner and most of the landed interest in the country, baying like their precious hounds, wanting nothing more than to tear this Bill into tiny pieces, and you with it.'

'I've defied their guns an their pitchforks up to now,' said George, with his habitual bravado, 'They'll not puncture me wi words, sharp as they might be.'

'Ah, but what you have to watch for is their tripwires. For instance, they are working up the question of speed, with the intention of equating speed with danger. Now I have heard you claim your railway engines can travel up to twenty miles per hour. When you give evidence you must keep your estimate well below that figure, or you will be regarded as a maniac fit for Bedlam and damn the whole thing.'

'Never fear, I'll cut it in half if you like, an damn the truth instead.'

When George was called in to the chamber and asked to take the witness position in front of the committee, he imagined Robert presenting himself similarly just a year ago, and he took heart from his success. For once, he was following in his son's footsteps, and he hoped not to let him down. Invited to describe his experience with railways to date, George felt on sure ground and started well, not particularly noticing the smirks and asides for his uncultured delivery from certain Members. It was not long before Edward Alderson was on his feet, assuring the committee that Mr Stephenson was indeed a fellow-countryman, and not a foreigner as someone in the room had opined.

'An engineer much respected in his corner of the North East where, as he has been trying to tell us, he has done so much of his important work.'

'Ah, but not just local,' George corrected. 'Some of our engines is sent all the way to France.'

'Congratulations.' Alderson said drily, and changed tack. 'It is your contention, Mr Stephenson, that the locomotive steam engine is superior to all other forms of transport?'

'Aye.'

'Much faster, you would say.'

'Speed's one advantage. There's plenty...'

'As to speed, what is your estimate of the speed that the engine might reach on the proposed railway?'

George hesitated fractionally, catching Henry Brougham's eye before he answered. 'My recommendation ud be not more un four miles an hour wi forty tons. An eight miles wi twenty tons.'

'Eight miles an hour?'

162

'Yes...' He could not help himself. 'I'm confident that much more might be done.'

Brougham sighed audibly, and leaned back in his chair. Alderson suppressed a smile as he pressed the point. 'Much more? How much more? Twelve miles per hour, say?'

'Oh, aye.'

'I am trying to imagine this locomotive rushing past fields at the rate of twelve miles per hour. Fields which the farmer might be attempting to plough. Surely the horse would be terrified and bolt at the sight and sound of your monster engine.'

'Oh, there's some horses scared of a wheelbarrow, but mostly they learn to take no notice of em. It's just a matter of use. At Killingworth there's cattle in the fields next to the line. They niver so much as raise their heads when the train's passin.'

A committee member spoke up. 'Suppose, now, that a cow were to stray upon the line and get in the way of the engine; would not that, think you, be a very awkward circumstance?'

'Oh aye, very awkward for the coo!' said George emphatically. He had the intended comic effect with the delegation, though his own counsel did not join in the general merriment. They were further discomfited by Alderson's next set of questions.

'You will agree, Mr Stephenson, that when a body is moving upon a road - or metal track in this case - the greater the velocity the greater the momentum that is generated?'

'Certainly.'

'What would be the momentum of forty tons moving at the rate of twelve miles an hour?'

'Very great.' George had failed to notice Alderson's subtle combining of the larger weight with the higher speed.

'Have you seen any railroad that could stand that?'

'Any railroad that could bear the weight at four miles an hour.'

'Do you mean to say that it would not require a stronger railway to bear the weight at twelve miles an hour?'

'Here's your answer to that,' said George, confident in his ability to explain the mechanics. 'I dare say every person who's been skatin on ice knows that the ice ud bear em easier at a greater velocity than it would if they had been slower.'

'I like your analogy - rail travel, ice skating,' said the barrister nodding as if in true appreciation, and he paused to reflect on it. 'How do you stop the train?' he asked suddenly. 'I believe there are no brakes.'

'On the wagons, there is,' said George, a tad evasively.

'Not on the engine or tender?'

'They're hardly needed. All the driver has to do to slow down is reverse the engine.'

'No easy matter, I imagine, when running at twelve miles an hour or more.'

'A good driver ull have no trouble handlin the operation.'

'A good driver...' Again Alderson let the phrase hang for a moment, then pursued his interrogation. 'What records are kept of accidents on the railroad?'

'I know of none that's occurred wi my engines.'

'No? Wasn't there one near Leeds, at the...' he referred to his notes, 'the Middleton Colliery.'

'Yon was a Blenkinsop engine,' said George, hackles up, 'and the driver was in liquor, as I heard it. He put a considerable load on the safety-valve so that on going forward...'

'The engine blew up and the man was killed.'

'True, but if proper precautions had been used wi that boiler the accident would never have happened.'

'I thank you for your expert opinion, Mr Stephenson,' said the lawyer blandly.

If the railway team thought the worst of the cross-examination over, they were mistaken. In the next session Alderson turned his attention to the details of the survey that carried George's name as author. He questioned the engineer minutely on his stated plans for bridges, crossings and tunnels; compared his measurements and estimates at various crucial points with those rechecked by William Cubitt. By the time he revealed that the track level of the proposed bridge across the River Irwell was three feet below the maximum flood level of the river, all pretence of politeness had vanished. Alderson was inquisitorial, openly hostile, and humiliation was piled upon the hapless George.

'What is the width of the Irwell here?'

'I cannot say exactly at present.'

'How many arches is your bridge to have?'

'It is not determined upon.'

'How can you make an estimate for it, then?'

'I have given sufficient sum for it.'

Alderson made a show of the piece of paper on which he had written in his own hand the sum that George had given for the cost of the bridge, five thousand pounds.

'So,' he said with no disguise of contempt, 'you make a bridge, perhaps fourteen feet high, perhaps twenty feet high, perhaps with three arches and perhaps with one, and then you boldly say that five thousand pounds is a proper estimate for it?'

'I think so.' George appealed to the Members who sat behind his assailant. 'I merely set out the line for other surveyors to follow.'

Alderson feigned incredulity. 'Did you not survey the line of the road?'

'My assistant did.'

George stumbled again when Alderson pressed him on the whereabouts of the original base line on which all the stated levels were calculated. It became obvious that he had no idea how the base line had been determined. The lawyer further challenged George's crumbling conviction of the survey's accuracy.

'You do not believe you are out on your levels?'

'I have made my estimate from the levels which I believe are correct.'

'Do you believe, aye or no, that your levels are correct?'

'I have heard it reported that they are not.'

'Did you take the levels yourself?'

'They were taken for me.'

'Other people have taken them for you and upon their estimate you have made your estimate?'

'Yes,' George admitted, wishing for the twentieth time that Robert had stayed to help him with the survey, wishing for the twentieth time that his son could be by his side to help cope under this relentless scrutiny.

By the third day, when Alderson was ready to sum up for the opposition group, that wish had been repeated a hundred times. By then Cubitt had been summoned personally to declare that George's measurements were not correct at any checking point. Another engineer Francis Giles had heaped criticism on both the costs and the methods proposed for traversing the notorious Chat Moss; the idea that George had come up with of effectively floating the engines across on a huge raft-like structure had been universally derided. Edward Alderson's final statement amounted to stamping on the body of his defeated opponent.

'This railway is the most absurd scheme that ever entered into the head of man to conceive. Mr Stephenson never had a plan. I do not believe he is capable of making one. He is either ignorant or something else which I will not mention. His is a mind perpetually fluctuating between opposite difficulties: he neither knows whether he is to make bridges over roads or rivers, of one size or another; or to make embankments, or cuttings, or inclined planes, or in what way the thing is to be carried into effect. When you put a question to him upon a difficult point, he resorts to two or three different hypotheses, and never comes to a decided conclusion.

'Was there ever any ignorance exhibited like this? Is Mr Stephenson to be the person upon whose faith this committee is to pass this Bill involving property to the extent of four hundred to five hundred thousand pounds when he is so ignorant of his profession as to propose to build a bridge not sufficient to carry off the flood water of the river, or to permit any of the vehicles to pass which of necessity must pass under it, and leave his own railroad liable to be several feet under water? He makes schemes without seeing the difficulties, and when the difficulties are pointed out, then he starts other schemes. He has produced five schemes all resulting in one estimate. I never knew a person draw so much upon human credulity as Mr Stephenson has proposed to do in the evidence he has given.

'I am told they are going to throw Mr Stephenson and his estimate overboard and to call upon the Honourable Members to decide without his evidence. Now, if they attempt that, it will be the strangest thing that was ever attempted in the House of Commons.'

Released from his duties as witness, George did not linger in the capital to wait under critical surveillance upon the fate of the Liverpool and Manchester Bill. He travelled back as soon as he could to the mitigating sympathy of his wife, to whom he simply said, 'It seems to me, Betty, that of all the powers above and under the earth, there's none so great as the gift o the gab.'

Neither did George write to his son: he left it to others later to advise Robert that the Bill was lost by a small majority, that although the projectors would try again they had appointed Charles Vignoles to replace his father as surveyor, and that the brothers Rennie, whose construction record was impressive and whose many friends in Westminster included the Duke of Wellington, had become the refined choice to commit a second application to Parliament.

*

No letters from home had completed their long voyage to Bogota by the time Robert arrived at the capital on his overland trek. Cheered by his achievement at reaching relative civilisation (and, truth be told, eager to justify his decision to travel), he immediately wrote a buoyant note to his father about the prospects for the company, for he was then only a short ride from what had been described to him as the thriving mining town of Mariquita. Days later, however, his instinctive pessimism returned as he journeyed on to Honda and saw, piled up on the banks of the River Magdalena, item after item of heavy equipment marked as the property of the Colombian Mining Association already beginning to rust as they waited in the sub-tropical climate for someone to move them, put them to use.

'Why has this machinery not been sent on to Mariquita, as directed?' he asked the local who was the nearest approximation he could find to a wharfinger.

'Because it would break the backs of our mules, *jefe*,' said the man. He smacked the heel of his hand against one of the pieces as if to assure the Englishman of its considerable solidity.

'Mules? I was told there is a good road to the place.'

'There is a road, *por supuesto*,' agreed the man. 'A mule road.'

The company's small advance party of miners had already struck out from the port and were making their way to Mariquita. Robert abandoned plans to dine with the Governor of Honda and rode out to join them, accompanied only by Walker and a servant. Even this lightly-laden trio found the way difficult. What may once have been a road passable by wheeled carriages had been despoiled by earthquakes and other natural wreakers of havoc, or acts of God as Robert's Aunt Nelly would have called them. In the past there may have been the political will and enough organised manpower to effect repairs, but the years of revolution had acted as another form of earthquake, ripping out the social foundations of the region. Long before they reached Mariquita, Robert correctly guessed what they would find there. A once-prosperous city of twenty thousand inhabitants had become little more than a ghost town. Two-thirds of the habitations were in ruins. Fewer than five hundred people survived among the rubble of once-magnificent churches and civic buildings. As Robert's mule picked its way along what would have been the main thoroughfare, two or three children clambered over broken-down masonry to stare at the stranger in the straw sombrero.

Walker pulled up alongside, and Robert spoke to him in a low monotone. 'Welcome to Eldorado.'

Yet the very next day Robert felt he had found, if not Eldorado, perhaps an outpost of Eden. Intent on exploring what remained of the mines of La Manta and Santa Ana in the hills above Mariquita, he was relieved to find the air becoming cooler. He was on an eastern slope of the Andes, and soon reached the first shelf of the table-land near the opening of the Santa Ana mine, where he had a full view of the Magdalena valley stretching out for miles below. Around him was a vast forest more surprisingly fresh and green for the contrast it offered with the rocky terrain that he had been labouring across for months. In the distance he could see the snowy summits of the Cordilleras, glittering in the sunshine.

Within weeks he was writing to his stepmother to tell her of the bamboo cottage with palm leaf thatch that his men had built for him there, yards from a deep tarn fed by the mountain river where he could swim and bathe every day, sometimes with a pelican or two for company. While he waited for the main body of Cornish miners to arrive in port, his duties were light. He supervised the making of a temporary road to Mariquita, and his small group were able to bring some of the lighter pieces of machinery to the mouth of the mine. Otherwise Robert busied himself with visiting the old workings, collecting mineral specimens, fitting out a small laboratory for experimentation, and exploring the forest for wildlife, which he found in abundance - exotic butterflies, fragile humming birds, mocking birds, parrots whose astonished squawks matched their stunning appearance, delinquent monkeys. Neither did he neglect the opportunity to foster good relations on behalf of his company with the local dignitaries. He became acquainted with the English-speaking doctor. He visited the Governor of Honda at his home, and even hosted a modest ball at Mariquita, his thoughts straying elsewhere as his eyes followed the swish of the *señoritas'* skirts. Despite distractions, he was diligent in his letter-writing, both to his employers (who ignored his pleas to refrain from sending more heavy machinery) and to his loved ones. Cool evenings on the veranda, watching the magnificent South American sunsets, were the best times for smoking tobacco (and occasionally more dreamy narcotics) in solitude. His one bedtime companion was Byron.

Between two worlds life hovers like a star,
'Twixt night and morn, upon the horizon's verge.
How little do we know that which we are!
How less what we may be!

Robert's idyll lasted a little under two months. One day in October his sleep was disturbed by furious knocking at his shutters.

'*Señor Stephenson! Vámonos! Vámonos!*'

It was the Governor's servant, and by the condition of the mule behind him it was apparent that he had arrived in great haste. His words came out in such a rush that Robert was forced to rouse Walker to interpret.

'He says, the Governor needs you in Honda immediately. The navvies have arrived.'

'Good. But why the alarm? They've long been expected.'

'*Les hombres están bebiendo, luchando...*'

'They are drinking and fighting in the town.'

'*...violando a mujeres.*'

'He claims they are... violating the women.'

'But are there no law officers to restrain them? No cells?'

Walker questioned the excitable servant further, and passed on his news that such law enforcement as there was had been overrun by the scale of the disorder. The navvies had erupted from the confines of their ship like lava from a volcano, spent their wages in a frenzy of drinking and whoring, and were now entirely ungovernable, drunkenly seeking out targets for their lust and aggression. The Governor had washed his hands of all responsibility for them, and demanded that *Señor* Stephenson, as *jefe*, come *pronto* to assume control over his men.

All the way down the mountain-side, leading only a small band of his trustiest workers, Robert was in anguish, dreading the moment he would have somehow to stamp his authority on the Cornish rabble. Though some were pitmen, many had been recruited for the hardest tasks of clearance, excavation and road-building from the ranks of itinerant labourers who had carved out the canals of Great Britain by dint of brute strength. At twenty-two, Robert had no real experience of the 'navvy' type, but he knew them by fearsome reputation, knew them to be quite a different breed from the North East miners he was used to. They seemed to owe no loyalty to any community but their own tribe of fellow-labourers (though that did not stop them regularly knocking lumps out of each other) and eschewed conventional morality for their own code of conduct, based on bravado, recklessness and the pursuit of animal instincts to satiation and beyond. They had been bribed with high wages to make this difficult and dangerous trip, and had obviously used what they had been paid so far to fuel their excesses.

Fortunately for Robert, the worst of the disturbance seemed to be over by the time he rode into Honda, for the simple reason that the money and the liquor had run out. Most of the men were asleep or nursing sore heads in one or another dark corner of the town. Robert realised that his only hope of establishing control and restoring good relations with the locals was to get the reprobates up the mountain away from temptation and set to work as soon as possible. He learned by enquiry that the navvies had an unofficial 'captain' whom they simply called Powder in token of his devil-may-care reputation with explosives during excavations. The moniker led Robert to imagine some dusty character with a face of a chimney sweep, but when he tracked him down to one of Honda's back-street bordellos he discovered Powder to be a fastidious and expensive dresser with neatly tailored moleskin trousers, double canvas shirt and a striking rainbow waistcoat. He was a lean but muscular man with a neat beard and an earring in one lobe that gave him a piratical aspect. He would seem rakishly elegant were it not for the heavy hob-nailed boots that stuck up from the bar table where Powder rested his heels in a display of cool arrogance as he watched his new employer's advance on him.

'Who moight this allish youth be, Powder?' The question came from his drinking companion, a navvy nicknamed Adam Anker either for his resemblance to a keg of ale or his capacity for one.

'Oi reckon he be the company clerk, come to pay our next week's fangings.'

'Ansum.'

Their exchange was deliberately loud enough for Robert to hear and be provoked by. He tried to remain calm; came to a halt near to the captain's shoulder so that he did not have to address him across his insolent boots. He stood erect, aiming to compel Powder to turn his head and look up, but the man declined to cooperate, steadfastly regarding the space in front of him with a half-smile. When Robert spoke the dryness in his throat betrayed him slightly.

'I am Mr Stephenson. You are Powder, I take it?'

'Kaboom,' from Powder, softly. Anker slapped his knees in appreciation, swallowed laughter with a noise like a donkey braying.

'I am, as I said, Mr Stephenson, and you are to work for me. I am charging you to gather all the men together ready to follow me to Santa Ana. We will leave from the Plaza del Mercado in one hour.'

Powder said nothing. His only movement was to change the anchorage of his feet so that his right heel supported them on the table rather than the left. Robert turned his back on the men, and made a slow (and what he hoped would be interpreted as purposeful) walk towards the door. Before he reached it, Anker broke wind noisily, and both navvies snorted like schoolboys over his retreat.

Robert waited with the company he had brought with him in the sunshine of the Plaza del Mercado. There was none of the usual bustle in this part of town. Every so often a straggler from the Cornish contingent would appear briefly, tottering across the square. One vomited messily into the fountain and continued his mazy progress, eventually vanishing down one of the narrow streets. Robert gave no instruction to round anyone up. The only intervention came when a distressed local girl came running from the direction of one of the bridges, her bare feet slapping on the dust. She stopped when she saw the group of men gathered in the square, cast a frightened glance over her shoulder, and ran off in another direction. Two navvies followed her across the bridge and gave chase, alternately laughing and jostling with each other and yelling lewd comments after the girl. Four of Robert's men of their own volition joined the chase and soon laid hands on the drunken pair. Having no means of imprisonment, they carried the would-be molesters down to the river and threw them in to cool their ardour.

The hour came and went with no sign of assembly. Robert returned alone to the bordello, where he found Powder and Anker more or less where he left them, now sharing a bottle of aguardiente and enjoying the lascivious attentions of two olive-skinned *putas*.

'I told you to gather the men together,' said Robert.

There was venom in Powder's response. 'We'll come when us good an ready.'

'Ar, St Tibb's Eve,' put in his mate, sniggering.

'Do you not want money?'

One of the girls looked at Robert with new interest, perhaps comprehending the English word *money*. Robert ignored her. Powder affected to ignore his question, but remained listening.

'There's double of first week's wages for every man who is in camp by Sunday.'

At that Robert turned on his heel and walked out, praying that this time his words would have their effect because, if they did not, he had no idea what he could do. He reasoned that by making the offer through Powder he was allowing the man to claim that he had negotiated the concession and thereby win some credit with the miners even as he persuaded them to go to work. It was a dangerous tactic, further elevating Powder's status in relation to his own, but he had no alternative. Robert sent his servant to assure the Governor the men were preparing to leave, and led his small group back up the mountain, trusting the rest would follow.

They came in ragtag fashion, mostly on foot though some had bartered, borrowed or stolen mules for the journey, all complaining about the *bros* as they called the fierce heat, though once they had rested they appreciated the cooler climes of the camp, with a few even splashing into

171

the mountain waters to refresh themselves. Robert put a guard on his own little lake, keeping a semblance of privacy and distance as the *maister*.

The day-to-day reality was a constant struggle between himself and Powder for the position of recognized leader. Robert had the respect of the established workers, and the general advantage of being paymaster. Powder aimed to undermine him at every opportunity and was openly scornful of his youth and inexperience, claiming this barely-weaned northerner knew nothing either of construction or of pitwork. In fairness Powder was a prodigious worker himself, and had earned his authority over the men, all of whom could put a mighty shift in when they were sober enough to stay on their pins; that is, only moderately drunk, which was their everyday state and no bar to ordinary labouring duties. Robert had banned the sale of alcohol from the tommy shop, but he was perfectly aware it was regularly smuggled up to the camp from Mariquita.

Apart from routine insubordination, the main problem Robert had with Powder was his lack of concern for his own safety and that of others. He regularly smoked his pipe while working with explosives and, since Robert upbraided him for it, made a show of striking at his tinderbox near the gunpowder barrel whenever his rival passed. 'Lookee yarn, jankin by,' he'd remark to his mates, depicting Robert as a scurrying coward. He also led his gang to take great risks with undercutting slabs of earth as they excavated the mountains, digging in to a lift of twelve feet or more before he would blast away the overhanging rock, not the six or eight feet that his orders and safety demanded. 'Knocking arf its legs, is all,' he would say when Robert complained; and on the day that he and half a dozen others narrowly escaped with their lives, throwing themselves out of harm's way at the last moment as fifty tons of rock suddenly cracked and crashed towards them, what he did was smirk, spit and say, 'Nice chance, thar one.'

As a diversion, the miners laid bets with each other on every occasion that offered, whether it be lizards racing up a cliff face or their own skill at directing piss onto the wings of a butterfly. Their favourite wagers involved feats of strength, bare-knuckle fighting, or outrageous dares. Powder often took the initiative, and was not afraid to put himself forward for a challenge. Picking up snakes that may or may not be poisonous. Standing yards closer than anyone else might risk to the seat of his own explosions.

About three months after the Cornishmen first arrived at the camp, Powder and his gang were clambering the cliffs above a re-opened mine-working, charged with sinking a new upcast, when one of their number almost stumbled down an old disused shaft half-hidden by vegetation. Cleared of plants, it revealed itself as an opening about ten feet across, with a sheer drop below. Tom One-Eyebrow, the navvy who had nearly fallen in, threw a large stone down the shaft, and they waited several seconds before a muffled sound told them it had reached the bottom. Tom gave a long, breathy whistle in imitation of the fall, thinking about what might have been.

'Durst aw jump it?' said Powder, on a whim.

'What, this girt? Blaamed if I will. I'm no antick, sure.'

'Yaller is what you is,' said Powder. 'Harkey, I'd do it, for a wager.'

'What coin?'

'Half a guinea.'

'Set it down ere, then. There's no gettin at it when you're down the ole.'

'Here's my wack, look yere.' Powder drew a leather pouch from inside his waistcoat and threw it on the ground,.'Welcome to it all an I miss my step. Are you in?'

'Oim in,' said Tom.

'An me,' from Punch Billy.

Without hesitation, Powder readied himself for the jump; took as long a run as he could manage on the uneven cliff, and launched himself from his right foot at the edge of the shaft. He seemed at first to stride across the gap, then to pitch himself forward, then roll so that he landed painfully on his left hip and leg against the rock at the other side, half-cussing, half-exulting. He stood up, balanced himself, and bowed to his mates across the shaft, who roared approbation, but for one.

'Easier than it looked,' said Tom One-Eyebrow, mourning his half guinea.

'Thinkst?'

'Now oi seen it done.'

'Well, then,' said Powder, irritated that he was not being given enough credit for his feat, 'my purse says *you* durnt do it.'

'It's bin done once, thars enough.'

'Not by you, it aint. Nor any but me. My full purse for any man ull follow us over ere.'

'No good asking me,' said Punch. 'Nor wi my porgy little legs. You can ha my half guinea, an welcome.'

'Thars honest, Punch,' said Powder, nodding. 'But Tommy, though, neither gick nor gack. Durst aw do it, or not? Easy done, you say.

Ay, an easy to craw. Well, thars my purse on it. There's above five guinea in tharn.'

Tom One-Eyebrow looked round at the gang of navvies waiting on his answer. It was not the prize at stake. He had no escape route. He had to make the leap, and show himself the man Powder was, or lose face forever. Fingers trembled as he plucked a small purse of money from his pocket; he had to close his free hand over it to silence the rattle of coins. Dropping his purse to the ground next to the other, he tried to speak, had to spit first to free the constriction in his throat, and his voice cracked as he called across the chasm. 'Thars yourn if I go, Powder.'

His captain raised an arm in acknowledgement. 'Brave. We'll be on the randy this night, you and me, Tom.'

Tom smiled grimly, and stepped back three or four steps, measured in heartbeats. Hurtling forward, he let out a loud whoop of bravado, desperation or anguish, and launched himself across the black hole. His legs kicked as one feeling the noose draw tight on his neck. His arms flayed forward, searching for something solid to grab onto. His whoop became a long scream, and the scream slowly faded as Tom One-Eyebrow fell head first, dropping like the stone he had tossed a few minutes earlier when, in idle curiosity, he had tested the depth of the shaft. The miners above heard the faint *crump* as he reached bottom.

Robert, informed of the accident, wanted to send a party of hewers through the labyrinth of old workings to discover where the disused shaft had been closed up, and have them hack through to recover the body. Powder was contemptuous of the plan - 'Tom's corpse ull be rotted ere we get him out thar way' - and in defiance of Robert's order tied a strong rope about his waist to be lowered from the top of the shaft, careless of the danger he was putting himself in. Twenty minutes after he disappeared into blackness, his signal came, and a chain of men at the surface laboured to haul back Powder and the broken body of his workmate.

They buried Tom One-Eyebrow with all the dignity they could muster on the mountainside. Robert was excluded, along with every other man who did not hail from Cornwall. In the absence of a clergyman, Powder himself solemnly performed the office, and Tom was winched into his grave with a piece of the same rope that had pulled him out of the pit shaft. Afterwards, Powder declared an unofficial holiday for the navvies, and sent a pack of men and mules to bring every last drop of booze from the township, 'For I promised brave Tom a randy, and a randy us shul have, god damn the clerk.'

Faced with such open revolt, and heavily outnumbered, Robert could do little but wait for the wake to run its course. Besides, he was at the time afflicted by a fever, and lay on his bed with sweats and cramps for two full days while the navvies caroused, sang, argued, spewed and sprawled around the camp.

Around midnight on the third day after the funeral, Robert was half-dozing by his open window (the night calls of frogs from the tarn prompting a memory of the nocturnal visit he and his father made to Brandling's lake to try the lamp that could burn underwater) when he was alerted by the sound of men's voices, much closer than the huts where they had been doing most of their drinking. Not just one or two either, but what sounded like a large and animated group. Robert raised himself from his bed to look out into the darkness, and discerned the lights from several torches or lanterns along the track that was the main approach to his cottage enclosure. He got up and splashed his face with water from the pitcher by the table, feeling a nerve throb in his temple. Some of the men were close enough now for him to make out what they were saying. 'Put that fool clerk in is place... Larn the beardless boy a lesson.'

Robert took down his white linen suit and dressed quickly, then sat on the bed, perspiring, unsure what to do next. Outside, the men were gathering, their shadows falling onto the veranda. A bottle smashed - either dropped or clumsily thrown, it was impossible to tell.

'So, this be the maister's cott?' someone asked.

'Nay,' came another. 'Ye've eerd tell the droll o the three little pigs? Yere be the thatch crow your runt o the litter made.'

'An yeres us to blow it down,' said a third.

'Or torch it.'

Robert stood up in fear. He glanced instinctively toward the roof, then tiptoed to the back window, peering out to see if the men were surrounding the house, cutting off his chance to escape. He could see nothing but darkness on this side. As he wavered he heard a voice he recognized as Powder's near the front door.

'Tharl be no torching. But if yon wants a lacing, Powder's game... who's cappun yere.'

Robert looked around the room. Not owning a pistol, he wondered what form of defence he might be able to come by, but there was nothing bar a pewter candlestick, which he left behind when he cautiously opened the door and stepped out onto the veranda to face the rabble, fifty strong. He could hear a growl of anticipation as he came into the light thrown by the torches, and he clutched the veranda post for support, using it to bring himself erect and appear more self-assured than

175

he felt within. All eyes were on him, but as he waited he noticed how several found it difficult to fix the object of their attention, their gaze wandering as if he were some fish swimming languidly before them, though in fact he had not moved one step from his post. To a degree, their inebriated state made Robert feel stronger (or steadier, at least) in comparison; equally, he appreciated how dangerous the condition was, how reckless men might become under the influence.

'I attend upon you, gentlemen,' he said, as politely as he could. 'What is it you wish to say?'

There was no immediate answer to this, even from Powder, for the truth was the navvies had no particular grievance, merely a general antipathy to authority which they had worked up in a drunken *randyvoose* to a march of vengeance on the incumbent. A lone voice from the back of the crowd filled the void.

'Tom One-Eyebrow is dead.'

'He is. I would like to have been with you to see him off, but I was... prevented. I hope you do not blame me for that.'

This caused a murmur among the mutineers as each discussed with his neighbour whether Stephenson could be blamed. There was some confusion about the subject of debate, with several arguing over his degree of responsibility for Tom's accident, others over his absence at the funeral, and a few insisting this had damn-all to do with the matter in hand. Powder cut through the noise with a loud declaration aimed directly at Robert.

'Powder aint yere to talk, youth, but to fight. Who's cappun yere? Oill fight ye for it.'

His challenge had the desired effect on the men, who hushed and drew closer to hear the young maister's response, focusing and unfocusing on his pale face at the veranda. Robert set himself against the chill running down both sides of his body. He felt the ache of tension and tried to imagine it as a belt, as armour. He clamped his eyes on Powder while he worked to slow the rhythm of his own breathing, and finally summoned from within a voice of such quiet authority that he hardly recognized it as his own.

'It won't do for us to fight tonight. It would not be fair, for you are drunk and I am sober. We had better wait until the morrow.' He paused, watching the effect on Powder. There was an almost imperceptible droop of the shoulders. Powder scowled at him, but it was as if he had spent the last of his energy on his challenge. Robert waited, and only when he saw his adversary blink - a long, slow blink - shifted his attention to the general assembly. 'So, the best thing you can do now is to break up this meeting and go away quietly.'

His brain added a silent, yearning *please*, and his body strained at every muscle, but outwardly he remained impassive. He played the part, even to the extent of lighting his cigar as a visible demonstration of aplomb. The smoke hung in the air, over Powder, who squinted at his shoes, over the sullen bunch of men until they, disconsolate, lacking a ready champion, gradually broke up and turned away. Robert leaned against the post, inhaling, exhaling, watching them drift in the direction of their huts. Several, including Powder, were unable to steer themselves unaided, so that they looked like walking wounded kept upright only by the weary shoulders of their fellows as they returned from the battlefield. Robert did not deceive himself that his victory was anything but temporary. He heard desultory cries of *One and all! One and all!* as the crowd receded, and he remained at his post for a while yet until his heart beat quieter and he was convinced that for tonight at least he would continue undisturbed.

The next day, being Sunday, Robert had his trusted men enclose the flattest area of the camp with stakes and ropes, and inside he placed a variety of objects, such as anvils and laden wheelbarrows, that could be employed in weight-lifting trials, as well as hammers for throwing. He started the competition by laying down challenges to his own prowess, acquitting himself well enough, then withdrew to the role of chief barker. In general the workforce needed little encouragement to take part, though the Cornishmen, whether they were still recovering from their drinking-bout or reluctant to mix with the other miners, were among the last to be drawn in. Once hooked, they proved the worthiest and eventually the most enthusiastic of competitors - the trials played both to their strength and their sense of pride. Robert saw Powder and some of his closest associates observing the action as it unfolded, but they resisted any attempt he made to have them join in, and seemed to melt away from the scene, which disappointed him.

By late afternoon, with most of the miners and navvies still enjoying the games, Robert left them, intending to pass a couple of peaceful hours working in his laboratory. As he neared his cottage he heard whoops and cries from the vicinity of the tarn. At first he assumed a tribe of monkeys had strayed from the forest, but as he listened more closely it became obvious that these were human rather than animal sounds. He turned off the path and walked near to the water's edge. From the shade of a tree he watched as three of his workmen disported naked in his private pool. Inevitably, one of the trespassers was Powder, the other two being the navvies he was with when he left the sports field. They were playing like children in the lake - launching themselves from the bank, creating tidal waves with their arms, splashing water into the faces of their friends - the chief difference being their regular recourse to a stone flagon jammed between two rocks, which Robert assumed to be liquor of some kind. He scrupled to interrupt. Not, he told himself, because he was afraid to do so, but because of a residual sense that he was unjust in keeping this natural treasure for his exclusive enjoyment. On the other hand, he was acutely aware that Powder was cocking a snook by this deliberate intrusion, perhaps expected and even hoped to be discovered so that he could find excuse for the confrontation he had walked away from the night before.

While he considered his dilemma, Robert saw Powder shin like a naked savage up the trunk of a tall wax palm tree that grew by the water. He was being watched, too, by his mates as they sat on the rocks and passed the liquor bottle between them. The trunk tapered towards the top and bent under his weight in the direction of the water. He stopped and crooked one arm around the trunk, leaning over with one foot jammed against it, waving at his friends, who laughed. His appearance put Robert in mind of Man Friday in the favourite book from his childhood. Would Powder had been so biddable a servant.

'Jump,' yelled one of the men below. 'Gor we windarly, lookin up thar. Jump aff.'

Powder waved again and suddenly let go of the trunk, pushing hard off his standing foot. He came down ungainly, dropping about thirty feet, and plunged into the water perilously close to the bank. The other two bathers stood on their rock to stare at the ripples formed by his entry, temporarily blocking Robert's view. When he shifted position he saw that Powder had not yet surfaced, and that the water was tinged with colour.

'Powder? Cappun?' called the one who had dared him to jump, still standing stupidly holding the flagon while his friend, with a mite more common sense, leapt into the pool to essay a rescue. Robert freed himself from his shoes and shirt, scanning the water where he knew the current flowed to an outlet. He fancied he saw something that could have been a head almost break the surface, only to disappear again immediately. Robert ran down to the bank, past where the other two were searching, and dived in half-clothed nearest to where he thought he had seen the head. He opened his eyes underwater, looked about, tried to make out any human shape. The water, usually so clear, had inky streaks he surmised to be blood. Powder must have struck something as he entered the water, injuring himself.

Robert swam another dozen strokes and was needing air when he saw something below and to his left. He quickly surfaced, keeping his mind on the place, sucked in a lungful of air, and dived again. It *was* Powder, unconscious or worse. Robert found great difficulty holding onto the naked man, and even more pulling the dead weight to the bank, but he managed it with a muscle-tearing effort, and some help at last from the others. Powder's eyes were closed, his face darkening, blood still seeping from a head wound, his life force ebbing away.

'Bring my shirt, it's under that tree.'

One ran to get it while the other helped him lay Powder flat on the granite surface. Robert had seen a demonstration of artificial respiration at the university in Edinburgh, but this was the first time he had to put it into practice. Kneeling in a pool of Powder's blood, he gripped the man's nostrils firmly between thumb and forefinger, and pulled his mouth open with his other hand. Eyes pricking with disgust, he covered Powder's lips with his own and blew evenly into his mouth, aiming to fill his lungs without bursting them. He raised himself up, pressing down on Powder's diaphragm, then stooped to blow again. At first the exercise seemed to produce no result, but after the fourth or fifth time of blowing and pressing Robert felt a convulsion under his hand, and water gurgled from the victim's mouth. Two or three more and Powder was coughing and spluttering, then cursing and throwing himself about so that the two navvies had to help keep him down while Robert ministered to him; finally succeeded in washing his face and bandaging the head wound as best he could with strips torn from his shirt. Colour was restored to the navvy's cheeks, and his eyes, though bloodshot, had the spark of life in them again.

'My uzzle's scrawed wiv retchin,' were his first oath-free words. 'Where's thar Samson?', sending Akker scurrying across the rock for the flagon of brandy and cider. 'An fetch my britches!' Powder yelled after him.

He slaked his thirst and then, refusing all further assistance, dressed himself and even placed his sealskin cap carefully on top of his home-made bandage. Robert stood slightly apart, looking on. When there was not a drop left in the jug, Powder motioned to his vassals and they started to make their way back to the huts. The *cappun*, though, lingered for a moment when he reached Robert's shoulder. Almost by stealth, as if it were part of a secret ritual, he shook him by the hand. They exchanged not a word, but favoured one another with a curt nod ere they parted. For

179

a few minutes the young *maister* stood watching the lake, smooth now as if it were in denial of any recent excitement. It was only when he stirred himself to return to the cottage that Robert discovered someone had stolen his shoes.

*

George, marooned in Liverpool by the Railway Committee, had no reason to believe other than that his son was making a grand success of things in South America. The thought made his own recent failure a more bitter pill to swallow. For the first time in his life, George was experiencing genuine self-doubt in his work. One Sunday, staring out of the window of their town house in Liverpool, he said to Betty, 'I wish we had a large garden here.'

'Do you, my love?'

'Or an allotment. I've an urge to grow my own vegetables again, as I used to in the old days, at the cottage.'

'*Il faut cultiver notre jardin.*'

'Eh?'

'Voltaire, I think. Something about looking after our garden. Though I understand he is referring to the need to attend to one's affairs.' She paused, then said, 'How goes the work on the Stockton and Darlington?'

'Oh, nowt but trouble. Since Robert left, the business has been in some disarray. And the Peases baulk at subsidising the losses. Can't blame em for that.'

'It would be a pity to see it fail,' said Betty quietly. 'I remember how exciting it was when you first revealed the plans to me. I could see it in the shining of your eyes. A proper stage for your locomotives at last.'

'It won't fail. Why would you say that?'

'Of course not, sweet.' Betty never let his tetchiness distract. 'I was merely reflecting on what you said about Robert's absence. It would be absurd of them to put any blame on him. But of course it won't come to that. Not with his father there to see things through.' She smiled at George as he turned to her, fathoming, and continued, 'I for one would love to see the look on certain faces when you ride the first train into Stockton.'

'And you will,' said George. He bent to plant a kiss on her forehead. 'I promise you will.'

Perhaps Betty was aware that her husband was due to meet with the Pease family on the subject the following week; certainly their conversation that Sabbath was still in his mind when he told his partners to prepare for the official opening by the end of September. Edward Pease, for one, was glad to see George's countenance lit up again, for he had worried not so much about the risk to his investment as the potential loss to society if this project were to fail at the last.

As fortune turned, Edward Pease was not able to be present at the grand official opening, nor were any of his family, though the promise was fulfilled to the extent that one locomotive was ready and the line was just about finished on time. On the eve of the celebration, while George proudly took the controls of *Locomotion* to take Edward and three of his sons for a trial run from Shildon to Darlington, twenty-two-year-old Isaac Pease was in bed breathing his last. By the time the others returned home, eager for the morrow, he was dead. Edward was devastated. George had to face this momentous day in his working life with neither Robert nor his friend and patron as witness.

There were plenty witnesses besides. The prospect of the world's first public railway had excited the imagination of thousands around the country. Long before the day dawned many of them were already on the move - walking, riding or being driven in carriages to claim their attendant place in history. *Locomotion*, waiting in the wings at Shildon, seemed suddenly too small to bear such magnitude of expectation, not to mention the thirty-three wagons and three hundred passengers it was supposed to pull along the ribbon of rail to their eventual destination in Stockton.

'How many?' George's brother James was watching from the footplate as arriving notables pressed through the gathering at the start, brandishing their tickets like the rod of Moses in a bid to part the human sea and get on board.

'Three hundred tickets given out,' said George below. 'Looks like they've all turned up.'

'Aye, an a few hundred more besides. We're like to be swamped.'

He had barely finished speaking when *Locomotion's* weight safety valve opened and shot out a complaining shriek of steam. There was an immediate surge backwards as those closest of the crowd turned to flee from the explosion they feared was coming. Several behind were knocked over, women screamed, and a general shudder of alarm spread quickly. George clambered up the wheels to stand on the engine's boiler in his top hat and tails, waving his arms placatory and calling out, 'All's safe! All's safe!' His cry was taken up by others, and pandemonium was narrowly averted.

From his new vantage point George could only now appreciate what his brother had already seen. There must be three thousand or more at this post alone, and most of them, once reassured they were not in danger, were pressing forward again. Many seemed determined to find a perch somewhere on the train: if not on the special coach *Experiment*, perhaps in one of the wagons that had been adapted to take passengers for the inaugural journey; or in one of the mineral trucks; or anywhere a foot could lodge, a hand could grab. Between the mob and the train a thin line of company staff, distinguishable by their blue sashes, was doing its best to hold back the ticketless boarders, while other workers struggled to finish the coupling of the wagons. In front of the engine, flanking the track, four heralds on horseback awaited a starting signal, each carrying a standard at ease. The two horses in front were alternately nodding and shaking their heads as if engaged in some equine debate about the enterprise. Beneath his feet George could feel vibration, but he could not tell if it was communicated from the boiler or from his own body, fuelled with anticipation and bursting to begin. He checked his pocket watch. Ten o' clock. He called down to his brother.

'All ready?'

'All ready.'

George slid down the curve of the boiler, sprang from the plate onto the trackside.

'Raise your flags,' he ordered the heralds. Their mounts' ears pricked as *Locomotion* let out steam, eliciting a delighted roar from the crowd, but no horse shied and all trotted primly forward when George waved the riders on. He stepped back to take in the sight of his convoy on the move before he jumped up to join James at the controls. Behind him, three hundred passengers joggled uncomfortably in their seats, another three hundred clung on to the precarious positions they had somehow secured, and the thousands left behind cheered to remind the future they were there at the start of it all.

Then anticlimax. On the first bend one of the wagons slipped off the track. James, alerted by yells and the clashing of metal on metal, threw his engine into reverse to stop. Carriages and trucks bumped clumsily into one another all along the line. George ran back to supervise and, with plenty of willing hands, soon got the errant wagon lifted back and into kilter with the others. A minute later a second derailment, involving the same wagon. George clambered out again to inspect.

'Damn wheel's shifted on its axle. What wi the weight of these extra folk, and all uneven. We'll have to shunt this wagon off.'

They limped to the first passing loop and began the shunting operation, but there was now so much unsolicited assistance that the work took twice as long. Worse, one eager helper stepped in front of the wagon as it rolled into the siding. Expecting to bring the tub to a stop by pushing at it, he was knocked flying by its impetus, fortunately just clear enough of the track to save his foot being sliced off by a wheel. George rushed to where the man lay prostrate. 'Are you hurt?'

'Proud to be winged in the course of duty, sir.' The injured man could have been addressing his general in the midst of battle. 'Fie, don't tarry for me. Keep her moving.' A few minutes later the volunteer was standing on the bankside, half-grinning, half-grimacing, waving a handkerchief with his one good arm as the journey resumed.

George was inordinately conscious of the time lost, and irritated by the early mishap. They had to stop again to remove a piece of oakum packing that had been sucked into the feed pump, and were almost an hour late into Darlington, where they dropped off six loads of coal for distribution to the poor, took on another coach full of worthies, and one containing the Yarm town band who were to provide musical accompaniment on the run in to Stockton.

Out of Darlington, the line ran close by the turnpike road. George noticed a number of riders trying to keep pace with their machine and a suspiciously light stagecoach that may have been specially prepared by the opposition to outstrip them and be first to reach Stockton.

'Right, then, we'll see,' he muttered, then aloud to his brother, 'Pressure up, Jemmy, let her out.'

Ahead of the engine, the heralds were already at a canter. The two hindmost riders glanced round anxiously when *Locomotion* began to nose her way through them. They saw George leaning out from behind the tank, gesticulating and yelling, 'Out the way! Out the way!' The heralds peeled off either side, and the engine picked up speed to break fifteen miles an hour, despite its eighty ton cargo, pulling well away from the unladen stagecoach on the parallel road, and from the sporting gentlemen urging their horses forward on the sward between. George craned his neck to look forward of the engine, careless of wind and steam in his face. Those passengers enjoying the relative safety of *Experiment* waved enthusiastically at the people ranged along the track to watch them go by. Others hung on where they could, their teeth set in concentration. Hats were lost, the band played faster and louder, and a workman fell backwards off the last coal wagon.

The entry over St John's Crossing onto Stockton Quay was triumphal. It is said there were forty thousand onlookers there, whose unbridled cheering could not quite drown out the peal of the church bells or the thrice-repeated salute of seven eighteen-pound cannon. As *Locomotion* came to a standstill, the band struck up *God Save the King*. Not that the titular monarch was there in person to greet the arrivals, but the patriotic note seemed entirely appropriate. Great Britain was once again showing the way to the rest of the world and, for today at least, another George was king.

*

Having travelled to South America with such high hopes, two years on Robert felt at best ambivalent about his continued employment with the Colombian Mining Association, and they with him. His intelligence was good, his reports detailed and meticulous, but all they really desired from him was a huge freight of silver, and he failed to deliver in any significant quantity. On his part, he acknowledged that he had learned a great deal, especially in the fields of geology and chemistry, and had become a competent manager of difficult men in the most trying of circumstances, but he knew his contribution was under-valued by the company, and he had to admit that his record of real achievement was modest. Nevertheless, he was determined to see out the three year contract he had committed to, despite the increasingly insistent calls for him to go home and pick up again the threads of the work he had left behind.

The letter that finally convinced him to return as soon as he could was not one of the affectionate, wistful ones from his parents, or those couched in half accusatory, half flattering tones from Edward Pease; it was that received from his friend Joseph Locke, then working as one of his father's assistants. Locke gave him the good news that, in the wake of his Stockton and Darlington success, George had been taken on again to complete the Liverpool and Manchester project, now that it was safely through Parliament. Locke pricked Robert's interest and envy with talk of his deep involvement in helping to overcome the problems thrown up by Chat Moss and the other natural hazards of the route. It was, however, the paragraph that told of Locke meeting and falling in love *with one of the most enchanting creatures under heaven* that brought Robert's homesickness to a head. His dream that night prefigured the firm resolution he made in the morning: that he must make his way back to England at the earliest date he could arrange for his release, begin to make his mark upon the world as a civil engineer, and marry Fanny Sanderson.

184

In fact it took another nine months of patient negotiation before Robert could finally close the door on his bamboo cottage for the last time, gift his loyal mule Hurry to Walker, and sit amongst his luggage on the bullock cart that took him on the much improved road to the Magdalena River where he could embark for Cartagena, the first staging point of his long journey home.

Frustration awaited him at the port, for the ship that was to take him initially to New York was delayed by two days, and the town was in the grip of yellow fever. Robert and his fellow passengers had virtually to quarantine themselves in the dilapidated hotel that had the dubious claim to be Cartagena's finest. There he had made arrangements to dine with Mr Gerard, another employee of the company *en route* to Scotland. As Robert sat at table waiting for his colleague to arrive, he heard two English speakers in earnest conversation on the other side of a wicker screen that divided the dining room from the hotel's excuse for a lobby. He did not mean to eavesdrop, was merely trying to work out if either might be Gerard before he joined them, when he found himself fascinated by their exchange. One who spoke in a Cornish dialect (though not with the crude vernacular of Robert's former workers) was apparently trying to sell something that the other (a Scot, so possibly Gerard) was reluctantly having to decline.

'You must believe, I ad em from Bolivar imzelf.'

'I ken that, Dick. The tale is well enough known. And its a shame you're forced to sell, but I just havenae the money to gi ye. Fifty pound, man... I wish I had it, I dae.'

'You saved me once, James. You could again.'

'And it was your life, aye, I would again. But I canna gi ye what I havena got.'

'Time was when I had siller enough to weigh down a ship...'

'I ken...'

'And now I can't purchase my own passage.'

There followed a defeated silence. Robert could not contain himself from knowing more. He had anyway the pretext of seeking out his dining companion, and he was sure the Scot must be he, so he rose from the table and walked round into the lobby where the two men were seated. He was struck by the contrast in what he came upon - a well-tailored respectable gentleman, short with kempt ginger whiskers, sitting opposite a long-legged, shabby figure, gaunt in appearance yet with the look of a man once powerfully built who had suffered privation. The ruff of the tall man's shirt was limp; his coat worn at the elbow and marked -

as were his trousers - by travel stains; his boots, expensively made, cracked and down at heel. His hands at first sight were above the table, clutching whatever he was aiming to sell, but as Robert approached he hid the object away in his pocket as if it were some secret, or something of which he was ashamed.

Robert smiled apology at him, and addressed the other. 'Mr Gerard?'

'Yes? Och, is it Robert?' He rose to shake hands. 'James Gerard, right enough. You must excuse me, I was on the road to ye when I was... An old friend. Let me introduce...' His pause might have been embarrassment or simply an instinct for theatre... 'Richard Trevithick.'

'Richard Trevithick?' Robert was unable to disguise his astonishment. This man who looked so... And to meet him like this after so many years... 'I... I believe you once knew my father, sir.'

'Your father?'

'George Stephenson. He is also an engineer.'

'I vary well know who George Stephenson is.' Now it was Trevithick's turn to show surprise; it brought him to his feet and there, towering over Robert, he grabbed him firmly by both shoulders. 'And you must be Bobby! I have dandled you on my knee, zir!'

'I'm told you did, sir.'

'My, but you've shot up since.'

They laughed together, and Robert was delighted to see animation in the face that had shown so careworn. But how could the great pioneer have come to this?

'You must join us for dinner, Mr Trevithick.'

'Oh...' His uncertainty returned for a moment, and he glanced at Gerard. 'I'm such a Jack-o-Lent...'

'Please do me a great honour, and be my guest,' Robert insisted.

'Well, my pleasure, I'm zure.' the other replied, recovering some dignity and confidence from the fulsomeness of the invitation.

The trio made what they could of the hotel food, much more of the wine, and Trevithick proved Robert's compeer in his enjoyment of a fine cigar, though he admitted it was a very long time since he had smoked one. Robert encouraged him to recount his adventures, and sat enthralled for an hour listening to Trevithick's reminiscences of draining the silver mines of Peru, being befriended by the national hero Simon Bolivar and having his horse shod with silver, enlisting in Bolivar's army and later being forced to abandon five thousands pounds worth of ore when his vessel came under enemy attack. He had made his fortune and lost it twice over.

186

'For, in the end, a zilver mine brings mizery, a gold mine ruin,' he drawled, in his cups now. His eyes went vacant for a moment, then lit on Gerard, whom he gripped by the arm fondly. 'No metal as precious as a true friend. This man saved my life, Bobby, on more than one occazion. Aye, from drowning once...'

Robert smiled as he listened; allowed in the pleasant thought that another Cornishman may remember *him* as his rescuer - not that he could imagine Powder ever waxing quite so sentimental, even in drink.

'And once from the jaws of an alligator. No droll...' (though Robert had shown no sign of disbelief) 'Tell him, James.'

'There was an alligator, right enough. We were out on a pig shoot. There was some ruction, some dispute with a local villager who set the beast on Dick in consequence. Och, I'm not sure about saving him from the jaws... I shot the bugger, that's aw.'

Robert laughed. 'You'll be able to dine out on these stories as often as you wish back home,' he remarked to Trevithick, 'and never have to put your hand in your...' He stopped, suddenly aware that he had inadvertently drawn attention to his gesture in paying for the meal and implied that his guest would be in need of such charity in the future. Certainly Trevithick seemed to cast a forlorn glance at him, and had turned morose by the time he spoke again.

'*If* I get home again.' He sighed heavily. 'I'm gone-in. I've walked right across this blarsded country to reach the ocean, and have no means to cross it.'

'How much do you need?' said Robert, though he knew already from his earlier eavesdropping.

'Fifty pounds.' Detecting Robert's interest, he continued, 'I'm not one to caadge, I have these...' He drew from his pocket a curious pair of silver spurs, tarnished, but of obvious quality; made doubly so when Trevithick added, almost in a whisper, 'I had these arf Simon Bolivar. Presented em imzelf.'

Robert inspected the spurs in awe, partly put on for Trevithick's benefit to bolster his self-esteem.

'Sir, I will give you fifty pounds, gladly. But please put away your treasures. I would not dream of relieving you of your valuable possessions, much less your memories. Take the fifty pounds for your friendship with my father. Without your encouragement, he might still be a brakesman at the pit, and glad of the work.'

'Then, for your father's sake I'll take it, an thank ee, sir. Though your father needed little encouragement from me. I always felt he would astound the world one day. Why, when I knew him he was near to

187

cracking the secret of perpetual motion. That would have been zomething, eh?' He grinned, albeit ruefully. 'But he will outlast me in reputation, zure. I've frittered away all I ever had, that's the truth of it. And I don't mean money. Money's juz money.' He paused, lightly tapped the table a couple of times with his fingers, seemed again to lose himself in abstraction, then soliloquised, softly. 'Perhaps with a bit more luck... I have not been the most fortunate of chaps, blaamed if I know why.'

Trevithick's luck may have begun to change for the better, as the next morning brought their delayed ship into harbour. The three friends set sail for their homeward journey on the serenest of seas. Too serene as it happened, for the ship was soon becalmed among the islands of the Caribbean. Robert grew agitated as the hours turned into days. Trevithick remained philosophical. Gerard brought worrying news from the sailors, or what passed as news among a crew that could read nothing as well as the weather and the movements of the deep.

'They say the stillness of the atmosphere betokens a storm's raged norward of us, on the open ocean. We may catch it yet.'

What they caught a few days later, as the ship laboured a few degrees north, was grim evidence of the storm's effects. Robert was alerted by a repeated 'Boat ahoy' from the lookout on the forecastle. When he got to the larboard deck he found both Trevithick and Gerard among the crowd of passengers craning for a view of the spectacle.

'What boat is it?'

'A wreck, is what,' said Trevithick. 'Looks like part of a hull, topsy-turvy.'

Robert pressed forward and saw for himself. 'Why, there's people on it!' though they seemed to him more like scarecrows or rag dolls, so limp and wasted they looked as they clung on to the remnant of the hull. Only one of the sixteen or so in this plight had the strength or a firm enough hold to raise an arm for attention, and none of them cried out, so it was at first difficult to tell if they could all be called survivors. For a few moments Robert had the strange sense that he and his fellow-passengers were audience to a tableau rather than the event itself.

The ship sailed as near as it dare to the broken bark - a delicate matter as there was always the danger of an accidental collision that might tip the luckless and exhausted into the sea - then members of the crew threw out a line in the hope that one of the desperate men could catch it. It took a dozen tries before one did and managed to hold on long enough for the wreck to be pulled alongside the rescue vessel. There was a dull thud as they met, and Robert gasped to see one starveling lose hold and slip as if poured from a sack into the deep water below. None of his fellows had the strength to make any attempt to save him, while the passengers and crew above could do nothing but watch until it was certain he would not reappear, when they turned their attention to those they could help.

The sailors lowered a rope cradle down the side and encouraged each man in turn to secure himself on it long enough to be lifted to safety. This operation took over an hour, and sometimes the crew had double the weight to haul up as a few of the sufferers were too weak to sit unaided on the cradle. A disturbing incident occurred when there were just the last two left below. As the cradle was lowered to them, one of the men crawled almost the length of the wreck to reach the other, who lay prostrate, face down and partly covered with a piece of sail-cloth. It seemed that the first man was going to help his stricken comrade to the cradle as some had done earlier, but instead he picked him up with a great effort and rolled him over the side of the hulk into the sea. As the waters closed upon his deed, the man left aboard sunk on all fours and, like a distempered dog, retched a stream of thin vomit before crawling slowly back along the hull to the dangling cradle.

'Why did you cause that poor man to drown?' the captain demanded of the survivor almost as soon as the crew had him pulled safely on deck.

The answer came in a croaked whisper. 'He was dead already.'

'Then the Christian thing would have been to bring the body on board and allow us to give him a decent burial at sea, not to cast him off like so much jetsam.'

The man tried to raise his head to reply to the captain respectfully, but the effort proved too much and it dropped back to the deck. Surrounded by his rescuers, he hid his face with his hands with a muttered 'Jesus,' then, 'I was... too ashamed to let you see what we had done to him,' before melting into helpless tears.

The captain learned the whole truth when some of the shipwrecked men had recovered enough to confess that, after nine days without food on the open sea, they had given in to the temptation of feeding off the raw carcass of the man who had died already from fatigue and hunger.

The voyagers experienced a far less comfortable journey from then on, not just because they had to make room for the extra passengers (who inwardly disgusted some, however courteous to the new arrivals they affected to be), nor because they secretly or openly feared shipwreck themselves, but also because they were indeed sailing into very severe

189

weather. Those that had been rescued told of a hurricane that had forced their ship against the rocks where it broke to pieces, and as the winds blew up anew they took fright against a second calamity. Among the established travellers there were some of a religious bent who claimed the storm was the work of an avenging angel in pursuit of the cannibals, and were all for sacrificing them to the deep so the virtuous might be saved. The captain and his men ignored all this and got on with the difficult business of navigating through the turbulent waters.

Robert was as sea-sick, wretched and wet as those around him, clutching himself in discomfort and fear, but he invested his faith in the crew, who remained as calm as they were stalwart, and in the vessel which seemed sturdy in its structure even while it was pitching and rolling, sometimes precipitous at the top of a wave, sometimes low in the valley of another.

'Land ho!' The longed-for cry came at last, just before darkness fell on the worst day of the storm. There was a pitiable cheer from the passengers who heard it. Some tried to make it to a vantage point to witness for themselves, only to be stopped by the first mate who cursed them and sent them back below decks.

'Fools an ye think we're safe yet. Get out the way, damn you!'

'Is it New York?' someone dared to ask. 'How far is it?'

'As far as eternity. Satisfied wi that? Now get below, or you'll be first to arrive. In Eternity, that is.'

Someone else boasted that they'd spied the land with their own eyes. 'It's close. Within gunshot range, I'd say.'

Whether true or not made little difference. The ship was still in a battle with the wind, and seemed to be making no further progress. The danger increased with the onset of darkness. Just before midnight there came a wrenching, tearing sound from the hull, and the ship shuddered its whole length.

'We've run aground!'

That was true, no question, and all aboard recognized it immediately. Panic swept like a second shudder through the ship. A mass of people surged towards the few boats on deck, where they were forced back by mariners bearing arms handed out by the captain. Some of the passengers had grouped to rush against the men guarding the boats when another blow from the wind shifted the ship against the rocks. A good part of the hull split and the vessel listed heavily. New orders echoed around the ship.

'Cut the rigging! Fell the masts!'

Robert's party, seeing the captain had left himself seriously short-handed by his assignment of a guard around the boats, volunteered their help. Soon they were hacking away at the sails and masts with whatever axes, knives and saws they could lay claim to. Their efforts were earnest, but to no avail. Below them the ship was breaking up rapidly, and water was rushing in. Inevitably the order came: 'Man the boats.'

Robert had not rendered assistance to the crew as a strategy for placing himself among the first to be allowed off, but perhaps he had a right to expect some priority. If he did, he was quickly disabused. The mate in charge of loading the boats selected whom he would, warning others back with the threat of his gun. Robert suspected bribery, yet some of the humblest sort were given the nod while most of the First Class passengers were held back. A petty trader from Cartagena who had been prominent in the card games on board was ushered forward and Robert, standing next to him, was denied. Better to be a friend, it seemed, than a gentleman, as Robert was presumed to be.

'What are we to do now?' he asked aloud, when the last possible boarder was squeezed in and the boats were being lowered, leaving Robert among others - including all the first shipwreck victims - on deck.

'Pray like buggery till the boats come back. *If* they come back,' from a voice, laconic, next to his ear. It was Richard Trevithick.

Robert retuned to his berth, expecting that at least he would be able to rescue some of his luggage while he waited, but there he met with further disappointment. His bunk was already entirely under water, his things dispersed or sunk. Robert sucked in breath and dived beneath, fully clothed. He tried to see, but sand and silt, churned up from the rocks, immediately attacked his eyes, and he was forced to resurface. He tried again, keeping his eyes closed and feeling his way by the contours of the bunk. He searched without result until, almost bursting for breath, his fingers felt canvas. He clutched, and rose for air. Back on his feet, he opened the bag to find, perfectly preserved, his collection of pebbles, stones and fossils from Santa Ana. Of the rest - his clothes, his diaries and letters, the precious Byron volume, his other specimens, and three years of careful savings - he could find nothing.

When it was fully light and the storm over, the passengers still on the sinking ship could see just how close they were to the mainland, yet they feared they might never set foot on it. The ship, more than half submerged, was listing at a crazy angle. Only its precarious perch on the rocks below was preventing it from toppling entirely into the sea. Everyone was by now crowded in or next to the forecastle, holding on to stop them sliding into the waters beneath. The captain, still on board, had warned that the vessel could give up the ghost at any moment. Under his direction, large spars had been chopped from the fallen masts, ready to be used as the last means of life support when the ship finally went down.

And then, and joyfully, the cry was heard. 'Lifeboat yonder!' Robert, damp yet in the clothes he stood up in, watched the distant moving shape and wondered if his vision was inferior to the others, who seemed so sure that this was their rescue vessel when it seemed so indistinct to him. Several minutes passed before he was reassured. In fact, following the traumas he had witnessed and suffered on this water, he retained a vestige of doubt long after he climbed into the boat, nursing it until the moment he stepped onto the dry land of New York.

'My father always wanted us to come to America,' he remarked to Trevithick as they took in their new surroundings. 'I expect if we had, he'd have used up all his savings, and we'd arrive as penniless as I do now.'

'Welcome to penury,' said Trevithick. 'Be grateful we arrived at all.'

'I am, trust me. Oh, I dare say if I seek out the company agent I might be able to organize some funds to be sent. What we are to do in the meantime, however, I'm not altogether sure.'

'Lucky you never took these arf-of me, then.' Trevithick felt in his pocket and brought out his famous silver spurs. 'Americans will pay a pretty price, I'm guessing.'

'Can you bear to part with them?'

'There's a time for zentiment, and a time to eat,' Trevithick said. 'I choose to eat. Please do me a great honour and be my guest.'

XI

Robert had not been deliberately avoiding George Hudson, but he certainly had not been seeking out his company. More surprisingly, perhaps, Hudson had not attempted to seek out his, though Robert guessed he had more than enough on his plate now that one railway board after another was setting up a committee of inquiry and demanding answers of their increasingly beleaguered chairman. They had not even been together in the House, but when Robert was called to a meeting of protectionist MPs at the home of their new leader Lord Stanley, he expected that Hudson would turn up. What Robert did not expect was that Hudson would be turned away.

'Gave the fellow short shrift,' announced Stanley coming back into the room with an evident air of satisfaction. 'Or rather my secretary did. Wouldn't stoop to speak to the bounder myself. No, just a curt note. Not wanted. That's all.'

'Quite right,' said John Herries. 'Not wanted. I've always considered the man disreputable, and a boor.'

At the far end of the table Disraeli's giggle hit the same bright note as the brandy decanter clinking against his lordship's glass. 'Did you tell him so when last at Albert Gate? If memory serves, you sat next to him at dinner.'

'Only in the course of duty.'

'Indeed.' Disraeli picked at his manicured fingernails and winked at Robert, who spent the rest of the meeting distracted by the import of the wink, and bothered by the fact that no-one bar Disraeli canvassed his opinion on any subject throughout the evening, or courted any favours, as they generally did.

Back at Gloucester Square, Robert was delaying his bedtime by answering letters he could easily have left to the morning when there was a timid tap at the library door.

'Miss Tomlinson, come in. I thought I gave you leave to retire.'

'You did sir, and I was about to when I heard a noise at the front entrance.'

'Late for a visitor.'

'Well, I tarried expecting a knock, but whoever it is seems to be just stood there, or in a fidget I should say. This man - he's breathing very loud, and, well, sort of muttering, to himself or somebody with him. I would have opened the door, sir, but I'll own I'm a little frightened. It's not a month since the Arthurs was burgled.'

Robert put down his pen. 'Are the hall lamps lit still?'

'Yes, sir.'

'Then go to bed, Margaret. I will investigate for myself. Don't worry, I have my gun.'

Once the housekeeper withdrew, Robert went to the drawer containing the caplock pistol he bought in Italy, satisfied himself it was charged, and moved quietly along the hallway to the front entrance of the house. He listened behind the door to what sounded like the snuffling of an animal. Keeping his pistol at the ready in one hand, with the other he stealthily unlocked and eased ajar the door, intending to spy through the crack. He heard sudden movement on the gravel path, hurled the door open to ambush any would-be burglar; instead found himself nearly collapsed upon by a stout figure groping at the air where the knocker had been.

'Hudson!'

He raised an arm to check the man's momentum. Hudson, misinterpreting the gesture, seized Robert's hand and held it close in a pantomime of affectionate greeting that turned to shock when he realised he had pulled a loaded pistol to his heart.

'Do you mean to kill me?'

'Of course not.'

Deflating like a bag of gas, Hudson slumped forward, almost knocked Robert off his feet as his slack mouth sought a confidant's ear to whisper, 'There's ose what would, though. I'd do it mesen, Rob, but for Lizzie, an that's the god's honest truth.'

His slurred mopings confirmed what Robert had already guessed from his unpinned appearance at the door - Hudson had been drinking heavily.

'You'd better come in for a moment.' With a certain impatience, Robert led the way along the hall. Hudson, struggling to keep up, bumped into one of the picture frames and stopped to steady it. Robert turned to see the man's squinted concentration upon the Lucas portrait of his father. He waited, and watched Hudson raise a brief apologetic hand to the painting before he followed his reluctant host into the library.

Robert hesitated about offering cognac; it was his personal need of it that overcame his better judgment, and Hudson was in no mood to desist. The proprieties of serving the drink allowed both a chance to calm themselves somewhat. They nursed their glasses and their own thoughts for a while as they sat in the recesses of their facing armchairs. It was only

194

Robert seeing Hudson on the brink of tears that forced him to break the silence, desperate to forestall him.

'I have not seen you in London for some time. I suppose you have been staying at Newby Park.' They both knew he meant *hiding*.

Hudson gazed dolefully at the man he still counted on as a friend. 'I came,' he said at last, 'to do my duty as a Member of Parliament. To do my duty...' He started to tail off, then came to attention like someone slapped. 'And I was turned away. By my own party. Turned away!'

He drained his glass of cognac, stared into it furiously. Robert made no move to provide him with another. Hudson talked to the glass. 'These people... I could buy em an sell em. Ave done, on many an occasion.' He looked up at Robert. 'What is it I've done wrong? I mean, out o the ordinry, what exackily am I sposed to have done wrong?'

In his head Robert made a tally of things he had known or learned recently about the shady side of Hudson's dealings - robbing the Peter of capital to pay the Paul of revenue, gross manipulation of shares and company accounts, buying materials on the cheap and selling them dear to his own companies, selling his own land in like manner, shirking his debts, dispensing bribes...

'I appeal to you, what have I done?' Hudson asked again. Receiving no answer from Robert, he supplied one himself, addressing the glass again. 'Nowt. No, not so long as I was coming up wi ten per cent dividend. No questions asked. Ha! They revile us now who fawned on us. Fail to deliver; on a sudden you're a swindler. They sharp forget who it was made a great business of the railway. Who had the talent to see all stretched before him. Stretched...' He liked the word, and liked better the next it suggested to him: 'El-as-ticity. Yes. Oftentimes, to summ... surmoun a difficulty here, a problem there, a little el-as-ticity might be needed in managing the affair. See... Robert, you know this... you don't get from A to B just wi picks and shovels, you know that... there's all sorts of obsicles to overcome, not wi tools only, but wi brain, wi guile, imagination, cunning. Eh? If that's all I'm being accused of, well, I plead guilty. Guilty.'

This speech energised him enough to take matters in his own hands. He stood up and marched to Robert's bureau, where he grabbed the bottle, splashed cognac into his glass, drank it quickly, and came back to fill up his host's. He remained standing, swaying slightly, using the bottle as a rhetorical device, thrusting it out to his audience of one as he said, 'Who stands before thee now?' Upward thrust of the bottle. 'Visionary?' Downward thrust. 'Or villain?' A few drops escaped onto the carpet.

'Or victim,' Robert said, without meaning to. Hudson nodded the neck of the bottle toward him in silent agreement, then tilted it to his lips and sipped the liquor reflectively while Robert contemplated the expanse of the man's waistcoat and wished he had not come. Evidently Hudson was thinking precisely the opposite as he next waved the bottle appreciatively and said, 'Summed up in a word. One word. Victim. You are... replete with unnerstanding, Robert. Why I came, my friend. *Mon ami.*'

He spread his arms as if to offer an embrace. Robert stayed where he was. Hudson swivelled, almost lost his balance as he made the gesture more public, as if he expected to find someone else in the room to enfold him. There being no-one, he sat down and turned lachrymose once more, the bottle trailing between his knees.

'Ye know what Zetland done? Made young Dundas break off with my Ann. They were to be wed this year. What's my pretty one done to deserve such cruelty, such spite? And all Elizabeth's plans dashed.'

Robert felt genuinely sorry to hear it. Against the biological odds, Ann Hudson was an attractive young girl, sweet-faced, surprisingly simple and demure. He remembered Fanny giving her little gifts when she was still a child in ringlets, accepting her kisses with quiet delight and exchanging sentimental glances with Robert. Ann's mother, Elizabeth, was the laughing-stock of polite society. The Hudson residences were all vast monuments to her appalling taste. Her *faux pas* and malapropisms were legendary - Robert himself once heard her reply, when asked if she would take port or sherry, *Ooh, a little of both, please* - but whatever the faults of the wife, he infinitely preferred that blithe object of ridicule to the snobs and tittle-tattles that made her so.

Hudson was still talking, leaning on his belly. Robert found himself unable to follow what he was saying while looking at him, as he could not dissociate him from the image of a toad, so he studied the spatters on the carpet and tried to make sense of the words spilling out from his visitor.

'One bi one, the doors is closing on us. *In* on us, and *agen* us. All them doors I myself opened over the years. Opened one by one. Before... You see, Robert, most folks know just either *in* or *out*. I've seen both sides o them doors. Like your father has. I'm his... I've known what it is to be poor, and to be rich. Same as him. I've made others rich, an if along the way I've profited some myself, is that not as it should be? Right and proper. I've opened them doors mysen, though they tried to bar em agen me. Not a person of quality? I'm a person of quality. What turned the key in the end, but my quality? The quality of genius. Same wi your father.'

'My father is dead.'

'Aye.' Hudson paused, thinking about this. Then, 'Respectably dead.'

Respectably dead. Robert was distracted for a moment, his mind on the conversations he had had with Edward Pease. When he again caught the loose thread of Hudson's ramblings to hear *And will rise again* he inferred his father was still the subject and was wondering where this idolatry was leading, when it dawned on him he was actually listening to a delusionist advancing plans for the Hudson resurgence...

'For I heard she's already consented to open the High Level Bridge.'

'Who?'

'Why, the queen.'

'Yes, what of it?'

'I'll tek the opportunity to present my wife to her Royal Highness as the world watches. Who will deny us after that? Oh, Robbie...' he said, warming to his theme, 'it'll be like old times again. Remember when we steamed into Gateshead, you an me an Geordie, flinging out the London papers to the crowd to prove we'd done the trip in eight hours? The parade... An never was such a banquet. It were Waterloo Day, I mind, with everyone at leisure. Band playing *Hail the Conquering Hero*. Yes, we must mark this occasion in the same way, or similar...'

'What are you talking about?'

'The Newcastle event. I'm sorry your father will not be with us, I am truly. He longed for the day.'

Robert stared across the room at his unwelcome guest. Hudson, pink with bleary nostalgia and doubly intoxicated by his inspirational plan - the *deus ex machina* to spirit away his disgrace - smiled back at him. Under prolonged scrutiny, however, he wilted. His chest sank back to mere fat. His eyes lost their glitter.

'Don't you think...?' he began. He stopped, pulled at the lobe of his ear. 'Don't you think... you owe it to me?'

Robert shook his head. Very slowly, very firmly. He did not speak until he was sure he had commanded George Hudson's full attention.

'Mr Hudson, I do not intend to cut you, or your family, to whom I trust you will pass on my best wishes. I would like to say that I hope you will not be ruined as a consequence of these investigations, though my greater hope is that others have not been ruined or irredeemably compromised by your actions. I would like to acknowledge the help that you have given me in the past, for which I am grateful and, having examined my conscience, am sure I have nothing to reproach myself for.

I'll say again, nothing to reproach myself for. I would also like to acknowledge your contribution to the growth of the railways in this country, which is undeniable however diminished by the exposure of your *modus operandi.*'

He stood up, kept his eyes on Hudson, who watched from his seat as Robert moved towards the door, where he stopped to finish his speech.

'I believe your right to be present at the opening of the Newcastle bridge or any other railway schemes in the future has been abrogated by your consistent failure to act in an ethical manner. I believe you have brought our profession into disrepute. For these reasons, our business acquaintance must cease as of this moment. Finally, I would be grateful if you would desist from boasting, as I have heard you do many times before, of your friendship with my late father. He dealt with you of necessity, sir, but in recent years especially did not wish to be thought of as your friend in any degree. He told me so emphatically, emphatically... And now I am telling you. Mr Hudson, please leave my house.'

Hudson remained motionless, gazing at the door. He seemed to be trying to take in what he had heard. After several seconds, he looked at Robert, as though about to say something, but did not. Instead he rose uncomfortably from the chair. His struggle for orientation lasted thirty seconds more, during which he could have fallen at any time, but he finally steadied himself sufficiently to move forward. As he started an uncertain walk across the room, his right foot brushed against the bottle on the floor and it toppled over slowly, leaking brandy onto the carpet. Robert ignored it - kept his eyes on Hudson as he opened the door and watched him through to the hallway. The Railway King managed to remain upright on his journey to the front door, and thus avoid a second collision with the portrait of George Stephenson. Indeed he did not seem to notice it on his way out.

XII

Robert's return journey from New York to Liverpool was completed in a first class packet named the *Pacific* and was both peaceful and uneventful. Only three individuals were disturbed by it; they were all firm and dry in England, but having heard what happened to their loved one's original ship nothing could prevent either Fanny Sanderson in London or George and Betty Stephenson in Liverpool existing in a state of trepidation until the side of the *Pacific* kissed the landing jetty at the Prince's Dock.

The Stephenson reunion was an occasion for tenderness and adjustment. As ever, Betty was the subtle intermediary in a reconciliation that might have been otherwise awkward, and this without saying anything. She merely held her husband's hand in one of hers, and took Robert's in the other, looking up with radiant affection at her two men until Robert completed the circle, enveloping both parents in a wordless embrace through which they could feel the strength and confidence he had developed over the three years away, and the warmth of the love he had nurtured for them.

Robert's maturity was evident: in the assured way he held himself; in his speech which was more resonant in tone and (Betty noticed) free of even the residual Northumbrian burr that had remained after his years of formal education; and in his careful attention to each of the myriad topics - personal and professional - they covered in their first hours of catching up on each other's lives.

Robert found his father much changed physically. He seemed older than his forty-six years, his hair prematurely white, lines etched into his face from the cares his work had obviously visited on him in these times. There were significant changes, too, in their relationship. George displayed greater equanimity in front of his son than he was wont to do. His pride in him had ripened into respect, and he had learned from Robert's absence how much he relied on his abilities and good judgment. Robert told him of the early troubles he had encountered in managing the men while he was away, and credited his father for teaching him the tricks and techniques that had helped him in dealing with them. He related the story of meeting Trevithick, and enjoyed watching his father glow to hear of Trevithick's continuing high regard for his old friend.

When Robert woke up in his parents' home, the morning after his arrival, he found on his pillow a beautifully designed and expensive watch and chain. Inside the case-door was an inscription *To Robert, from your loving father George Stephenson.* His smile, as he ran his finger down the chain and felt the weight of the watch in his hand, was partly for the memory of his younger self being upbraided by George for wearing *chains and fang-dangs,* partly for the idiosyncrasy that made his father include his full name on the inscription, and partly because the gift was solid silver, the elusive object of his search during their separation.

'Sir, where would the company find me most useful?' he asked at breakfast. He was anxious to start work again, for himself and to repay the partners for allowing him to travel abroad. 'At Forth Street, I suppose?'

'Ay, well Newcastle's in a mess, if you want to know the truth on it, but I wondered if you'd also like a project of your own. What would you think on the Canterbury?'

'The Canterbury and Whitstable line?' One thought immediately struck Robert, and his face registered it.

'Ah, that pleases you, eh? As I say, it's good to have summat you can see through from start to finish.'

'Especially when it's so convenient for London,' Betty added. Her expression was all benevolence. Robert grinned and, despite his acknowledged maturity, betrayed some spots of colour on his cheeks.

He allowed himself a full week at the temporary office in Canterbury, and walked the proposed railway route every day to acquaint himself fully with the work, before he sought to reacquaint himself with the pleasing features, the gentle manners, the life-quickening touch of Miss Sanderson. She was not much changed from the girl he had kept warm in his memory; her hair a little longer, her lips a little fuller.

'I am sorry that I lost all your letters at sea,' he said.

'There was nothing much in them, anyway. My life here has been very boring compared with all the adventures you have had, and the things you have seen. I expect you found them tedious to read.'

Robert, sensitive to a fault, detected a hint of censure in Fanny's reply, and aimed to win her over. 'I promise you, my greatest excitement was in the arrival of your letters. I did not find them tedious at all, and I tried my best to save them when the ship went down.'

'I suppose there is something romantic in the notion of my letters lying at the bottom of the Pacific Ocean.'

'The Atlantic.'

'Oh.'

'I came back in a boat named the *Pacific*. Possibly that's what confused you.'

'I'm easily confused. Especially about geography. Did you read many books while you were away?'

'Only those I had the opportunity to take with me. Mainly scientific ones. And some poetry. Byron.'

'Oh, I love Byron, though I ought not to. *Mad, bad and dangerous to know*. What about novels? Have you read Miss Austen?'

'I'm afraid I don't know her work. Perhaps Mama does; be sure to ask her when you meet her.'

'I hope I might soon.'

Fanny met first with his father when he came south to visit the Canterbury works and Robert brought him to Broad Street unannounced. Fanny was flustered by the visit, but overcame her nerves sufficiently to impress. 'Intelligent and gracious, like your mother,' was the verdict George delivered to Robert. 'I mean, like your *mama*.'

Three weeks later, the young man proposed and was accepted. That is how short a time the couple needed for each to be certain that their feelings for one another had ripened naturally even (or especially) through the darkest hours of aching for the absent lover, not artificially induced during their separation by mere romantic fantasy. For Robert, all too aware of his own addictive traits and chronically self-distrustful, this understanding came as a great relief.

Through the early period of their engagement Robert continued to divide his time between Canterbury and London and, in the words of his favourite poet, all went merry as a marriage bell, until George, facing another crisis of criticism, dragged his son back north for support.

'Telford's been here, poking his nose in.'

'Why?'

'We need a hundred thousand loan to finish the Liverpool line on time. The Exchequer won't countenance it until their tame engineer meks his report.'

'Didn't he like what he saw?'

'Oh, he had plenty to say about the way the jobs is priced, an chuntered about how we should bring in contractors apart from our own company, but who can I trust better than my own men?'

'Yes, but you need to be seen to accommodate him, Father.'

'Oh, aye, I understand all that. But I'm not sacrificing my locomotives, no matter what he tells em.'

'Why would you have to?'

'Telford's weighed in with the stationary engine lobby. Affects to believe the line's not suitable for locomotives. He wants the wagons hauled by ropes every inch of the way. What does he know, when all his experience is roads an canals? Where does his real interest lie, that's what I want to know. But he's managed to put doubts in the minds of those wi the purse strings. I'm taking them on, but. I've asked em to send a group to see the Stockton and Darlington working.'

'Is that wise? There's been a deal of problems running that line.'

George opened a palm as if to deflect objection. 'I've told Pease I'm sending you across to help with the case. The future... Our future is in the steam train, son. Is that not right?'

'I believe so, sir... if we can make it more efficient and less ugly.'

'Time ull come to bedizen her up, once we've made sure of her very existence.'

If Robert was to any degree frustrated by this evidence of George reverting to his old ways - peremptorily taking his son away from his work at Canterbury (and from Fanny) to direct him where he chose - the young man neither baulked nor displayed irritation, perhaps appreciating more fully now his place in the wider scheme. He was not encouraged, however, by what he found when he inspected the Stockton and Darlington operation. The Pease family were still having to subsidise the scheme, which had not turned a profit in three years. A bewildering variety of carriers was making use of the line - with the steam engines only being used for coal, and passenger trucks still pulled by horse power - and all the carriers were at each other's throats, particularly when it came to establishing precedence. Just as Robert had feared from the start, the single line with passing places was a daily cause of obstructions and arguments. The morning he arrived he witnessed a fracas when two horse-drivers refused to allow a steam train to pass, with one on the main line and the other on the passing loop. The engine driver worked up such indignation that he started to shunt his way forward in a threatening manner. One of the horses panicked and shied, overturning a passenger coach. Those who escaped without injury immediately jumped up intent on causing injury to others, and within moments fists were flying amid accusations, counter-accusations and some of the most colourful language Robert had heard since his return from South America.

He met afterwards with Timothy Hackworth, who was taking day-to-day responsibility.

'Surely,' Robert argued, 'the answer is to lay down a second line as soon as possible.'

'Funds will not allow.'

'Then it must be done in stages. Let's begin by extending the passing loops at least, before our visitors arrive. What else should I know about?'

'Fire damage to the fields caused by the chimney sparks. Mr Fowler up at Preston Hall is complaining to all and sundry that his plantations are ruined.'

'Well, what are we doing about it?'

'I now have fire-beaters stationed along the line, ready to put out any flames that might occur.'

'You mean, there are men paid to stand... No wonder there are problems with funds. Clearly the fault is with the engines, and that's where the solution should be looked for.'

Hackworth bridled at this. 'Don't you think I'm trying to mek a better o the engines? Ye might have forgotten, what with being abroad an all, but I've been working on steam traction for as long as your clan, if not longer. The *Royal George* is my own work, an more efficient in my book than either *Locomotion* or *Hope*. The plain truth on it is, we've had so much trouble with all the engines, some of the directors here are champing for a return to the horse for freight as well as passengers. If it weren't for Mr Edward keeping faith they might ha done so already.'

'What kind of trouble?' Robert was beginning to suspect that his father's reports may have had something of a rose-coloured tint.

'Well, two drivers killed for a start-off. Gillespie and Cree.'

'How?'

'Boiler explosions. Judgin when to top up the water's largely a matter of guesswork, and sometimes the drivers are that keen to keep moving they neglect it. That's likely what happened in these cases.'

'Isn't there a safety valve?'

'Aye, but there's a temptation to tamper with it - just tie down the safety arm, I've seen that done many a time.'

And done little about it, Robert thought, but did not say. This was no time to be upsetting the locomotive superintendent. They had enough difficulty besides.

On the eve of the deputation's arrival, Edward Pease wrote to Hackworth, *Have the engines and men as neat and clean as you can, and be ready with thy calculations, not only showing the saving, but how much more work they do in a given time. Have no doubt wilt do thy best to have all sided and in order in thy department.*

Which Hackworth did, under Robert's direction. Some rapid improvements (and even more cover-ups) had been made in preparation for the day, and fortunately there were no obvious altercations between rivals on the route while the visitors, Messrs Walker and Rastrick, were being towed along it by the company's most proficient driver, George Chicken. The engine, having already benefited from some modifications by the younger Stephenson and, by his instruction, burning coke rather than coal, released no stray sparks from the chimney, or not enough to cause a conflagration in the fields. Robert was pleased in general with the interview that concluded the day, though the visiting engineers were in possession of some unflattering statistics on the relative running costs of locomotives and stationary engines, partly countering what their hosts were aiming to demonstrate. Robert felt he dealt with the interrogation well enough, and by the end was untypically hopeful of a happy outcome.

The Walker-Rastrick report was delivered by the end of March. The directors of the Liverpool and Manchester Railway invited both George and Robert to the boardroom to learn what the consulting engineers had advised. Chairman Charles Lawrence tapped his finger on the copy in front of him.

'It is a diligent study. A well-written and interesting report.'

'And...?' from George.

'And in my opinion, comes to the wrong conclusion.' Lawrence's finger ceased tapping. He spread his whole hand over the title page. 'Walker and Rastrick, after careful consideration, recommend fixed engines for the Liverpool and Manchester.'

George erupted. 'Telford's toadies!'

Robert was no less angry, but more measured in his response. 'I do not understand how they could advocate a system that, should it fail in one place, would bring the whole railroad to a standstill. By contrast, when a locomotive fails, one just shunts it out of the way.'

Henry Booth also had his copy of the report on the table. 'In fact, they admit so much themselves. See the passage I've marked.' He passed the document across the table to Robert who read aloud: *The one system is like a number of short unconnected chains, the other resembles a chain extending from Liverpool to Manchester, the failure of one link of which would derange the whole.* While the committee assimilated the point, Robert turned leaves in the report to discover a drawing of Benjamin Thompson's proposed method of trains changing tracks at railway stations. 'Can anyone make head or tail of this?' he asked. 'If not altogether impracticable, it is certainly very complex.'

'Unworkable,' from George.

The Chairman called the meeting to order. 'What are we to do? In the light of our need for public support, we cannot be seen to be flying in the face of independent opinion.'

George snorted at *independent*. Robert was passionate in defence of his position. 'Locomotives should not be cowardly given up. I will fight for them to the last. They are worthy of the conflict.'

'I think I see a way forward.' Booth motioned for the return of his copy, and thumbed his way through to another passage he had carefully marked. 'Walker says somewhere there are more grounds for... here it is... *for expecting improvements in the construction and working of locomotives than of stationary engines*. That being the case, gentlemen, I propose a competition.'

'A competition?' from Joseph Sandars. 'You mean, between a fixed engine and a travelling engine?'

'No sir, I mean between locomotives. A trial, if you will. Let us see if any of our eminent railway engineers - present company included - can devise a locomotive that would satisfy the strictest of criteria for operation.'

'Capital idea,' said Lawrence. 'If we can find a locomotive that passes the tests, and does so consistently, all opposition to travelling engines must surely melt away. What do you think of it, Mr Stephenson?'

'I think we will win,' said George.

Robert loved Fanny sincerely, and would continue to do so throughout their married life (and beyond), but their honeymoon in Wales after their quiet wedding at the Parish Church of Bishopgate was for the bride disappointingly short. In making his excuses to her, Robert was a shade disingenuous, hinting that his father was to blame for stoking the urgency to return to work in Newcastle; in truth he was just as hot to get back to the race to be ready for the locomotive trials. While George was in Liverpool concentrating on the major works to be completed on the line, Robert was in charge at Forth Street, working on the engine that was to carry their hopes. The new Mrs Stephenson's consolation was a neat house at Greenfield Place in the west end of town (not far from the works), and the transportation of her precious piano all the way from London. Otherwise she could look forward to an occasional stroll with her husband across the Town Moor, though he had a tendency to walk too fast as he waxed on the theme of railways, rehearsing vexations and visions while Fanny waited patiently to ask where in Newcastle she might purchase sheet music, red flock wallpaper, lace doilies.

The trials were to be held along a level stretch of the company's line at Rainhill. One of the three men appointed to act as judge was

Nicholas Wood, who visited Robert at Forth Street to discuss the conditions.

'The engine must weigh no more than six tons, though we would prefer one of less weight.'

'Including water?'

'Including water; and the pressure of steam on the boiler must not exceed fifty pound to the square inch. The load it must carry can be proportionate to the engine's weight, but say it is six tons, then it must be able to draw twenty tons after it, on each day of the trial, at a speed of ten miles per hour.'

'If any engine can manage such consistency, it will be a Stephenson engine. Has there been much interest from others, since the trial was advertised?'

'Much interest? I should say so. You would not credit some of the claims we have had. Letters sent from as far off as America by supposed engineers and inventors none of us has ever heard of. I say *engineers* - at least one describes himself as professor of philosophy - and the methods they outline range from the weird to the wonderful: columns of water, columns of mercury, a perfect vacuum, and of course that old mythical favourite, perpetual motion...' (Robert nibbled at a finger, remembering his father's early experiments.) 'One correspondent boasted that the friction on his carriages will be reduced so low that a silk thread would draw them.' Wood laughed. 'I'm afraid you'll have no chance against such spectacular forces, Robert.'

'And apart from these mountebanks and charlatans, any serious contenders?'

'Oh, certainly. Your father's old sparring partner Vignoles is backing an entry from a Swede, name of Ericsson, who is to partner with the steam fire-engine man, John Braithwaite. One of our former Board members, Tom Brandreth, is working on some contraption, though how serious it is I'm not sure. There's Burstall from Leith, very experienced, and of course the other North East entry.'

'The other North East entry?'

'Why, your colleague, Timothy Hackworth. I saw him yesterday and he tells me his plans are well advanced. He expects to have some of the parts made here in your workshop.'

'I see. He did once give me his opinion that his travelling engines are better than ours, so this is his chance to prove it, I suppose.'

'Well, and the chance to win five hundred pounds. It's a tidy sum in anybody's language.'

'The prize is much greater than that.'

'Aye, daresay it is.'

Wood provided more details of the Rainhill terms and left his former apprentice with a final reminder. 'You must have your engine delivered, complete and ready for trial, at the Liverpool end of the line no later than October the first.'

'Trust me, we will be there,' said Robert.

His apparent breezy confidence was shot through with anxiety, like a cheerfully waved handkerchief faintly specked with blood. Progress on the *Rocket* was far from smooth, and Robert was pained by every reverse. He found comfort in writing almost daily to his father to report developments and ask advice.

George was in good heart, buoyed by a public event that marked the completion of his great tunnel into Liverpool - an illuminated procession through the work headed by such local lights as the mayor and a former government minister, the Right Honourable William Huskisson. Chat Moss was still proving a challenge. George's persistent belief that he could carry the railway across it rather than circumventing it with a long detour attracted few disciples, so he was delighted when he received Huskisson's enthusiastic support. Robert's letters came as a pleasant diversion from the politics and economics of big capital projects, an invitation to mull once again over the intricacies of steam engine improvement. George chuckled as he read the latest at home in the evening.

'Ha! Water, water everywhere.'

'Coleridge,' Betty noted absently, then looked up from her crochet work. 'What are you saying?'

'Robert's flooded out at Forth Street.'

'Dear me. Has the weather been so bad in Newcastle?'

George thought this an even better joke. 'Nay, lass. It's *Rocket's* boiler. Booth had the bright idea of inserting a host o metal flue tubes to make the water heat faster. Nowt wrong wi the theory, but when Rob's come to carry it out he's ended up wi hot water shooting out at every joint. Summat more like a fire engine than a railway engine.'

Betty was torn between sharing in her husband's amusement and worrying about her stepson. 'Will he be able to do anything about it?'

'Oh, aye, it's easy fixed,' said George. 'He's been using brass screws for the work when what he wants is to bore clean holes in the boiler ends, fit his copper tubes as tight in as he can, solder up and raise the steam. The copper will expand wi the heat an that should mek him some nice watertight seals.'

Robert followed his father's good guidance, adding stay rods of his own devising, and the result was a far more efficient multi-tubular boiler for the engine. By the same principle of collaboration between the Stephensons and others involved in the work - not least the factory superintendent Mr Hutchinson, whom Robert called his *oracle* - vast improvements were made in design and construction, from the water-jacket firebox and repositioned cylinders to the boosting of pressure by way of the blast pipe in the chimney, with one end in sight: to ensure that *Rocket* lived up to her name.

Robert entertained some curiosity about the progress of his rivals, but was both too busy and too scrupulous to make enquiries even of his colleague Timothy Hackworth. Others were less circumspect. One afternoon - with *Rocket* nearly ready for her trial run at Killingworth and already greased for action - Robert was working alongside his draughtsman George Phipps in the office above the factory floor when Phipps said, 'Who might that be, Chief? A customer?'

Robert, peeking through the glass where he sat, could see only the movement of a top hat below the level of the mezzanine. He left his desk and stepped out to the balcony rail for a closer look. From there he could see the stranger - a gentleman about his own age in a single-breasted frock coat with white shirt and black bow tie - making a slow circuit of the *Rocket* as if it were part of his itinerary on the Grand Tour. His exaggeratedly casual air (almost a promenade) was provoking, and contradicted every few moments as his attention was caught by a particular feature of the locomotive, when he would prod it or trace its outline with the walking cane he carried. He affected to be oblivious to anyone watching him until Robert came down the stairs to ask, 'Is there something I can help you with?'

The young man remained cool, bordering on supercilious. 'Aye, well... Are you one of Stephenson's lads?'

Robert had not been in Edinburgh for five years or more, but he had no trouble recognizing the accent.

'Which Mr Stephenson are you looking for?'

'Oh, Robert... Of Robert Stephenson and Company.'

'That would be me.'

'Aha.'

Robert endured the disdainful sweep of scrutiny; repeated, 'Is there something I can help you with?'

'Timothy Burstall... Junior,' said the other, presenting his card, which Robert did not trouble to study. 'My faither asked me to look you up.'

Robert was politely sardonic. 'Look me up? Or look my engine over?'

Burstall turned to take in another view of the *Rocket*. 'She looks gey smart, I'll gie ye that. *Genty*, we say in Leith. Do you have a name for her yet?'

'*Rocket*.'

'Ours is *Perseverance*.' He extended an insouciant hand. 'May the best engine win, sir.'

'Oh, I am sure it will,' said Robert. 'Now, pray excuse me, Mr Burstall, some of us have work to do. I trust your visit was instructive.'

'In that I have learned there is nocht to learn, ay, it was. Good day, Mr Stephenson. We'll meet again at the trials, nae doubt.' Burstall tilted his cane by way of farewell, and sauntered out of the works.

George Phipps clapped a hand at Robert's shoulder and said into his ear, 'Should I follow and give him a good kicking, Chief?'

'No, don't bother, Mr Phipps. We'll do that at Rainhill. Or our *Rocket* will.'

The days were disappearing as fast as the ballast his father was tipping into Chat Moss, but Robert's efforts gained extra impetus from the Burstall spy mission, and he advanced his plans for the Killingworth trial. He left the choice of driver to his Uncle James, expected James would take the controls himself, and was therefore a little surprised, the morning of the test, to see his relation climb up to his vantage point on the spoil heap near the colliery to watch the *Rocket's* progress in his nephew's company.

'I give the job to a younger man,' James explained. 'There'll be long days driving at Rainhill, and I'm not as fresh as I was once.'

They soon heard the steam blast from the colliery yard, and watched for *Rocket's* emergence. She was pulling five wagons in addition to a borrowed tender, and forty pitmen had volunteered to ride in the tubs for her trial run. Some of them waved as they passed the spectators on the slag, and James waved back while Robert consulted his silver timepiece.

'Puts me in mind of the *Blücher* fifteen year since,' said his uncle. 'But look, the old lass could never manage that incline - we had to haul her up nearly all the slopes.'

'What's the gradient there?'

'Well, it rises may be twelve feet in the mile.'

Robert eyes flicked between the train and his watch until the ascent was complete. 'By my reckoning, about eight miles an hour.'

'Pullin steady all the way. That's a canny rate. She'll be quicker by half on the level.'

Robert's timekeeping confirmed the accuracy of his uncle's prediction, for *Rocket* easily reached twelve miles per hour, outward and return, on the flatter stages of the three mile route. 'And that's not trying the boiler above one twenty,' Robert said as they walked along the track to meet with the driver. 'I'm satisfied she can do more than they have set out in the stipulation.'

The driver, a muscular sort in his thirties whom Robert did not recognize, climbed down from the footplate as they approached. He stayed close to the engine, rubbing his hands with an oily rag and watching James as if awaiting a signal.

'Have you come across our man, Bob McCree?' James inquired of his nephew.

Robert started at the name, and could not help but study the face closely, almost rudely, looking for a resemblance. 'McCree? Not... No relation to Dick McCree, the enginewright?'

'He was my father, sir. I was junior apprentice to him when... when the fire took him.'

'I'm sorry I did not know you, Mr McCree, forgive me. I was but a boy when your father died, though I was at the pithead that night.'

'I saw you there.'

'Well.' Robert nodded and reached out his hand, which McCree took a little hesitantly, perhaps afraid of transferring grease onto it. 'And you are to drive the *Rocket* for us at Rainhill?'

'If you'll have me, aye, I'd like to.'

Robert paused, thinking what his father might have to say, and (he was ashamed to admit to himself) fighting off an irrational and indeterminate sense of foreboding on his own part. Then he said, with forced cheeriness, 'Of course you must. Excellent driving, Bob. What do you think of her?'

'I can barely credit her pulling power. She was well within herself today.'

'That is just as it should be. Don't want to draw the strength out of her on pit work. The test is yet to come.'

'The best is yet to come,' quipped James, managing to ease the tension that had somehow caught the present in its grip.

Two weeks later a small boy, sitting cross-legged on a coil of tarred rope, hunched himself against an early autumn wind coming off the Mersey as he waited the arrival of the Cumberland steamer. Mr Stephenson was paying him eightpence a day to watch; his only further duty was to run straight to the railway workshops at Crown Street to let them know there when the ship was come in, or to Upper Parliament Street if it should land in the evening. Cold though he might be, the lad was happy enough to have earned thus far a full two shillings without a sighting of the vessel.

Robert was very far from happy. Not that he begrudged the urchin his money, but he was mad with anxiety over the fate of his engine. He had been meticulous in his planning and organisation. As soon as *Rocket* had completed her trial at Killingworth, he had personally supervised her dismantling and the hoisting of the parts into wagons bound for Carlisle. Before the week was out he had received confirmation that the engine had been successfully transported by lighter from the Carlisle Basin to Bowness, and transferred without mishap to the steamer. From there it should have been only one day's sail to Liverpool, where Robert had travelled to meet her and to oversee the manufacture of her tender at Crown Street. But *Rocket* had not arrived, and there was no word on the whereabouts of the vessel save some worrying reports of stormy weather at sea. Robert was all too aware of what that could mean. He appeared unperturbed in public but (Fanny being left in Newcastle) fretted in the company of his mama.

'Suppose we have lost her? What then?'

'Please do not distress yourself before you have cause. They say no news is good news.'

'But she should have been delivered days ago.'

'And will be, just as you came back to us despite the danger you were in. I am sure everything will be all right.'

Such comfort as Robert found in Elizabeth's words supported him until the next morning when he went to visit Henry Booth in the Railway Office. On his way in, he was surprised by another brief encounter with Timothy Burstall Junior, who was hurrying out of the building in far worse humour than he had displayed the last time they met. The young Scotsman scowled at his rival as if he were the cause of his trouble, and left without a word exchanged between them.

'Burstall looks as if he has lost a shilling and found sixpence,' Robert remarked to Booth.

'He has had news which could mean our competition's loss as well as his own. The *Sans Pareil* has met with some sort of accident on the road from Edinburgh. It has been badly damaged and will not be able to take part if we stick to our proposed dates.'

'I would find it hard to sympathise were I not presenting a similar case.'

'Has your *Rocket* still not fetched up in Liverpool?'

'I'm afraid not.'

Booth's forehead drooped low enough to threaten his desk. When he spoke he sounded so mournful that Robert was half-inclined to take his request seriously. 'You may shoot the man that had the notion of this trial.'

'I believe that was you, sir.'

'It was.' Booth sat back in his chair with a sigh, his expression pale and pained. 'It was done to establish once and for all the credibility of the locomotive over horse and stationary engine. Now, what are we left with? From dozens of statements of intent, we have the grand total of five declared entries. Of these, two are either damaged or vanished. The third, Mr Brandreth's...' He groaned. 'That man is a shareholder and a friend of your father's; what does he think he is doing?'

'What *is* he doing?'

'Making mischief. You will see for yourself; damn fool has already set up camp, as it were, at Rainhill, with his *Cycloped*. Of the others: Hackworth for all his promises is struggling to complete on time; Braithwaite and Ericsson are at least on their way.' He sighed. 'I see no alternative but to delay the trials by a week. The *Mercury* will hound us for it, but otherwise we'll have nothing to show.'

'My party can be ready in far less time, once our engine is in harbour.'

'Hmm.' Booth looked sceptical. 'How long since she left Bowness?'

'Three days ago. Well, this will be the fourth morning.'

'Do you have insurance?'

'Through Lloyds, for five hundred pounds, but that's...'

'I would go and see them, if I were you,' said Booth. 'You will find their agent in Norfolk Street.'

Robert did as recommended, and thus became perhaps the most reluctant individual ever to be offered five hundred pounds. The agent, having already entertained other claims in relation to the missing steamboat, was certain that *Rocket* must by now be lost and was ready to settle immediately. Robert was so disheartened by his promptitude that he left the office forthwith and, not willing to face his colleagues at Crown

212

Street, hired a hack to ride out ten miles to Rainhill where his father was helping prepare the ground for the trials.

He found George among a cluster of men gathered around a strange contraption - somewhat between a platform and a treadmill - mounted on the railway line, and with two horses standing on its boards. Robert surmised it was a version of a device he had seen in operation at Stockton, that allowed the working horses to ride the train and rest on the down slopes.

'Some kind of dandy cart, is it?' he asked his father.

'Well, here's the feller that give us the dandy cart.' George introduced Tom Brandreth. 'Now he hopes to beat us with his *Cycloped*.'

While the small crowd watched, Brandreth demonstrated his machine by the simple expedient of cracking a riding whip across the animals' haunches. As they broke into a trot, they moved the platform beneath them, which in turn moved the *Cycloped's* wheels by virtue of a cog arrangement underneath. With no wagons or passengers to pull, the horses effortlessly reached a speed whereby it was difficult for their minder to keep up with them.

'But this is not by any stretch a locomotive,' Robert complained in his father's ear. 'Surely Brandreth will not be allowed to compete.'

'I'm not sure he's all that fussed. He fell out with the Board when he set himself agen locomotives. This *Cycloped's* his way of gettin back at em - trying to prove a point, I reckon.'

Certainly Brandreth enjoyed showing off his invention, which continued to impress until the horses made their own Combination Act and mutely declined to take another step until hay and water could be brought to them. George and Robert left during this hiatus and kept each other company on the ride home, making themselves a miserable pair through gloomy contemplation of their prospects. Even George was thoroughly cast down by Robert's report of what transpired at the insurer's office.

'All is lost, then. We canna find an engine to answer now. Not if we do get a week's delay. Or a month's.'

Betty herself opened the front door. 'Did the boy find you, Robert?'

'The boy?'

'Poor mite ran his heart out from the harbour to Crown Street; then, when he could not find you at work, ran all the way here to tell you the news. I gave him an extra sixpence for his trouble.'

'What news? What news, Mama?'

'Good news, dear. The Cumberland steamer has docked at last. Your *Rocket* is safe. Did I not tell you it would be so?'

Robert's answer was to reach across and embrace his stepmother so eagerly that he fully lifted her from the hallway over the step. Betty's excited protests encouraged him further and he danced her a little way down the street, while George enjoyed the comedy of his elegant wife transformed to a marionette and made to kick her dainty heels in girlish abandon.

With the trials about to begin, Rainhill became the living embodiment of its name; people flowed down all the roads and lanes about and collected there, suffusing the green void. For race goers, the sensation was as the opening day at Royal Ascot - the air of anticipation, the splashes of colour from fashionable ladies and dandies competing with the runners for attention, card sharps and hawkers, the eager buzz of a large crowd. Wooden grandstands had been erected at the starting-point for the use of gentlefolk while *hoi polloi* milled around the various stalls and amusements that had sprung up like mushrooms at dawn, listened to the bands, or found themselves viewing-places somewhere along the mile-and-a-half of track. Robert guessed that the gathering must be well in excess of ten thousand, but amongst the blur of faces he had no trouble in spotting Fanny, who had surprised him by making her own way from Newcastle to support his efforts and was now seated with her mother-in-law, the two of them chatting amiably as they waited for proceedings to come under orders.

The judges seemed in no hurry to start. They had been in conference about the rules all morning and continued to debate, perhaps procrastinating in the hope that the Burstalls' *Perseverance* might yet arrive. The one adjudication they had made was the simple one of disqualifying *Cycloped* from the competition, but that did not deter Thomas Brandreth, who started parading his equine treadmill at first light and had since recruited fifty passengers from among the onlookers to test his invention with a full load.

'Let us see what horse-power can do,' he called out to the crowd. 'Witness the nobility of these beasts against those dirty, ugly, belching steam devils.'

Robert was stung by the insult. No-one could in justice call his *Rocket* dirty. He had ordered fresh livery for the occasion and the locomotive, parked three hundred yards from the grandstands, could easily be picked out for its sunflower yellow and its gleaming white chimney. Ugliness is more subjective. He had to admit that the public

214

seemed taken by the appearance of Braithwaite and Ericsson's *Novelty*. It was a much lighter construction than the Stephenson engine, with a vertical boiler that put Robert in mind of a milk churn on a cart. Its single driving cylinder, mounted along with mechanical bellows directly above the wheels, gave the impression that the engine had virtually no moving parts. This, and its polished copper cladding, lent the *Novelty* a sleekness that attracted appreciative attention.

'She is the people's sweetheart,' Robert said to his father.

'Ay, bedizened up to the nines, but lacking guts. Mark what I say, she'll flatter to deceive, like most females o that sort. There's our hardest opposition.' George pointed out Timothy Hackworth's *Sans Pareil*. His was a more conventional engine, not unlike his *Royal George*, but with four coupled wheels instead of six.

'The question is, how much of it can Hackworth call his own?' Robert said. 'We ourselves made the cylinder at Forth Street, and the boiler is Longridge's.'

'It ull be Hackworth's own if he comes out on top, mek no bones about it. Mind, she looks heavy, though. Aint she above the weight?'

'Well, if the judges ever show their faces we might find out. I just wish we could begin.'

Brandreth had to give up his place in front of the spectators when one of his horses put a hoof through the treadmill board and put an end to *Cycloped's* mischievous display. For want of further immediate entertainment, two farmers strapped themselves into harness and pulled along six passengers in a wagon, to the great delight of the crowd who worked up a chant: *The prize, the prize. Give em the prize.*

The Stephenson engine was ready to be tested. 'Come on, Rob,' said George, champing at the bit. 'Let's show em what a real steam engine looks like.'

'But the judges are not in place yet. Besides, we don't have precedence. *Novelty* is first to be called, then *Sans Pareil*, then us.'

'Neither of em is stoked up, an the crowd's restless. Howay, just for a first run out.'

Bob McCree was summoned, steam raised, and *Rocket* trundled along towards the grandstands and the main body of the crowd. 'Take her easy,' Robert cautioned, running alongside at the start. 'The proper trial is not yet begun.'

Applause rippled along the line as *Rocket* made its first pass, but there were cries of consternation too, and some of the ladies who had been sitting in prime position near the track made a hasty retreat, beating at their skirts so vigorously that their crinolines swayed like bells. The

215

Stephenson women remained where they were, but Robert saw his mama take out a handkerchief to rub discreetly where Fanny demurely offered her blackened chin.

Robert, turned to his father, perplexed. 'Why are we blowing out so much filth, when we're burning coke?'

'It burns slower on the mix,' argued George. 'We don't want to run out too quick.'

'So you've added coal?'

'It's better wi coke an coal mixed, trust us.'

Robert bit his lip. He doubted whether the spectators nearest the track would agree. Moreover, the judges had decreed the engine must *consume its own smoke*. No question, his father was one of the country's most inventive engineers - and one of its most inveterate meddlers.

Rocket continued to perform without mishap up and down the line, pulling thirteen tons behind at a steady pace, covering ten miles all told in a little less than an hour. Some of the more vociferous among the fashionable set carried on objecting to the dirt from the chimney, and there was the odd alarm when a red hot cinder landed in a lap, but in general the onlookers seemed impressed. *Novelty* was relegated to a siding, Charles Vignoles aboard and fuming like his engine, but his old adversary refused to surrender his ground until the judges belatedly arrived to take up position and Nicholas Wood ran over to assume control. '*Novelty* is first in our order, George. You must give way.'

Instructed accordingly, McCree began to move the Stephenson engine forward, expecting *Novelty* to reverse out of its siding and allow *Rocket* to take its place. Instead Vignoles advanced so that his smart little rig came face to face with its heavy opponent. Robert, watching, was reminded of the confrontations he had witnessed at the Stockton and Darlington. George had a different analogy to offer.

'It's like David an Goliath,' he muttered to his son. 'Only for once, we're cast in the role o Goliath.' George spat on the ground, fully conscious of where the crowd's sympathies would lie. He was right. As *Rocket* was forced into reversing past the grandstands to the passing loop on the farther side - an awkward shunt that made this locomotive appear even more cumbersome in relation to her rival - she was jeered on her way. Many in the audience waved handkerchiefs, which were immediately afterwards thrown into the air along with hats as the steam heroine of the moment was wildly welcomed onto the stage. Robert glanced across at his wife, watching *Novelty's* arrival with interest. His stepmother caught his eye and lightly touched Fanny's arm to draw her attention to Robert, who was rewarded with a little smile and wave.

216

George brought him back to the contest with another muttered grumble. 'Is she to pull her own tender, just? We had a full load on.'

'I heard Vignoles ask if he could try her for speed only on this run,' Robert said. 'The judges must have agreed.'

'Why is Wood trying to make us look bad?'

'I'm sure he is aiming to be fair to all. He will be anxious to show that everything is above-board.'

Braithwaite and Ericsson were publicly introduced and they jumped up onto *Novelty's* platform (for she had nothing so locomotive-like as a footplate or a cab) to acknowledge the cheers before leaving Vignoles to get under way with a crowd-pleasing, 'Ladies and gentlemen, I give you the future; I give you *Novelty*.'

The fireman applied himself to the bellows, the wheels rolled languidly a couple of revolutions, then picked up speed so abruptly that Vignoles was hurled against the copper boiler and almost toppled over as the engine shot off to a roar of approval that echoed down the line.

Wherever watchers gathered along the track, *Novelty* spawned an instantly devoted following that sighed as she disappeared from immediate view, and hummed in anticipation of her return. She made several journeys to and fro, most triumphantly past the grandstands where most of the important guests, politicians, scientists and press observers were gathered. At the second pass, the representative from *Mechanics Magazine* jumped onto his table by the marking post and announced, 'Twenty-eight miles an hour!' At the third he leapt up in even more excitement, waved his chronograph. 'One mile in one minute and fifty-three seconds!' At each declaration there was a collective gasp, followed by spontaneous applause, whoops and a very loud *Bravo!* from one of the two Honourable Members for the rotten borough of Newton.

Robert spoke quietly to his father. 'I thought you said Hackworth would provide our greatest competition.'

'He may yet - who knows what's in store.' George was grim-faced and decidedly downcast. Rain started, as if to accompany his mood, though it could not dampen the spirits of the elated crowd.

Novelty pulled up in front of the grandstand, where Mr Vignoles invited Messrs Braithwaite and Ericsson back onto the platform to accept the plaudits. After a while Braithwaite raised his arms and, with some difficulty, commanded silence in order to make a speech.

'We have given you merely a taste, a *soupçon* of what *Novelty* can do.' (More cheers.) 'Imagine, if this railway line were finished...' (*If ever!* someone shouted, to George's obvious annoyance) 'If, as I say, the railway were finished, why, at this rate we would have gone nearly the whole way from Liverpool to Manchester within the hour!' (*Bravo!* from the inebriated Member for Newton.) 'I give you this undertaking,' Braithwaite continued, 'indeed, I am prepared to stake a thousand pounds on it, that as soon as ever the railroad be opened, we will perform the entire distance in that time!' He grabbed Ericsson's hand and together they bowed from the waist. The audience applauded and the rain seemed to take up the sound, adding dramatic punctuation.

Robert was by now as visibly upset as his father. 'How dare he talk so, when the trial has barely begun.'

'I'll tek im on for his thousand pound, an no mistake,' said George, 'supposin I give it to charity. Let me up there.'

'Leave it for now.'

'We've a right of reply.'

'The best way is action, not words. Let us see how he answers in the trial proper.'

As if to rehearse their response, Braithwaite, Ericsson and Vignoles all accompanied *Novelty* into a siding where the wagons awaited coupling, and the spectators sat patiently in the rain to witness her performance under full load. The judges waited in a little more comfort under a canopy, but half an hour later a message came from the siding to the effect that *some inattention to the supply of water and coke* was the reason for the delay; they would be some time yet. The judges invited Timothy Hackworth to bring *Sans Pareil* to the fore, but he also sent back to say he was not quite ready. Indeed anyone passing by his engine for the last three hours could have seen Hackworth contortionate with hammer and wrench, trying to effect some repair to its innards.

'So now we can take our turn again,' said George, cheering up. 'Uncouple her an we'll show how we need not be beat for pace.'

Rain drummed furiously on *Rocket's* boiler as the Stephenson party prepared for her re-entry. Bob McCree was back on board and ready to roll when Nicholas Wood appeared from the murk, waterproof cape at his shoulders, eyes squinting to make out which was George. He raised his voice to be heard.

'We have called a postponement. There is nothing to be gained from carrying on in this weather, not with two of the three engines out of action. Come back at ten o clock tomorrow morning.'

George was irate at missing this chance to pit *Rocket* directly against *Novelty* under inspection. It was all Robert could do to persuade him to go home, for he was determined to stay and strip the locomotive down to its bare essentials in search of more speed. The cheers his opponent had received rankled and provoked him. He stopped working only when he saw that the spectators had left the field.

'We'll come back at daybreak, then,' he said, when he had finally been cajoled into the barouche with his family. 'She mun not be found wanting.'

'Dad, there is nothing that needs to be changed with *Rocket*. Remember, this is a trial, not a race. What we have to do is fulfil the conditions, and do so consistently, mile after mile, under full load. It is the others that will be found wanting, not us.'

George sat in the barouche, picked at the white ribbon in his button-hole, and glowered through the window at the rain. Betty leaned forward and lightly stroked his hand where it rested on his knee. Fanny, next to her, observed the tiny gesture and smiled at her husband opposite. George subsided, but still wanted the last word.

'I think you should drive tomorrow,' he told Robert.

'Why? I thought Bob's driving today was very good.'

'He's a McCree. That's a family don't put itself out much.'

Nonsense, Robert almost said out loud, but stopped himself, to avoid openly contradicting his father, and because he was ashamed that such thoughts had crossed his own mind when he first heard the driver's name.

For all the sleep he got at home, Robert may as well have agreed to go back with George at dawn, or indeed to have stayed in the field throughout the night. As it was, the two of them had an unplanned early breakfast together and were back at Rainhill before eight in the morning, where the ground was still wet but the morning fair. Robert remained anxious. George had recovered much of his optimism.

'Let's give the folk an early day ride. A *Catch-Me-Who-Can* in Trevithick's honour.'

The Stephensons coupled *Rocket* to a coach that could hold thirty passengers and, as visitors arrived they were indiscriminately invited to step aboard for a trip to the end of the course and back. Lord sat with labourer (or at least in the same vehicle), lady with laundress, and George himself took the controls, pushing the engine further than Robert had allowed Bob McCree to do the previous day. By reversing out and heading back, he ensured the grandstand view would be of the locomotive in its full glory. At each pass he raised his hat, revealing his shock of white hair and cheeks heightened to a toby jug glow.

Excitement built with the coming of the crowd; there was a clamour to be part of the pleasure rides and George was happy to oblige.

He became more adventurous with each trip so that he could return quickly to pick up the next party. Robert stayed close to the start, and saw there the reporter from *Mechanics Magazine*.

'Now, sir, will you put your watch on the next return, see how she does?' he asked.

'This is a diversion only. I am here for the official trials.'

'It is no more a diversion than your favourite *Novelty* undertook yesterday, and at least our engine is carrying weight. Pray oblige me, sir.'

The journalist reluctantly stationed himself by the marking post and watched down the line, chronograph in hand, for the returning *Rocket* to reach the distant marker. It let out a shriek of steam as it did, quickening Robert's pulse as he glanced across to check the watch had started. The reporter nodded firmly, put out to be scrutinised thus. Some in the crowd pressed forward almost onto the track in their eagerness to see the train coming, then stepped back in alarm as it rushed by with a velocity none of them had ever encountered. They stared at the people inside the coach as if they expected to see faces torn away in the rush of air, but they were met with expressions touched only by gaiety and exhilaration. Robert's eyes were on the reporter, whose own were shining despite himself, and who turned to say something that was lost in the roar of the engine.

'What was that?' Robert strained his ears as the man shouted it out a second time. *Thirty miles an hour!* he heard upon the wind.

George cleared the line, satisfied that he had redressed the balance. For all the excitement about *Rocket's* performance, however, there were many who felt that *Novelty* would eclipse it, and they whistled their support when their champion returned to compete on the track at the head of a regulation load three times her own weight.

'Now we'll see,' said the *Mechanics* man to Robert. He did. *Novelty* had travelled not five hundred yards east from his position at the rail when the reporter and hundreds around heard a dull explosion, and a moment later witnessed smoke, steam and fire issuing from where *Novelty's* bellows were located; saw, too, Vignoles leaping from the platform and rushing for water to douse the flames. There was a moment of stunned silence among the crowd, then they bubbled over in chatter and speculation, each one describing to his neighbour exactly what he had seen, as if the neighbour had not been present to see it for himself.

'It's a blowback,' said Robert, to anyone who cared to listen.

One of the judges, Mr Rastrick, ran along the track to investigate, and ran back a few minutes later to confirm Robert's diagnosis. 'A blowback from the furnace has burst the bellows,' he said. '*Novelty* will have to be withdrawn for repairs.'

With Timothy Hackworth still unable to present *Sans Pareil* in competition, and in the continued absence of *Perseverance*, the judges conferred at length again, and came to the painstaking conclusion that each engine must be given every opportunity to prepare properly for the trial. *Rocket*, as the only locomotive fit for examination, was listed for the morrow.

'Why not today?' asked George, perfectly reasonably.

'The morrow,' was the reply.

Fanny arrived soon after by coach to watch the proceedings, and was mystified to find the bulk of the visitors already on their way out. Robert walked across to tell her of this second postponement.

'What a shame for you,' she said, 'still not able to show how *Rocket* can perform.'

'Well, we were able to, a little. Some of the people have enjoyed short trips with us, up and down the line. On one occasion, Father got her up to thirty miles an hour.'

'That sounds very fast.'

'Fastest ever, I would think.'

'Oh, I wish I had been here to see it. Or better, to enjoy the ride.'

'Really? You would like to try it?'

'Of course.'

'Then, why should you not? Come with me.' Robert felt his heart beating. Like a smitten youth on a fete day, he took his new wife by the hand, helped her negotiate the dangers along the line to where his crew were tending *Rocket*. Bold as he seemed alone with Fanny, he was bashful when he brought her in front of the men, and then disappointed to find they had already uncoupled the passenger coach and removed it from the track. He hesitated to make them go to all the trouble of reuniting coach and engine merely on a whim. Robert considered the footplate and tender, contemplated his young wife in her fine clothes.

'I cannot make you passenger, but... Would you care to drive with me?'

'You mean, up there?'

'Yes, well, no, it's a foolish thought...'

'If you would like me to. If I would not be in the way...'

Robert climbed first on the footplate to examine the possibilities. 'Would you be able to sit here?' He indicated the platform space between his position and the water tank. For answer, she stretched out her gloved hand. Robert helped her up and she sat sedately behind him throughout the preparations, even remaining calm when the steam blasted and the wheels rolled forward on the track.

Robert drove cautiously at first, but when he looked round for the first time, as they passed the empty grandstand, Fanny's composure was such that he dared to let *Rocket* open out. The steam valve yielded easily to his touch; the engine responsive, eager. He glanced back, anxious for his charge. Fanny, keeping her bonnet secure with one hand, signalled to him happily with the other. Robert let the steam pressure build to fifty pounds and gave the engine full regulator. A minute more, a touch at his sleeve. Fanny was standing with him on the narrow footplate, as close as an embrace. The speed increased. He could feel her excitement as she slipped her arm under his, her breath warm on his neck.

'Such sensation,' she said. 'We are like birds.'

'We can fly faster.'

'Yes.'

The breeze was tugging at her bonnet. He watched her undo the lace with one hand, twist it round her fingers and toss her head in release. The wind whipped at her long dark hair, pressed down her eyelids. She turned her face to his cheek. 'Oh,' she said, and cleaved to him. He felt a quickening within. Prosaic metal softened, rails smoothed to silk. Divine fusion of a husband and a wife; lovers liquid in the ethereal stream.

Though Robert and Fanny never spoke of it in quite those terms, they intuitively recognized this as the moment their marriage truly began. Years later, when he sat with her cold hand under his and slipped into a trance from an hour of numb despondency, he conjured the vivifying wind through her hair and the thrill of her intimate embrace in a swirl of steam.

For the present, he was hers entirely. Once the brief and delicious honeymoon ride aboard *Rocket* was over, they had a craving for closeness in each other's company that could not be satisfied by an immediate return to the parental home. Fanny knew where she wanted to go.

'Do you know Madame Tussaud has returned to Liverpool? Why do you not take me there.'

'Of course.'

The coachman was directed to the Pantheon in Church Street where they had to wait for almost an hour to pay their shillings and join the promenade around Madame's saloon. 'I suspect many of those whose day was cut short at Rainhill have come here to seek their pleasure,' said Robert.

'Yes, but Madame's collection is popular wherever she goes. Have you heard which pair are newly represented?'

'Mr George Stephenson, and his handsome son Robert.'

'Perhaps one day. No, the West Port murderers. The body snatchers.'

'Oh, Burke and Hare. Interesting.'

There were other attractions to take in before they reached the plinth that supported the notorious Irishmen. Many of the wax figures were carved from life and were reputed to be the perfect mirror of the originals, though Robert and Fanny, like most of the visitors, had to study the labels carefully to determine who was standing before them, having seen relatively few engraved or otherwise illustrated, and almost none in actuality, except for Wellington, whom Fanny had twice observed in a private box at London performances she had attended, and whose striking profile adorned many of the Waterloo keepsakes that were still on general sale. The couple played the game of guessing whom it was on the next plinth before they were close enough to read the inscription, with mixed success. Napoleon and Josephine were easily recognized, as were Henry the Eighth and Mary Queen of Scots from their costume, and the present king from his girth, but they could not distinguish between the Lords North, Liverpool, the Pitts or the other politicians displayed, without recourse to the written descriptions.

They picked out Shakespeare from the literary tableau, made a correct guess at Chaucer and a wrong one at Milton (*Daniel Defoe* from Robert). Sir Walter Scott defeated them. 'But see who this is!' cried Fanny. 'Your favourite.'

'Lord Byron; I was going to say so from his noble look. At least there is a place for him here. Westminster Abbey refused him for Poets' Corner.'

'On what grounds?'

'Well... questionable morality.'

'Oh, yes, I suppose...' Fanny said nothing else for a moment, as she studied the image of the poet; then... 'Your eyes are like his.'

'Glass, do you mean?'

'Don't tease me.' Fanny tapped at his wrist, a little too tenderly for a scolding. 'But where is my Miss Austen? All the ladies here are queens or courtesans.'

She blushed suddenly, realising she had spoken this out loud, and put her fingers to her lips. Robert leaned over to whisper softly in her ear, 'And none as pretty as you. Wax or otherwise.'

In the Adjoining Room, next to the depiction of the Reign of Terror (a bloody guillotine and a glut of severed heads) there was a large crowd around the models of Burke and Hare, which made the viewing difficult and the air about particularly stale. The Stephensons paused only to read how Burke had permitted a mask of his face to be taken on the eve of his hanging, and the informer Hare on his early release, before they retired to take tea and enjoy the music of the promenade band.

'I counted over forty figures on display,' said Robert, 'and barely a scientist or an engineer among them. Benjamin Franklin only, and he more by virtue of his political career.'

'Perhaps you should invite Madame Tussaud to Rainhill, so she might see something that attracts a crowd other than monarchs or murderers.'

Such a visit might have been instructive for the venerable Frenchwoman. There was no diminution of interest in the trials the next day; indeed the numbers spectating seemed to grow larger and to arrive earlier. Perhaps none had travelled so far as the two gentlemen who introduced themselves to George as representatives of the *Albany Evening Journal.*

'Weren't they Yankees?' he said to Robert afterwards.

'Indeed they were.'

'It's rum, eh? All them years I said we'd go to America to mek our fortune, an now they're coming to us.'

What the New Yorkers saw on their visit incited them to write later of *a magnificent prospect, an unparalleled opportunity.* For their counterparts on *The Scotsman* the demonstration supplied *a greater impulse to civilisation than it has ever received from any single cause since the press first opened the gate of knowledge to the human species at large.* The man from the *Derby Mercury* was convinced of the immense practical potential: *When the Liverpool and Manchester Railway is completed, and the Locomotive Carriages are plying upon it, we shall undoubtedly possess a mode of conveyance superior to any that the world has hitherto seen, and one which must be pronounced a noble monument of mechanical genius and commercial enterprise.* More succinct was *The Times,* quoting verbatim an exclamation from the terraces, *The power of steam is unlimited!*

The Stephensons carried all before them. *Rocket* did everything that was asked of her. Bob McCree drove tirelessly most of the day. With a full load, they covered thirty-five miles of track in the first three hours, and the next thirty-five in less. For the amusement of spectators they detached *Rocket* from the wagons and sped along the course at half a mile a minute. They tried the gradient beyond the level Rainhill track, and *Rocket* coped with ease. Towards evening, with George taking a spell on the footplate, he passed Isaac Cropper, one of the company directors, waving his top hat and declaiming enthusiastically, though engine noise prevented the driver from hearing his speech. Robert told him afterwards that Cropper had shouted, *Now has George Stephenson at last delivered himself.* This from one who had been the staunchest advocate of stationary engines.

One by one their rivals left the stage. The public's darling *Novelty* made another bid for glory, but had to withdraw when an accident to her steam pipes caused hot water to fly in all directions to the great peril of anyone who came near.

'They never would take my thousand pound,' said George.

There was a flurry of excitement (and anxiety from Robert) as the Burstalls put in a surprising late appearance amid much waving to the crowd, but such bravura simply deepened the sense of anti-climax when *Perseverance* could manage only five or six miles per hour at best, a limp show that ended with father and son pretenders retreating in shamed silence.

Only *Sans Pareil* seemed liable to threaten *Rocket's* position. Once Hackworth had succeeded in getting her fit for trial, and the judges had chosen to ignore the fact that the engine was significantly overweight, she started off briskly and returned a time for her first run of just over five minutes. Succeeding runs failed to match her initial speed. It became obvious that she was consuming too much fuel and that Hackworth, manning the regulator, was fighting a losing battle with a faulty feed pump. Returning from a fifth run, immediately in front of the packed grandstand, *Sans Pareil* ground to a halt in a vaporous cloud. Lack of water in the boiler had caused the lead plug above the fire to melt. Her immobility was such that a chagrined Hackworth was forced to call upon volunteers to help push the heavy locomotive to the blacksmith's shop at the end of the course.

Robert went to offer some help to a former colleague. He found him disgruntled and bitter. 'This is your doing,' Hackworth said.

'What are you talking about?'

'Yon cylinder's cracked, that's where the trouble started. The cylinder made in your workshop.'

'I can assure you...'

'Strange, that. But mebbes not so, considering what you had to lose should my engine prove superior to yourn.'

'Damn your insinuation.'

'Not enough, were it, to have the dice loaded already? - your dad already installed as engineer on the line, and one of your directors as judge.'

Hackworth was failing to appreciate how tolerant the judges had been over his many delays and his flouting of the rules over weight;

225

failing to note that his *Sans Pareil* had proved manifestly inferior to *Rocket* in almost every aspect of design; failing to acknowledge that if the cylinder was indeed cracked as he claimed, then the most likely cause was the excessive strain placed on an altogether inadequate engine. Furious in his disappointment, all thoughts were of injustice and sabotage. All he could see were enemies.

Robert was beside himself. It was as much as he could do to refrain from snatching up the blacksmith's hammer and knocking the man's block off. He had not been so provoked since his early encounters with Powder and crew. Hackworth's spiteful expectorations had curdled the cream of his success. With the greatest effort, he confined his response to words.

'You're like a mewling infant, sir, that falls over and blames the world for it. There's no conspiracy against you - look to your own failings before you find them in others. Your engine just ain't good enough.'

He turned on his heel and walked out of the shed. There was a metallic clatter behind him. Robert forced himself not to look back; if, as he suspected, that sound was of something like a wrench thrown in his direction, he could not know it and keep from committing murder on Hackworth.

He feared George might act likewise, which is why he tried at first not to mention the argument to him, but Robert's mood was so low, in the midst of all the celebrations over winning the prize, that he eventually had to answer for it by giving a full account. He was surprised when it failed to disturb his father's sanguinity.

'Ah, let him grow lean on it,' George said. 'An envious man never wants woe.'

'I just hope he does not spread a rumour that we spoiled his chances. It would hurt to have our integrity questioned.'

His father placed a hand lightly on his shoulder, a gesture rare enough for Robert to remember it afterwards. 'Summat you'll have to get used to, son. When people like us stick out from the common sort, there's allus those ull want to beat us flat again. I've had my share of it already, an now the world's eyes are on us.' His hand moved from Robert's shoulder to his arm, and he guided him a few paces to where they could see the silhouette of *Rocket* against the evening sky. 'Know what I like best about what we do, you and me?' Robert shook his head and smiled, appreciating the warmth of his father's *you and me*. 'I like that it's solid. That it's there in front of you, to look at, an touch. An to show other people. Well, we don't have to be present, of course. *Rocket* ull still be here, solid as ever, when we go off tonight, an here for people to look

226

at when they come back in the morn. Things don't go away when our eyes is closed.'

'No. I like that too. I mean, about what we do.'

'An that's our answer, when the knocks come, like they're bound to,' said George. 'I'm tellin ye this partly so you can remind us of it, as I do forget at times. I know I'm not allus in this fettle.' Robert could see the gleam of him even in the encroaching darkness. 'So just remind us, whenever some jaw-jaw starts his carpin - some barrister, or shiny-arse, or peer - to take em where our work is to be found an say, *Here, have a look at this. Or this, or this. There's your answer.*'

Robert's gaze followed along the line of his father's pointing finger to where *Rocket* rested at the end of the track. He could still make out her contours, if not her colours. She seemed like a statue of herself. And yes, she looked solid. Solid and dependable.

XIII

While George Hudson's fortunes drained away, leaving the wreck of his reputation exposed in its slime, Robert, having freed himself of association, was pleased to receive what he took as a token that he had recovered his own position. Shortly before he was due to return to Newcastle for the royal opening of his High Level Bridge, he learned that he had been elected Fellow of the Royal Society.

Many distinguished scientists had lectured at the Society and Robert had attended when he could. Following his election, he determined to make an early appearance, and selected a talk from its intriguing title in the prospectus: *The Secret Diseases* to be given by the doctor and author William Acton. He did not realise at the time of his choosing what an effect the two-hour presentation would have upon him.

It was as well, Robert mused as Dr Acton warmed to his theme on Monday night, that women were ineligible to be members of the Society, for such a lecture could not have been delivered in any respectable female's presence without causing acute embarrassment. Even this normally sedate male audience was discomforted by the doctor's frank description of the causes and symptoms of the condition he referred to as *blennorrhagia*, by which he meant the manifestations of the various forms of venereal disease. Like others in the room, Robert listened with horrified fascination to the speaker's graphic account of the three stages of syphilis, complete with illustrations projected onto the wall by magic lantern. At a later point in the lecture he became more disturbed still.

'The next form of blennorrhagia I am about to describe, as it exists in the male, is gonorrhœa. My mentor Dr Philippe Ricord calls it urethral blennorrhagia; some French writers denominate it venereal catarrh; in England it is vulgarly known by the name *clap*, derived from the French word *clapier*, signifying a filthy abscess; and in France the common people call it *chaude pisse*.' The doctor paused, seeming to anticipate though he did not openly acknowledge the constrained chuckle that went round the room, and his expression remained unchanged when he continued: 'As the term gonorrhœa is generally accepted, I shall employ it, and at once proceed to treat of the conditions which tend to its development.'

His seriousness of tone commanded respect. His audience fell silent once more as the doctor described the transmission and symptoms of gonorrhœa in its acute form, and explained how the disease could also persist in chronic form, sometimes without the patient being aware of it. Robert paid close attention to the example of the military man who presented with complications thirty years after being originally infected, his condition only coming to light as a result of his consulting the doctor when his wife's failure to bear children eventually caused him to become anxious about his own potency.

'He was found to have inflammation of the epididymis - the structure in which sperm is manufactured and stored - and despite belated treatment by the application of twenty-five leeches to the perineum and daily immersion in a warm bath, was unable to recover his fertility. The patient subsequently died of Bright's Disease, perhaps the ultimate revenge of his long-neglected gonorrhœa.'

Robert was still in deep reflection on this case when Acton abruptly departed from the purely scientific line he had been pursuing to take a moral path, deploring the high incidence of prostitution and its attendant evils in garrison towns and close-packed cities, not least in London itself. 'Prayer and lamentation will not cure them,' he said. 'Sackcloth and ashes will not arrest the deterioration of our national fibre. The schemes of Reformatories, Maids' Protection Societies, Vice and Obscene Book Suppression Societies are but paltry, peddling scratches on the surface of evil. A grave, internal malady lurks within the body social, and if society will not hear these words of mine the patient will be extinct before the disease is eradicated. Let us be clear - by ignoring the evil we do not abolish it; it walks abroad; it is a vice as patent and as familiar as drunkenness. The streets of London are an open book that we may all read plainly, would we not avert our eyes. It is a mistaken and cruel policy to allow vice to grow so desperate and reckless, as you must surely now appreciate, gentlemen, from my illustrations of the dire consequences.'

More than one of those present could by now be described as shame-faced. Several seemed to be examining the floor below the speaker's podium; others pulled at their ear lobes. Robert seemed to be in a state of abstraction, but he looked up sharply when Dr Acton essayed a response to a member's question about the prevalence of the 'secret diseases' among London's prostitutes.

'It would be vain and unsafe, sir, for me to attempt any estimate in the absence of reliable statistics, but by comparison I can advise you that in Paris, where the authorities examine all those who come under police arrest, the extent of syphilis among unregistered prostitutes is more than one in five of the women, and in plain fact gonorrhœa is

229

considerably more common. There is no reason to believe that Britain is superior to France in that regard.'

He went on to describe the 'progress of the modern harlot', who might entertain up to fifteen or twenty clients a day. 'Many, perhaps most, of her liaisons will not be with men of her own impoverished class, but typically the wandering, hotel-sick country man of business whose footsteps stray at night to where she waits unafraid to beg shillings for her services. She is a sort of whitewashed sepulchre, fair to the eye, but full of inner rottenness. Beware this siren that beckons in our streets.'

At the end of his lecture, Dr Acton was generous in the time he allowed for responding to more questions from Royal Society members, but one Fellow who may have been most desirous of answers was left in a state almost of insensibility, unable to ask anything. He remained in his seat for several minutes, staring into space. When the others transferred to the tea room, Robert slipped unnoticed out of Somerset House through the courtyard and onto the Strand. It was the coincidence of his passing the Adelphi Theatre (presently advertising *A Most Unwarrantable Intrusion*) that shook out from his mental paralysis a memory suppressed for the last twenty-five years.

The night that began with Robert taking Fanny to the public demonstration of laughing gas had not ended with the young man's first inhalation of opium at Mr Chung's den. He lay still in his stupor on the low mattress and became only gradually aware of a shadow moving across the strange, swirling light. In the far distance - from the dark side of the moon or the antipodean depths of a tunnel - an echo of a human voice. The dark shape bent over him, and he smiled in dreamy anticipation of a goodnight kiss. 'Mama.'

'Not your mama, friend, but I will find you soft company, depend on it.'

The voice was male. Robert opened his eyes. The nose and eye-holes of a mummer's mask, refracted by shards of coloured light, resolved at last into the face of his new companion, the man in the opera cloak; he could not remember his name.

'Did I not tell you that the coolie's black was good?'

'Good,' Another voice that seemed familiar; Robert made an effort to attend should it speak again. 'Good.' The voice sounded something like his own.

'Best in London - trust Frederick Travis to know. And now for Salisbury Square. The walk will do you good. Come.'

He allowed himself to be picked up by the shoulders, and he leaned awhile against Travis, recovering his balance. Mr Chung stood by the doorway with a candle to light the way, bowing his head as they left. Robert glanced back to say goodbye to the little servant girl, but she was not to be found - perhaps sleeping in a corner somewhere. Outside, the dank air rendered him nauseous. Travis gripped him by the waist and helped him negotiate the worn steps to the main thoroughfare. There he faced him up for inspection.

'Can you stand unaided, sir?'

'Of course.'

'Splendid.' Travis reached inside his coat for a brandy flask. He drew the cork out with his teeth and offered the brandy to Robert who took a long draught while the older man looked on, the cork between his teeth giving his grin a vulpine quality. Travis drank in turn, draining the flask before stowing it once more inside his coat. He patted himself down, exhibited disappointment in the result. 'Are you still in funds, friend?'

Robert had to rax the muscles of his face, clamping and unclamping the jawbone before he could answer distinctly, 'I have money, yes.'

'Excellent.' Travis steered him by the shoulder and fell into step, walking easterly.

'Where we going?'

'As I told you, soft company. Chung's place is all very well, but lie there too long and the damp gets to your back. Mrs Hodges supplies comfort and pleasures of a different kind. You said you had money?'

'Yes.'

'Perhaps I should look after it, being a habitué. Strangers do get gulled; sad but true. Though she has a tender heart,' he added, clapping Robert's shoulder in reassurance as he took charge of his purse.

The place they headed for lay to the south of Salisbury Square. It had the appearance of a boarding-house that seemed shut up for the night. Travis neither knocked nor tried the door, simply lingered outside with his charge until a man emerged from the shadow of a nearby cut. He was out at elbow, with a menace about him that had Robert stepping back for fear of assault, but the vulgar fellow offered nothing worse than a cold stare. With a flicker of recognition to Travis, he inclined his head towards the door. Travis took a coin from Robert's purse, pressed it into the man's ready palm, opened the door himself and drew his companion inside with him.

Light and the sound of voices came from behind another door to their left. Travis was reaching for it when it was opened from the inside by a woman in an excess of green velveteen. She gave out a theatrical squeal and a 'La, gents, what a turn... Oh, mister, is it you? Delighted, I'm sure.' She clasped Travis's hand in both of hers and lifted slightly on her toes to blow kisses from puckered red lips. Robert guessed her to be, beneath the paint, a woman in her late fifties. Moving her skirts to allow them entrance to the room, she gave off a heady fragrance of perfume and kippers.

He was by now aware he was in a bawdy house, a brothel. Yet more novelty. He tried to take stock of his position, as far as he was able to in his altered state. Somehow he had been plucked from everything and everyone he knew, and set down here. It was quite other than his life, his family, his relationships. Something indefinably exciting, alluring. A flavour, a scent, a figure beckoning from a secret world. Soon all would vanish, and he would be back among his own kind; a boy returned from adventure. For now, there were no connections. He would wait and see what might befall.

He and Travis were secreted in a plump-cushioned pocket of the large room. Mrs Hodges brought them brandy and water. Robert could hear the low murmur and laughter of other men (presumably seated in some other snug, screened-off area) and now and then the lighter notes of women younger than Mrs Hodges, mere girls to judge by their voices. He was trying to catch what they were saying when Travis struck his knee to attract his attention.

'You must meet Jenny. I will give her up to you tonight.' He called out. 'Mrs Hodges, where are you, woman? Bring Jenny here, and another; the little dark-haired beauty, the new girl.'

Mrs Hodges popped her head around the screen. 'They will be with you directly, gents. Jenny and Mona.'

'I'll make her moan, surely,' laughed Travis. He nudged Robert with his boot, partly to remind him his brandy was on the table.

After an interval there was some rustling behind the panel, some whispering too. A brace of girls appeared, ushered through to the men by Mrs Hodges. Something about their dress and the way they held their chins reminded Robert of dancers he and Bidder had watched betimes from the stalls of the Edinburgh Theatre Royal. They seemed to pose, then the fair-haired one bent to give Travis a peck on the cheek. He held her naked wrist, enjoying an expanse of bosom before he relinquished her.

'Jenny, you must keep company with this young gallant tonight.'

232

He beckoned Mona to him while Jenny perched herself on the arm of the chair next to Robert, a natural position from which to play her fingers through his hair and down the nape, which she did immediately, and he found no objection to. He was wondering whether it would be considered good form to smoke, when she said something. 'Sorry?'

'Can I have a sip of your brandy?'

'Of course. Please, allow me...' He reached forward with her, and in doing so brushed the side of his face accidentally against her breast. 'Oh, I beg your pardon.'

'Not at all.' She giggled as she accepted the tumbler, and over his head exchanged an impish glance with Mona, who was already wrapped lasciviously around Travis and he round her. Robert sat back in the chair, unable to think of anything more to say. Jenny occupied herself between ruffling his locks and tasting his brandy. Eventually, she put the glass to his mouth, coaxing him to have something. As he demurred, a drop or two of brandy escaped across his lips and down his chin. Jenny stopped the trickle with her free hand, and sucked the liquid off her finger. Seeing him watch her do so, she smiled, then deliberately dipped her finger into the brandy and sucked it again, watching him. She dipped a second time, now to smear his mouth with brandy, teasing his lips open with her wet finger. He half-tasted, half-kissed the finger. Jenny, encouraged, bent down and saluted him full upon the lips, then slicked her tongue between his teeth to leave him in no doubt of her passion. At last they broke off. Robert, shocked into self-consciousness, stole a sideways glance at Travis and Mona, similarly engaged. Jenny, still watchful, leaned in to whisper in his ear.

'We can go somewhere, if you would like.'

He nodded, and she stood up, holding her hand out to him like a mother to her child. Robert took it, and Jenny led him away quietly out of the room, up the stairs to the seclusion of a private chamber.

So we'll go no more a-roving
So late into the night,
Though the heart be still as loving,
And the moon be still as bright.

For the sword outwears its sheath,
And the soul wears out the breast,
And the heart must pause to breathe,
And love itself have rest.

Though the night was made for loving,
And the day returns too soon,
Yet we'll go no more a-roving
By the light of the moon.

Robert's walk from the Strand back to his home in Gloucester Square took an hour, but he was entirely unconscious of it, his brain seared with the memory of his only sexual encounter outside marriage. He felt again the guilt that he had repressed until the evening in Newcastle and the intimate conversation with his mama, when he had confessed his love for Frances Sanderson and so released within him a silent torment that had contributed not a little to the irrevocability of his decision to leave the country. Finally it was shame that sent him away.

On the voyage to South America, he had experienced a stinging sensation when passing water. He mentioned it to the ship's doctor, a phlegmatic type who made no comment other than to prescribe nitrate of silver (a theoretical prescription, as it transpired there was no stock on board) and advise swabbing his member regularly in warm water. Eventually the sensation ceased, whether through the water treatment or naturally, and he gave the episode no further thought, having put the condition down to some effect of the lack of fresh provender.

Of course there had been temptations aplenty in Colombia, but Robert had not once fallen prey to them (not carnal ones, at least), nor ever again in England or abroad. His faithfulness to his wife diluted his sense of guilt by degrees, and it had been many years since he had brought to mind that single transgression of his youth. Until Dr Acton brought it forcibly home. The doctor's account of the soldier who had chronic gonorrhœa for years without knowing it, and had subsequently proved impotent, shocked Robert particularly for one detail - the swelling around the vas - for Robert, sometimes when washing, had detected just such hardness of the tissue at the base of his private parts, only to dismiss it as normal in a man. Acton had also said the disease could be passed on to the female without her being aware of any alteration, and that too could cause infertility. The notion that he might unknowingly have infected his sweet, respectable, virtuous spouse was horrifying to Robert. The possibility that their childlessness - oh, profound regret -was caused by one foolish, sinful deed committed a quarter of a century ago threw him into a despondency deeper than his vision of hell.

XIV

Mr Ebenezer Buckle of the Hare and Hounds, a coaching inn situated on the Manchester Road about a dozen miles out of Liverpool, would surely have scoffed two weeks ago had one of his customers suggested Buckle would be present at the official opening of the Liverpool and Manchester Railway and indeed would travel the route as a special guest, holder of a light blue ticket, on the famous *Rocket*, driven for the occasion by Joseph Locke and Bob McCree. Had such a prophecy been made by one of his regulars - Clancy for example, or Fred Trotter; one of those he did not have to squander politeness on - Buckle would have cussed, and gobbed into the nearest spittoon to show what he thought of the idea. The railway, after all, could spell the end for his business. Yet here he was at Crown Street, ticket at the ready for inspection, craning his neck over the mass of heads in search of the light blue flag that would show which of these eight panting locomotives was the *Rocket*.

Ironically, his opportunity had arisen in consequence of his disparaging the railway project just a few days earlier as he stood behind the bar at the inn. A coach party had recently arrived, but the rush of orders had ceased for the moment and he had just lit his pipe as he caught a moment's relaxation.

'Yull not have time for smoking next week,' someone said.

'Why would I not?'

'All the folks fetching up for the opening o the railway. It's said there'll be hundreds ont road. Thousands, may be.'

'Mek the most of that trade, Abe,' said Clancy. 'For it might be just you, me an Trotter as the future goes.'

Buckle's pipe was not drawing; he rapped the bowl against the bar in irritation.

'There's no standing in the way of progress,' said Clancy. 'No sense getting your dander up.'

'I aint. I aint feart about the railroad, and I'll tell thee for why. Let em come next week, the more the merrier. Let em go ride the steam trains. Cos I'll tell ye straight, you will see on opening day how they will all smash into the Moss. Aye, and that will be the end of that.'

'Chat Moss is secure,' came another voice from beyond the bar.

'Impossible. The Little General himself couldn't make his way over it.'

'Don't speak to me about him. George Stephenson has done what Boney could never do - drove a railway line from Liverpool all the way to Manchester, through Chat Moss an every other obstacle in his road.'

'And who might you be to say so?' demanded Buckle, standing on his dignity as proprietor.

'George Stephenson.'

The group around the pumps turned as one to the advancing figure, and simultaneously parted either side as if to give space to some invisible surrounding aura. Not one of them knew the man except by name and reputation, but that enough gave them liberty to stare. George had the dust of travel on him, but he stood impressive, tall and self-possessed. He placed one hand on the bar and seemed to address them all while he made further answer to Abe Buckle.

'Chat Moss is conquered by its own materials. Brushwood an heather laid over the spoil. Sand, earth an gravel binding together. Cinders. Safe as a bird on its nest. My engines is floating across the bog.'

'Sounds owt but safe to me. Floating...'

'I can assure you, friend. Nay, you should experience it yoursel. Compared to yon death trap...' George pointed through the open door at the stagecoach waiting to take him on to Liverpool, 'travel by railroad is as safe as lying in your bed.'

'You haven't seen his missus,' Clancy joked, and was rewarded by a laugh from the company. George hauled back their attention with an expansive flourish; produced a card from his inside pocket and held it out to Buckle.

'Here, you can tek your place on opening day as a guest of George Stephenson. First Class - Come an see history made from the best seat.'

'Oh, well...' Buckle eased his neck from his collar - he felt both flattered and caught out - 'I don't know, twill be a busy day at the inn...'

'Pish,' somebody snorted, 'there's plenty hands here. Take your chance when it's offered, Buckle. Or are you really feart o getting drowned in the Moss?'

'Well, I don't know, I...'

'Go on, take it. Who knows? You might get sat next to Wellington, or Peel.'

'The new king's coming, I heard,' said another.

'And them twins from Siam. The stuck-together ones.'

'Chang and Eng? Nay, they're to go on show in the ballroom at the King's Arms. They ant here for the railway, just to milk off it.'

'I'd sooner see the steam engines. How about it, Abe? Surely you'll take the gentleman's invitation.'

236

'Well, may be,' Buckle conceded, reaching across the bar to take the card, 'May be I will go, I'll... have to see.'

The publican's seat on the train was not in fact near to any of the luminaries mentioned by his customers (certainly nowhere near King William, who stayed at home) but next to an accountant from the railway company, who helpfully pointed out the splendid carriage that had been provided for the Prime Minister. It was sitting on a separate track parallel to *Rocket* and the other locomotives, and was to be hauled by the lilac-painted *Northumbrian*, driven by George Stephenson himself.

'I know him personally,' said Buckle.

'The Duke?'

'George Stephenson. My that's a carriage and a half.'

'See the gilded pillars with the Duke's gold coronet on top?' said the accountant. 'That canopy's been cleverly contrived so when a tunnel is reached it can be lowered for the carriage to pass under.'

'It's some sight altogether,' agreed Buckle. 'And some size.'

'Thirty-something feet long, I believe. And eight wheels, look. You never see a coach with eight wheels.'

'I dare say you don't.'

Buckle felt in his pocket for his pipe, and thus startled a quaint old couple at his shoulder who were trying to steal a glimpse of this wonder that was being talked about. They were mortified to be caught away from their allotted seats; scuttled back in some confusion. The publican held up a hand to settle them. 'Come, come and look at the Duke's carriage.' They crept back like the timid creatures they were and watched through the window, chirruping softly at each other, while Buckle assessed them professionally as he did strangers to his inn. He quickly surmised they must have been married forty years, had those Sunday best clothes at least thirty, and did not get about much. 'I don't suppose you work for the railway company,' he said by way of angling when they resumed their places.

'Och no, we ken nothing of railways,' said the man.

'Friends of Mr Stephenson? Family?'

'Friends, aye. We're nae kin to the gentleman.'

'Hardly friends, Lachlan. Dinna claim to be whit you're not,' said the woman. To Buckle: 'We met him once over, and that was twenty-four year sin.'

'It said friends in the letter, didnae? *Dear friends.* An he's paid our way here. We've not once had to put a hand...'

237

'He found us out again, see,' she started to explain to Buckle. 'Though how he remembered over all the years... We took him in out of the dreich, that was aw; anybody wid.'

'Aye, he were drookit, that night,' Lachlan confirmed.

'He was just a young man, then - why, he still is. Walking to find work...'

'In Montrose.'

'In the dark, in the wet,' she said, finishing her thought. Buckle imagined they held all their conversations like this, trading one with another.

'And he remembered your kindness?'

'Said then he would ay mind us,' from Lachlan. 'For the braw brose she made and how we widna tak a mite for bed and board. Said he wid return the favour some day. Why, we thocht nae more about it...'

'And now look at this,' said his wife with a tilt of the head to mean the grand occasion. 'Wid ye credit it? And for him to gang an aw the fash of seeking us out again...'

Buckle sensed they were about to embark on a repetition of their story, so he gave them a benign nod of finality to let them know he was suitably impressed, and returned his gaze to the window, sucking at the stem of his pipe.

Well away from Buckle's view, in a private area of the company yard, Robert and his father awaited the arrival of the special guests. They were not especially talkative; even George was visibly feeling the strain, which he expressed by frequent wanderings from his post to the archway that gave him the best sight of the crowd gathered for the spectacle. Men from the 4th King's Own Regiment were on hand to keep order, but the mood was carnival. George observed there was almost as much interest in the souvenir stalls selling mugs, pocket handkerchiefs and other knick-knacks with images of the locomotives printed on them as in the steam-breathing originals tethered to their carriages on the iron rails. Booth and Walker had produced a pamphlet of facts and figures about the making of the railway, but George was not sure whether copies were on general sale or reserved for the use of distinguished visitors. He turned back to check if Robert knew, but before he could ask they heard the clatter of hooves echo around the yard, and four confident grays drew up with the Marquess of Salisbury's open carriage.

Salisbury's flunkey flew round to open the carriage door and lower a respectful head. The Marquess gave precedence to his two illustrious fellow-passengers: first, the Prime Minister. He was dressed in black (still in mourning for King George) and drew about him a long Spanish cloak. No doubt he expected a journey by railroad would involve a fierce battle with the elements; or perhaps he felt the cloak added a certain *élan*. (*Sir Gorgeous*, the Duke was sometimes called behind his back, the name coined by ex-minister Huskisson for the amusement of his friends.) Sir Robert Peel stepped out next; cheerful and handsome, despite the beginning of a paunch. One of the pair seemed rather pleased to be introduced to the Stephensons; the other practised silent *hauteur* until someone (George) should provide escort to his ducal conveyance.

Robert stayed to greet the remainder of the important guests and their wives. There were the Lords Grey and Melbourne, enough earls and viscounts to fill several pages of *Burke's Peerage*, and as many from the House of Commons, including the influential Huskisson, Arbuthnot, and Calcraft. Should Ebenezer Buckle's fear be realised and the trains did smash into Chat Moss, what a void would open in the political landscape. Here were ambassadors and diplomats, bishops, civic dignitaries... not to forget the country's leading engineers including some (Vignoles, the Rennies) whom Robert hoped to steer well away from his father, at least until the Stephensons proved they had carried the day.

Many of this select body had lilac tickets, which placed them in carriages directly behind the Duke's. For some, their final seat allocation represented either a little victory or a defeat in their delicate negotiations with Henry Booth's office, and not just for the pleasure of sitting on the crimson-coloured ottoman that ran down the centre of the coach drawn by the *Northumbrian*.

'Moves afoot,' Booth whispered to Robert.

'Sorry?'

'Members rarely gather without someone pressing for the advantage of office. In this case, all hopes are pinned on a *rapprochement* between Huskisson and the Prime Minister.'

'Aren't they both Tories?'

'Yes, but not necessarily in the same party,' Booth said, gnomically, then, 'Politically estranged. Personally antipathetic. Until today, perhaps. Interesting to see who makes the first move. This may do us some good, Huskisson being the Liverpool man. Keep an eye open.'

The female Stephensons were more than content with their green tickets that entitled them to sit in the front carriage of the *Phoenix* which Robert was to drive, the first of the locomotives on the northern track. The women, joined by Robert's Aunt Nelly, waited patiently until he could prise himself away from the pernickety demands of the privileged classes, and they all walked together to their train. Fanny squeezed

Robert's arm as they passed the lines of people being loaded into their respective compartments, 'like bullets ready for firing through that chamber,' she said. Her eyes were on the tunnel at the far end of the station.

'Well, there will be guns of a sort. We are to go at the sound of a cannon.'

George, having deposited the Duke, was ready on the footplate of the *Northumbrian*. He waved to his family as they approached, and Betty called out, '*Bon chance, bon voyage*'. Once the women were safely inside, Robert crossed the few feet of space between the tracks and held up his hand to his father, who leaned across to grasp it.

'All ready?' from Robert.

'Oh aye,' said George. 'I've just been waitin for the world to be.'

Inside the carriages a momentary silence - of respect, excited anticipation, or alarm - followed the blast of the big gun. Outside, the roar of the cannon released another; a chorus of halloos and hurrahs from those crammed into the station, from the grandstands just without, and from every bunch, row and pack of spectators hanging over bridges, teetering on slopes, scrimmaging for space or clinging on anywhere a vantage point could be found, from the heights of Olive Mount to the tow-paths and canal boats under the Sankey Viaduct. The ribbon of sound unfolded ahead of the locomotives as they struck out on their historic journey, pushed through the stone chasm of the Olive Mount cutting, up the Sutton incline and over the viaduct at nearly twenty-five miles an hour.

Sometimes the *Northumbrian* nosed a little in front on its lone track, sometimes the *Phoenix* at the head of its convoy; whichever engine appeared first at a viewing-point set off a riot of hat-hoisting and handkerchief-waving. Some spectators carried flags or banners which, at this stage of the journey, were mostly optimistic in tone, brought along to add innocent colour and gaiety. If any trouble was to be expected, it would be at the Manchester end, where memories of Peterloo still rankled, hatred of Wellington was endemic, and reformists with no voice in Parliament were active beyond virulence.

Each passenger, surviving the initial assault of wonder, developed a peculiar perspective, which they shared with others or kept to themselves. Elizabeth Stephenson, tracing the hewn red sandstone walls of Olive Mount up and up, thought of Orpheus. Fanny nodded her sympathy when Aunt Nell confessed she was afraid to peek too far out of the carriage for fear of seeing a giant hand pulling them along from above. Two trains further back, the accountant (for the first time looking upon the result of the work his office had been concerned with for the last five years, and for the first time fully aware of the human endeavour that had gone into the construction) felt puny under his new suit. Ebenezer Buckle was putting off his worry about Chat Moss by reading, at every station they drove through, the fresh-painted signs advertising the fare to Manchester, and taking pains to inform the rest in his compartment: *Closed carriages, four shilling; Open carriages, three shilling*, his announcement as they passed Kendrick's Cross. Opposite him, Lachlan remarked again that they had not been asked to pay one penny towards their trip, while his wife tried to draw his attention to a single reaper in a field scything oats to his usual rhythm with nary a glance at what was going by, as if his world had not changed a whit. In the ducal carriage, Wellington was another who affected indifference, only deigning to turn and look outward after discovering how the rush of scenery made his window eye rheumy when he stared straight ahead.

At four minutes short of the hour, just past Wynwick Church, *Northumbrian* began slowing for its one scheduled stop at Parkside, seventeen miles from Liverpool. The intention was for all engines to take on water before the final leg to Manchester. Joseph Locke, in drawing up the schedule, had added ceremony to function: the Duke's train - the state coach, as it were - should wait on the southern track for each of the seven locomotives to parade by on the northern line so they could make a kind of obeisance before the journey recommenced.

Everything was going exactly to plan when George pulled up at Parkside. Some worsening in the weather seemed to be the likeliest threat. With a glance upward, the driver clambered onto his tender, heedless of his expensive clothes, to watch the other trains go by, and to be seen by his guests. First through was the *Phoenix*. It seemed to George that it was not just his family who waved more enthusiastically at him than at the Duke and his entourage. He kept his eyes on the *Phoenix* until Robert came to a stop further along the track, making ready to lead the second charge, then he turned his attention to the next train coming through; the *North Star*. More cheers and waves. George saluted his brother at the controls. After that, a hiatus.

William Huskisson MP, one of thirty distinguished guests squashed onto the ottoman in the carriage behind the Duke, was feeling his gout. He suffered in silence until he noticed several of the male passengers - Prince Esterhazy and Sir George Drinkwater included - leaving the stationary train in search of ease from their own cramps.

'Well, if we are to be here for some time,' Huskisson said to wife Emily, 'I think I will go and stretch my legs.'

'The pamphlet instructs that we should on no account leave our seats.'

'Dear, I am sure that only applies when the train is in motion. I tell you...' he said, standing up and testing it, 'this limb has never recovered from the king's funeral. All that kneeling and praying.' He made his way gingerly to the door of the compartment and, opening it, registered a slight shock at the eighteen-inch drop to the ground. (The step he expected to find was hanging at the rear of the carriage, having been removed once the passengers were safely in.) Huskisson glanced back to where his wife was seated, and almost resolved to return, except that William Holmes now appeared at the trackside to help him out.

'Thank you. Splendid.' Huskisson landed a little heavily on the cinders, grateful that Holmes was there to prevent him stumbling further. He did not immediately relinquish his hold, the ground so rough underfoot; placed his free hand on the arm in affectionate manner; took stock. 'Well, Billy, what are your thoughts about travelling by the power of steam?'

'Very exciting. Is it the future, do you think?'

'Undoubtedly. I expect to see at least the beginnings of a transformation even in our lifetime. And how gratifying that it is Liverpool leading the way.' Huskisson raised his eyes and felt suitably visionary, though his moment was all but spoilt by a chance sight of the town mayor relieving himself against a wheel at the far end of the train. It aggravated an urge that was already becoming insistent in his own bladder. Blessed distraction came with a touch at his elbow. Holmes had turned conspiratorial, spoke in a furtive whisper.

'The great captain is looking your way.'

Huskisson risked a glimpse past his friend's shoulder. It was true. Wellington was sitting in the front corner of his carriage, leaning slightly out of the window with a definite object in view. When he saw that he had attracted his ex-minister's attention, the Duke made a movement of his hand that might be interpreted as a courtly salute and gave a nod that was perceptible only by those watching for the merest hint of favour. Holmes could detect it in the lift of Huskisson's chin. 'Now is the time; go to him.'

Huskisson picked his way carefully across the cinders. Arbuthnot and Calcraft, enjoying a smoke together in the open air, exchanged glances as he passed. Just as he reached the Prime Minister's carriage window, with Wellington on his feet and leaning out to acknowledge him, a warning came from distance: *Engine approaching. Take care, gentlemen.* Huskisson, alarmed, aborted his greeting, peered down the track. His leader took umbrage. 'Sir!' Demanded attention, and won it.

'I... Your Grace, good day to you, sir.' Huskisson looked up, extended an uncertain hand and the Duke, leaning further out, shook it firmly. He followed up with a few words, formal and well-modulated, but Huskisson could not properly hear them against a noise closing down on him; a steam engine in full cry on the other track. Now both men were impelled to watch it nearing and apparently increasing in size. Other passengers were clambering back inside the parked train. Someone - Arbuthnot perhaps - took fright and ran across the bare metal rails to the far embankment. The Duke belatedly recognizing danger, pointed to his carriage door.

'Get in, man. Get in.'

Huskisson, close to panic, edged along the outer wall of the carriage. Before he could get to the door a person reached from behind him and tugged at the handle; someone prepared to nudge an inferior aside in his rush to open the door and scramble in. It was Prince Esterhazy. Huskisson tripped on gravel, and the door slammed shut. He gasped. His senses entered a tunnel. He could see only Holmes, further along, pressed up as if stuck against the side of the *Northumbrian*, and above him, the pale face of Emily looking out through a window. His ears under attack; a thunder of metal crushing space. And the Duke barking the order.

'Get in, you damn fool!'

Huskisson leapt up and made a last desperate grab for the handle; made it. The door swung open with his weight and tossed him across the gap, beneath an unforgiving wheel of Stephenson's *Rocket*.

'Whit the ding was that?' from Lachlan inside.

'I think we've hit summat,' said Buckle. He stood to look out of the window, but as he did so their coach collided into the one stopped suddenly in front; Buckle was launched sideways into the Scotsman's lap. From another carriage came a woman's scream, and somewhere in the distance a clanging sound, like bell metal struck repeatedly with an iron bar. Commotion outside, shouts and men running, converging on one spot. The accountant stuck his head out of the carriage.

'I think there's something gone under a wheel,' he advised the others. 'A sheep perhaps, or a dog got loose.'

'Oh, poor creature,' cried Annie, Lachlan's wife.

Buckle recovered his feet and joined the railway man at the window. 'A lot of fuss over a sheep,' he said. 'Look, that's George Stephenson on his way over. Feller with white hair.'

'I know which is he,' said the accountant.

From his viewpoint at *Northumbrian's* tender, George had not observed Huskisson's panic but, moving in position to wave as *Rocket* went by, witnessed what he thought was a heavy object thrown from his train towards the other. It slid under a wheel and was dragged a few yards before the locomotive could stop; and only then George recognized the thing as human. He jumped to the ground and ran as fast as he could across the clinker, meeting first with Bob McCree at the footplate of the *Rocket* - the driver immobilised by anguish over his part in the accident. George choked off the instruction he was about to give, instead commandeered his fireman. 'Run back along the tracks an warn the other trains. But, tek care, look. We want no more mishaps.'

A knot - almost a queue - of people was already forming where the victim lay. 'He lives,' someone said as George forced his way to the front. He looked down and saw Huskisson trapped half under the train, staring in revolted fascination at his right leg crushed and deeply lacerated at the thigh, as if it were some anatomical exhibit not his own. He seemed for the moment in no obvious pain, though the leg was convulsing, causing blood to spray randomly, but he was convinced of his fate.

'This is the death of me.'

'I hope not, sir,' from George.

'Yes, I am dying. Call Mrs Huskisson.'

In fact the lady was even then at the back of the crowd, pleading, resisting the solicitations of those who would prevent her from seeing her husband in distress. Huskisson heard her protests and called out, 'Emily.' Joseph Parkes, a Birmingham solicitor, had the presence of mind to remove his coat and cover the injured leg before Mrs Huskisson was allowed a passage through. Nevertheless, she screamed when she saw him, fell to her knees in a soft cloud of perfume, covered his face with tears. He tried to talk to her but his voice (chronically weak, from a childhood infection) suddenly gave out, and he was left mouthing words without sound until she was persuaded to withdraw while a makeshift tourniquet was applied to her husband's leg by Lord Wilton.

Robert arrived, and was immediately dispatched on an errand by his father.

'There's a storeroom here. Run an see if you can find summat we can use to carry this man on.'

'To go where?'

'Anywhere he can get properly seen to.'

'Back to Liverpool?'

'I...' George's reluctance was palpable. 'Nay, we must go on. It's no further to Manchester than Liverpool from here. I'll tek him.'

Robert went in search of a board while the patient was comforted as far as humanly possible by friends. George organised the uncoupling of *Northumbrian* from all its carriages except a flat-bed wagon behind the tender (meant for the band to sit on as they played triumphant music on the run-in to Manchester). The Duke's carriage was shunted into a siding, where he took counsel and privately fulminated. It was as if he felt Huskisson had staged his accident deliberately to inconvenience his rival.

By the time Robert returned with the storeroom door, ripped from its hinges with unconscious strength, all eight trains were standing at Parkside. A trio of doctors had presented themselves from among the passengers. One who took charge was Dr Joseph Brandreth, brother of the man who had aimed to make a mockery of the Rainhill Trials with his horse-operated *Cycloped*. 'For pity's sake, give the man some air,' he yelled at the bystanders, and sent them back to wait in their carriages while he and another doctor improved on Wilton's tourniquet and fashioned a splint using walking canes and knotted cloths, including two of the souvenir handkerchiefs bought earlier in the day. Robert laid the board beside the patient, saw up close for the first time the extent of his wounds, and the question of death in Huskisson's eyes as the man searched his own for corroboration. Robert looked away, watched for his father's return.

'That's as much as we can do here,' Brandreth reported when George came back. 'Mr Huskisson needs a surgeon as quickly as possible, though....' confidentially, 'I fear we are really too late.'

'Niver too late. There's no speedier transport in the world than what you see around you.' George gestured as it were to cargo at his feet. 'Here, help us get him to my train.'

He pushed the makeshift stretcher closer in to the injured man. Robert knelt opposite to help him lift, and two of the doctors did likewise. Their male fingers unnaturally interlocked under Huskisson's back and buttocks. Robert could feel the scrape of loose spoil on his knuckles, wetness running into his palms. Huskisson was wracked with pain by now, but his response, whether through fatigue, the fortitude of an English gentleman, or the continued paralysis of his voice-box, was more strangled whimper than scream. Once he was safely lifted and set

245

down all four bearers had to wipe their hands discreetly on the ground before they could hold on, without fear of slipping, to their corner of the door. They carefully carried him across to the *Northumbrian*. A memory came unbidden to Robert, of his grandfather brought home like this from his accident at the pit.

Once installed on the flat bed of the wagon, the patient may have had a temporary loss of consciousness, for he lay still, breathing shallow. His wife was brought to hold his hand, Lord Colville to cradle his head, and the three doctors sat or squatted around him, morally ready though not technically equipped to minister to his needs. George was in solitary place behind the engine, where Robert spoke to him briefly.

'What about the Duke?'

'That's your job for now, welcome to it.' Then, in a gentler tone, 'You're best suited to deal with him anyway, Rob. Only don't let him sound the retreat.'

His son took a step away as George coaxed the locomotive forward, hand gripped firmly on the regulator. Robert observed a quickening under his chin, the merest hint of agitation suppressed. No-one on the wagon acknowledged the young man as they passed; their eyes were fixed either on Huskisson or on the way ahead. Robert followed in their wake, scrunching along the trackside even after the *Northumbrian* faded from view. His present need was to be away from the press of people at Parkside. Somewhere down the line he stopped; stared along the slick new metal track that stretched out so confidently across the fields. He was fighting nausea and dizziness. Several minutes passed before he collected himself sufficiently to return to his family, still sitting obedient if anxious inside their carriage. They seemed quietly relieved to see him.

'What will happen now?' asked Fanny.

'I do not know. It is to be hoped that a surgeon can be got quick enough to save the poor man's life.'

'And will the day be... lost?'

'Really, I am not sure. Father and I had no chance to discuss what is to be done.' He felt as ill-equipped for decisions as he had when he first arrived in Mariquita. His mama leaned forward and placed her fingertips on his.

'Perhaps you need to ask the Prime Minister what his wishes are,' she said.

'Yes. Yes, of course. That is what I must do.'

It took him some time to make his way along to the siding where the Duke's carriage had been left, not only because the *Phoenix* was the most advanced of the stationary trains, nor because he was still feeling faint, but because so many passengers, no longer subject to Dr Brandreth's censure, had spilled out of their compartments to walk between the tracks or sit on the embankment while they waited on whatever would happen next. There were the perplexed, the inquisitive, the angry, the aching, the lachrymose, the stoic. Some needed, like the railway engines, to take on water, others to run it off. Several were looking for diversion, to hear and recount what had happened, what they had seen or believed they had. A crowd had once again congregated at the spot where Mr Huskisson fell, including Ebenezer Buckle who knew that his customers would expect him to relate every lurid detail of the incident when he was once more behind the bar at the Hare and Hounds. Buckle watched one who had seen it all from the *Northumbrian* demonstrate exactly how the victim had been jettisoned from the carriage door to end up beneath the wheels of the oncoming train. He pulled a face with the rest when an unfastidious passenger scooped up a remnant of human flesh from under the offending wheel and offered it for all to see.

'He had some nerve, calling stagecoaches death traps,' Buckle said aloud, thinking of his first encounter with George. 'And we ain even got to Chat Moss yet.'

Robert felt some inhibition about entering the carriage where the Prime Minister was sequestered in conference with Sir Robert Peel and other ministers of state. He hung back irresolute for several minutes, until Henry Booth and Joseph Sandars joined him outside the door.

'We have been summoned,' said Sandars. 'The Duke has something to say.'

He followed them into the sanctum. When he saw the Duke of Wellington starched into his golden armchair, he could not help thinking how like his waxwork he looked.

'Our sense is that we should return to Liverpool,' was what the Duke had to impart once they were gathered deferential around him. 'In the light of what has happened, it would be bad form to proceed.'

'Very bad form.' Peel acting echo.

Sandars and Booth looked at each other; both wanted to protest and neither wanted to be the one to face up to the Duke. Eventually it was Sandars, as the senior man, who said, 'Your Grace, we admire your sense of propriety, and of course we sympathise with the plight of Mr Huskisson, God save him; but pray consider, sir, the import of any cancellation... that is, the message that would be sent by it to the British people, and to the world.'

'What message? Speak plainly, man.'

'Well, I hope you will agree that up to the point of this unfortunate accident, our demonstration of the technical superiority of this new form of transport was proving entirely successful. If we were to abandon it now, then we would be abandoning our opportunity... our duty, sir, to complete that proof.'

'And it is not as if... what has occurred here was any fault of the railway,' put in Booth.

Sandars closed a button on his coat. 'Not at all. But it might appear so, were we to allow it to put us off the track, so to speak. Travellers would be persuaded by it that the railway is unsafe. Investors would be put off, to the detriment of the nation's wealth.'

Wellington repeated the phrase, 'The nation's wealth.' He examined his fingernails. 'You may have a point. Let it not be said that I am insensitive to the needs of commerce. However, gentlemen, my chief concern is not with the good standing of your company but with the reputation of this government.' By which he meant his own. 'On balance, I am still for going back.'

It seemed that was to be the last word on the subject, but before they broke up there was a knock at the door of the carriage. It was the Borough Reeve of Manchester, Mr Sharpe, who had some disturbing news just brought to him by an official on horseback. 'Your Grace, ill-founded rumours are already spreading along the route, occasioned by the delay here. Some claim you have perished in a railway disaster, others that you have stopped here afraid to face the people of Manchester.'

'Preposterous. The French did not frighten me, and by God...'

'Indeed, but the situation is volatile and such poison is pervasive. An unsatisfied crowd can easily become a mob. It is my duty to advise that only the sight of you in person would prevent a riot.'

'But neither do we want to be caught up in a riot,' said Peel.

'I give you my word, you will be well-protected, sir.'

'Then, of course we must go on,' said the Duke, as firmly as if that were his original resolution. 'I will brook no more delay - the populace is waiting to see me, and by God they shall see me.'

Robert spoke up for the first time. 'Er, there is one technical difficulty, your Grace.'

'Meaning...?'

'We have no engine to pull your carriage, as the *Northumbrian* is presently being used to carry Mr Huskisson to the surgeon. Moreover, all of our other engines are standing on the other line, and there is no practical way at this depot of effecting a transfer. We could of course place you in one of the coaches on the northern track...'

'Impossible. The Duke must travel in the ducal carriage.'

'Of course,' from Sandars. 'No question about that. Have no care, sir; we will devise some method of pulling your carriage, and preserving the dignity of your office. It will be done without further delay.' He bowed, then turned to look at Robert, his eyebrows raised. Robert gave the slightest shrug of the shoulders, nodded his respects to the Prime Minister and retreated from the carriage, his mind already on the task.

George had not yet reached Manchester, despite having driven at a speed that created an eddy of excitement among onlookers, who imagined they were being treated to a form of cavalry charge before the main advance. He slowed only when he heard shouts from behind the tender. He turned to see Brandreth, hatless, gripping the edge of the truck, fighting against the rush of air to be understood.

'This is too much for him - we must stop as soon as possible.'

George acknowledged the doctor, and faced into the wind once more, calculating what to do. There was a soft roll of thunder, and he could sense the threat of rain to follow. He thought of the Reverend Blackburne, whose house at Eccles was so close to the track that he was among those who had required special appeasement. Perhaps Huskisson could rest there until a surgeon was brought to him.

A mile and three quarters further, and George was able to ease the *Northumbrian* to a halt by Eccles bridge. Around and about were only a few houses other than the vicarage, but even here the bridge was in use as a viewing point, the spectators rewarded for their long wait by a locomotive stopping directly beneath their toes. As George dismounted from the footplate, he glared, irritated, at the party on the bridge, mistaken into believing someone there was throwing down pebbles. It took him a moment to realise these were actually hailstones. Unusual weather for a strange September day.

He went back to the wagon that contained Huskisson. 'If we can carry him to the vicarage here,' he explained to Brandreth, 'I can crack on myself an fetch the surgeon. How is he bearing up?'

'Surprising well, all things considered. He is still with us - I mean, he is conscious.'

Brandreth bent over the patient to explain what was intended, and Huskisson was able to respond in an almost voiceless whisper, 'Yes, pray do so. Blackburne... is a friend. I am sure he will be kind to me.'

While George made ready to continue his journey alone to Manchester, the other four men in the group each took responsibility for a corner of the door Huskisson lay upon. They lifted him so gently from the wagon they hardly disturbed the hailstones that had landed on him, but he could not contain his moans, or the tears he squeezed onto his wife's hand which he clasped to his face for comfort as they carried him as steadily as they were able across the scree, in full view of a curious gallery.

No-one in attendance on the patient had appreciated that Blackburne was among the guests still stranded at Parkside. Fortunately his wife had been left at home, and she was able to offer the front room sofa for her incommoded visitor's comfort as well as a generous measure of brandy to assist, along with the doctors' laudanum, in easing his pain. Mrs Blackburne was compelled to leave the room while the doctors cut away his right boot and the leg of his trousers, being unable to bear the sight of broken bone poking out from torn flesh; she was thus spared for now the ruin of her slipcovers and cushions. Mrs Huskisson stayed at her husband's side throughout, taking her courage from his. After the cutting, a fresh application of the tourniquet, and a passage of concerned whispering among the medical men, very little was done or said in that room for the next hour while everyone waited the arrival of the surgeon with his tools of amputation.

Robert was once more at the head of a convoy of locomotives, but the procession that left Parkside was extraordinary in a different way to the one that had arrived ninety minutes earlier. He had coupled his engine to the *North Star*, and from their rear extended a chain across to the southern track to pull the engineless carriage containing the Prime Minister. The other locomotives followed in their proper order a respectful distance behind, like mourners at a funeral.

The continued cheers of spectators along the route seemed incongruous now to the subdued passengers, but further along the line gatherings were more sporadic as settlements thinned and the weather worsened. Before long the travellers were looking out on a scene more appropriate to their present mood. Something less than rural: bleak.

'Chat Moss,' Abe Buckle said, half to himself.

'Chat Moss,' Robert said, entirely to himself. He could detect the change of tone under the wheels and felt, with a quickening of his gut, the slight sideways motion of the engine as it left *terra firma* for his father's floating platform. On the Moss proper the train quietened, as if holding its breath. Robert could see the darkening woods to his left where George had scrubbed the brushwood to lay across the bog. His thoughts went to his youthful days of surveying: how William James had almost drowned himself here; how in rainy weather the Moss would swell and rise at the

250

centre. He heard again all the authorative voices raised in opposition to the scheme; recalled the delight in George's voice when he told his son how William Huskisson had expressed total confidence in his plans for defeating Chat Moss.

Robert looked behind him, and over to the opposite track. Through the mizzle he could just see the chain, and of the Duke's carriage a shape without definition. He could do nothing in the case of a collapse. Of course his father had put his construction to the test many times. But with vehicles on both tracks at the same time? Three in such close proximity? And another four following close behind; a total of six hundred passengers to be ferried across in the rain.

His well-beloved wife, his aunt, his uncle, his mama among them.

At his seat Ebenezer Buckle did enough praying for them all, and perhaps that is what kept them safe across, though Buckle, not in general a religious man, invoked the name of the devil as often as God. Robert preferred to credit the practical genius of his father. The passage over Chat Moss was in the event the smoothest of the journey thus far.

When they arrived without further incident at Eccles bridge, George and his engine were waiting for them. Father and son embraced as if they had been separated for years.

'How is Mr Huskisson? Is he...?'

'Here at the vicarage. I've just took the surgeon in to him. The leg ull have to come off, but he's in no state to steel himself to it. I don't suppose he'll see the morn.'

'It is a dreadful business.'

'Aye.' George seemed about to say something else when an emissary from the Duke appeared, to ask why they had stopped again - His Grace wanted to get on, to do his duty by the people.

'Tell him, I'm just coupling up,' said George, then in an undertone to Robert, 'though from what I've seen he's ridin into enemy territory. Not so much *Hail the Conquering Hero* as *Hanging Johnny*.'

The situation was worse in Manchester than when George had left with the surgeon. For all Reeve Sharpe's good intentions of shielding him from danger, he ultimately heightened the threat to the Duke's safety. The instruction Sharpe sent back to deploy soldiers to control the masses at Liverpool Road station was acted upon as soon as it was received, and with no little vigour when it met any resistance. With the disaffected calling loud attention to any evidence of brutality, half the crowd surged away from the line of military and, having nowhere else to go, escaped in large numbers along the railway tracks.

George and Robert, matching their respective engines for speed so they might make their entry like Castor and Pollux, were surprised by an onrushing wave of people hemmed in by the deep cutting outside the station. As Robert admitted to Fanny afterwards, it was miraculous that not one among the swarm was killed or injured before the two drivers could slow their vehicles to a crawl. It soon became obvious that it was the rail passengers who had more to fear, especially those in the carriage easily identified by its elaborate design as the one the Prime Minister was in. That coach was besieged.

'Where is the Duke?' was the cry. 'Show us your face!'

George tried to keep his engine on the move, pushing through the stream of bodies, for he could only imagine what might happen if he stopped altogether. To left and right he could see placards demanding *The Vote* and *No Corn Laws*, and *Remember Peterloo!* He caught a glimpse of a *tricoleur* swaying over heads. Some in the crowd had stones - he was sure of it this time - and no doubt there would be clubs, pitchforks... perhaps, who knows, guns. He looked across at Robert, driving likewise, his jaw set, but it was only a momentary glance; his eyes were needed everywhere.

The Duke stayed behind his crimson blinds until, enraged by the noise of folk banging against his coach and trying to climb on it, he raised a blind, intending to impose his authority. He was startled by an arm thrust through the window.

'Shake my hand, sir, shake my hand.'

The man had hauled himself up and was clinging onto the window frame with his other hand. His face was all delight to be in the presence of greatness, and the Duke was surprised into accepting the proffered handshake. As he did so, an object hurtled through the open window, just missed his head. It rattled against the inside of the carriage and dropped with a dull thud to the floor. Waterloo's hero looked down in shock, half-expecting the sight of a cannonball. It was a large turnip. Wellington slammed his fist hard down on the intruder's fingers. His face disappeared from view. The Duke sealed the carriage once more and pressed himself back into his seat, wrapping his Spanish cloak around him in a storm of temper as the boos and catcalls swelled outside. Peel, opposite, made no comment; kept his eyes on the turnip as it rocked back and forth dropping fragments of soil onto one of the gold coronets woven through the ducal carpet.

The locomotives inched their way across Water Street bridge and arrived at the station, where a semblance of protection was given by the military making themselves a human barrier between the crowd and the trains. The noise redoubled, bouncing off the roof, so that the passengers

252

felt encircled by menace. To Robert it was like being trapped in a jar of butterflies at the hands of urchins with torture on their minds.

According to the schedule, distinguished guests were to repair to the new goods warehouse where a lunch had been awaiting them these last two hours. Wellington refused to move a muscle.

'Bring my food to me,' he said. 'And prepare for our departure.'

While the noble lion fed in his cage, and the two Stephensons rushed around organizing the shunting of locomotives from front to back, more than a few of the passengers decided they had already had their fill of the delights of the day, deserting the party in favour of good old-fashioned stage coaches or hackney carriages to take them home. Ebenezer Buckle, inured by his trade to the occasional threat of violence, picked up one of the discarded luncheon tickets and sallied through the throng of protestors to take one of the many places now available in the warehouse. The Scottish couple stayed where they were, as did the accountant. In the carriage behind the *Phoenix*, the ladies discussed lunch, but decided that as their men were too busy to accompany them, the wiser course was to remain seated.

'Well, at least we got here,' said Fanny as brightly as she could, and looked out of the window as if in anticipation of the best entertainment.

'Oh, I see why Robert loves you so,' said Elizabeth, and Aunt Nelly gave a little nod to show that she did too.

At the vicarage in Eccles, another devoted wife was supporting the hand of her husband as he attempted to sign a codicil to his will, painfully dictated by him over the past hour. The codicil was simple enough, giving over to Emily all estate that had come to him since he had last expressed his final wishes. The couple had no children.

The signature was made and the document folded away when Huskisson lifted his hand with the pen still in it, seeming to indicate that he wanted to add something. Emily smoothed out the paper, and laid it again on the low table by the sofa. She offered her hand once more for support, but her husband managed without her; stretched his arm to the table and, with precision that belied the effort it cost him, placed his customary dot between the W and the H of his signature. Mission complete, he dropped the pen into Emily's open hand, and fell back upon his cushions with a sigh. There was to be no amputation.

The journey back to Liverpool was a tortuous one for all who made it. In the confusion of shunting locomotives from one end to another and dispatching some to take on water, several had switched tracks, engines had separated from their carriages and could not be reunited because others had got between - a muddle partly created by Wellington's insistence on leaving Manchester as soon as possible to get away from the demonstrators, and his refusal to allow his carriage to be sent back there while the mess was sorted out. As a result, guests faced even more hold-ups, and it was a strange combination of engines and coaches lashed together by rope in a long line that eventually crawled homeward. Only the Duke's carriage escaped delay, and he got off at Roby, returning to the Marquess of Salisbury's house with a festering hatred for the railway.

Night had fallen long before the last of the trains pulled in to Crown Street station. Along the route firemen had jumped down from the engines and tried to light the way ahead by burning tarred ropes, but they provided nothing more than a glimmer. In the darkness, the *Comet* demolished a wheelbarrow left accidentally or on purpose in the middle of the track. A second human tragedy was narrowly avoided just past Rainhill where the convoy accelerated down the incline and almost mowed down a group of uniformed men trying to follow the rails back to town; these pedestrians made to run for their lives were the bandsmen that had been abandoned at Parkside after they gave up their flat-bed wagon to the injured William Huskisson.

Yet the gloom was lifted in the deep cutting at Olive Mount. Despite the lateness of the hour, thousands of spectators had stayed behind to watch the trains return. Many of them brought candles and lanterns, which they waved in unison as each locomotive saluted them on the way through with a cheering blast of steam. The mount was alive with moving orange flame. Fanny, looking out of the window of her carriage, thrilled to it more than to any of the light spectacles she had seen at the Vauxhall Gardens Cascade, something she reported to her husband afterwards as he sat low-spirited at their table in the ballroom of the Adelphi Hotel.

'And the tunnel too, all lit up with gas; and to emerge at last to all those people cheering and singing in the station. It was wonderful, Robert.'

He held her hand and smiled, but could not help but look past her at the many unfilled places in the room; the stage, empty of the band; the top table missing the Prime Minister, the Marquess, Peel, Huskisson...

'It was not the day I dreamed it would be.'

'Love.' She kissed his hand, scolded him gently. Across the table, he saw his mama watching them in stirred abstraction, like one following a dance of lovers at the ballet. The seat next to her was empty for the moment. He scanned the room for sight of his father, and discovered him standing by the doors, talking in his usual animated style to a man Robert did not know. George happened to glance across at their table, waved, and a minute later brought the stranger over.

'Son, this chap is Francis Ogden, the... er...'

'United States Consul,' the man supplied. 'Francis B Ogden. Honoured to make your acquaintance, sir.'

'Do you know, Rob, Mr Ogden was just tellin us, he was the very first man to sail a steamboat in the sea.'

'My claim to fame, I suppose,' said Ogden, playing bashful against type. 'Lots have done it since. It was in quite a gale, though. But hey...' He snapped back his shoulders as he moved into speech mode, addressing them more formally. 'You gentlemen, what you have done today, and leading up to today, well, it's nothing less than earth-shattering. You are going to change the world, I mean it, you are going to change the world.'

'I believe that's true,' said George. He grinned proudly at Betty as he motioned the consul to sit down with them.

'Thank you for being so kind,' said Robert, once the ladies were introduced.

'Well, it's not just words. Let me tell you, there were more than twenty Americans in attendance today. They were all here for one thing, and they got it in spades; that is, to take inspiration for their own project, the Baltimore and Ohio Railroad.'

'That sounds like some undertaking.'

'Nearly three hundred miles, all told, when complete. And it will be. That's what they are all saying to me now, and they'll do it quickly too. After today, they can't wait to get on with the work.'

'Despite all the problems they have seen..?'

'Hold it; listen.' Mr Ogden pulled his chair closer, confidential. 'I'm an American; forgive me for speaking plainly. You can't be responsible for every damn fool who gets himself killed: it happens. As for the rest of the shenanigans, that was politics, nothing to do with your project. I'd stake one hundred dollars, Wellington will be out of office this time next year.' He squeezed Robert's arm, and turned his attention to Fanny, who had been leaning across her husband to hear what was being said. 'Mrs Stephenson, you are a very lucky lady.'

'I know I am.'

'And you are going to be a rich one also, if your husband has anything to do with it.' He straightened up and said more loudly, 'Very rich. You too, George. Take my country, for instance: as well as the Baltimore, I know for certain that Louisiana is putting in an order for

British rails to take a line from Lake Erie to New Orleans. Then there's the engines, and of course the expertise... The world is your oyster. You might need to take on a few more business partners.' He patted at his pockets without success, then said expectantly to Robert, 'Say, you wouldn't happen to have such a thing as a cigar, would you?'

Huskisson's death was confirmed sometime after midnight, when all but a few of the company had already retired. Drinks had been taken on. Robert went out for air, and his father met him when he came back into the hotel lobby. They sat down together.

'There's summat I been waiting to tell you about what happened after the accident,' said George. 'I mean when I drove Huskisson to the vicarage.'

'What of it?'

'Well, it's fifteen mile from Parkside to Eccles bridge. I timed the run exactly at twenty-five minutes.'

It took a moment to assimilate the information. 'That's... That's more than thirty-five miles an hour.'

'Man's never gone faster.'

They looked at each other. Circumstances forbade congratulations. Robert simply nodded twice, allowing his father's chest the right to swell a little. They sat a little longer, and George said, 'You mind when I told you an John Nixon that the railroad ud become the great highway, meanin the King's highway?'

'I remember that.'

'I should have said the world's highway. After what we've heard tonight, we mun believe it.'

'Why not, indeed.'

'I'm proud of what we've done. There's nowt wrong wi that, surely?'

'Of course not. I am proud of it. I'm proud of you, Dad.'

'Likewise. What more can we want if not to make our families proud? Never mind what the American says, there's more than riches. It's what your mother... I mean, your *mama*, what Betty said to me when we finally got together, that she was proud of us.'

'Fanny is too.'

'Of course, as your children will be, I'm sure; our grandchildren... For we've just got started yet.'

'We have.'

George rose from his chair, stretched an arm across his son's shoulder and drew him in. Robert submitted to the embrace like a child at bedtime, pressing a cheek to his father's breast as if for the reassurance of his heartbeat. George's voice resonated through their kindred bones.

'When you was just a bairn, when Old Bob had his accident at work, your Aunt Nell had Betty write a letter to bring me home from Scotland, an it took a week just to reach us. I never felt so far away from my family. That won't be the case for the next generation. I mean to have the mail run between London and Edinburgh by locomotive. If I can succeed in that afore I die, well, that ull be good enough for me. That ull fettle it for me.'

'I mean to help,' said Robert. 'And so Amen.'

Later that same morning, the first booked train left Liverpool Crown Street for Manchester with a full complement of one hundred and forty passengers. It reached its destination in two hours - that is, precisely on time. Within the year, the Hare and Hounds closed its doors as a coaching inn forever. Ebenezer Buckle managed to secure a new job on the railway.

XV

The train that brought Robert Stephenson and George Parker Bidder north to Newcastle arrived - like the first public service into Manchester nineteen years before - precisely on time. True, the Central Station was not quite finished, but the salient point was, the train arrived in Newcastle. Had they chosen to do so, the travellers could have arrived by road and crossed the Tyne at the same point; Robert had designed the bridge for both rail and road, on two levels. It was a stunning contribution to the architecture of his home city and, along with his new viaduct at Berwick, fulfilled his father's dream to connect London and Edinburgh directly by rail. In two days, the royal train would follow the route south from Scotland, bringing Queen Victoria to the official opening of the High Level Bridge.

The two engineers had arrived early because Robert had conceived a desire to show his friend some of the places of his childhood. He had been thinking of these a lot lately. They stayed the night at the Turk's Head in Grey Street and next morning hired a hansom cab to take them to Killingworth. Robert asked the driver to deliver them into the centre of the village. By chance, they alighted outside the Three Tuns public house.

'This is the window ledge my daddy sat me at while he went hunting for someone to take his place in the militia.' Robert applied his forehead to the glass to check if the interior of the place had stayed the same; as he did so the cab moved off with a groan of wheel, wood and leather, prompting a memory of the carriage that drew up behind him that night with Aunt Nelly in it, and the graceful woman who was to become his stepmother. He turned. Bidder stood close by, smiling and engaged, for he had heard the story from both the father and the son.

'Come on, I will show you Dial Cottage,' said Robert, plucking his sleeve, and they walked off in the direction of West Moor. Everything was closer than he remembered, his legs so much longer now. Halfway along the crushed path, he could see the wheels turning at the pithead, and heard soon the distant rumble of coal tubs on the surface line. The place seemed grimier than the one in his head - the spoil heaps grown into black mountains - and he was thus pleasantly surprised, once they came in sight of the cottage in Paradise Row, that the fence surrounding it gleamed with fresh whitewash, as if the royal visit was also expected here. The garden was trim, with both trees in good order. There were flowers and a lawn where his father had grown vegetables; no need now of a mechanical scarecrow.

'Ar, the famouz zundial,' said Bidder, running the words into one.

'Indeed. It was the first thing we ever worked on together.'

They inspected it from the gate, as Kit Heppel had done the day it was put up. While they waited for a cloud to clear from the sun (so they could check the accuracy of the dial) the front door opened, and a neat little woman stepped out. She must have seen them from the window for she showed no surprise that two strange men were staring at her house, or perhaps she was used to it being an object of attention; she said, approaching them down the path, 'I suppose you know who lived here once over?'

'*I* did, in my childhood.'

The woman looked at Robert with new interest. 'Oh, when was that?'

'Forty-odd years ago we came, and I must have been past eighteen by the time we left.'

'He yelped his father make thar zundial,' said Bidder.

The woman looked behind her, as though seeing the device above her lintel for the first time; turned back in some astonishment. 'You're not one o Geordie Stephenson's children?'

'I am, the only one.' He checked himself. 'The only one surviving, I should say.'

'Is it Robert?'

'It is.'

'Well, I never did. Come in, come in - the kettle's on the hob.'

Robert followed her up the path, his friend close behind. 'We will not trouble you for tea, mam, but I would like to take a peek inside, thank you very much.' He had to stoop slightly at the threshold. He paused just behind the door to run his hand up the wall into a recess above his head. 'There was glass here in our day, where we kept a pet blackbird.' His eyes adjusted to the change in light. 'And here used to be the one room we lived in, but for a tiny loft above.' In the middle of the room was a table occupying the same space as their old table that had served both for meals and for his father's workbench, and once for supporting the deal box where his mother lay. He felt too tall for the room now, like Trevithick with his long legs.

'I'm told this bookcase belonged to George,' the householder was saying.

'It did, it did,' said Robert, almost chasing around the table to get to the bookcase, which he touched with a degree of reverence. 'And so did this.' In the corner next to the bookcase was a dilapidated writing desk, stained the same dark brown. 'May I?' As the woman watched, he ran his fingertips along the back line of the patterned inlay that bordered the writing surface. Near the centre he stopped, pressed down on a whorl in the pattern, then with palms flat, dragged at a section of the desktop, which slid away, revealing a shallow compartment beneath.

'I had no idea that was there,' said the woman to Bidder, who shook his head as if to say neither had he, though he had never before set eyes on the desk.

'And look what is here yet,' Robert said. He reached into the secret compartment and picked out two objects, souvenirs of a boy's life. One was a silver button from a redcoat's tunic. The other was a key, made to fit a very large door. He showed it proudly to his friend and the householder. 'This was Old Bob's - my grandpa's. I borrowed it for an experiment, and to my shame I never did give him it back.' He placed the key in his top pocket, and carefully stowed the button once again in the secret drawer. 'Now, Bidder, I have something to show you at the back of the house.' He started to lead the way, then remembered himself. 'If you don't mind, madam...'

'Not at all.'

'Thank you. This is all new to Mr Bidder.'

He found his way easily to the back door and out into a plain garden at the rear overshadowed by the branches of an apple tree. Robert climbed onto the fence at the bottom of the garden, helped his heavier friend up beside him.

'The mineral line runs straight past the house, and there on that track *Blücher* was completed and put through her paces. You've heard us talk of *Blücher*?'

'From the day we firz met in Edinburgh. Six tons in weight and er could pull a load up to thirty ton at four mile an hour.'

'GP, figures stick to you like burrs.'

He lingered at the fence, seeing in his mind's eye the locomotive steaming on the track, a horse in the field beyond, two boys flying a kite. When they returned to the house they found tea poured out for them despite their protests.

'Does John Tate still live in the locality?' he asked, as they sat companionable.

'John Tate? No, can't say I know that name. Not since we've been here. Did he work at the pit?'

'Man and boy.'

'Happen he's moved away, then, or died mebbes. There's a John Heppel.'

'Kit's son? I met up with Kit again just last year, at the time of my father's funeral.'

'Well, Kit stops under John's roof now. I'm sure they'd want you to call on em, if you've got the time. I can show you where.'

Twenty minutes later, Robert was embracing his father's old friend, and again being urged to take tea, this time by Kit's daughter-in-law.

'I knew you'd sure to be up for the bridge openin,' said Kit, 'but I didn't reckon on you comin back to this mucky owd place.'

'Why not? I lived here long enough.'

'Aye, an the morrow you'll be hob-nobbin wi the queen. Eh, Bobby.'

'Will you come to the opening, Kit?'

'Oh, aye, we thought if we set off early enough we might get a decent place down on the quayside, see the royal train coming over the bridge.'

'I'm sure I can get you closer than that. Come along to our hotel tomorrow morning; I'll arrange for you to be one of the platform party.'

'No, no. Haven't I told you afore, it wouldn't sit right wi me, being in that sort o company. No, I'll be more than happy on the quayside.'

Robert knew the man was talking sense, but the residual guilt he still had about his failure to make Kit an official guest at George's funeral spurred him to cudgel a solution from somewhere. 'Listen, I have it. In the morning, please go to our manufactory in Forth Street. I will send instruction that you are to be included in the workforce that is to be lined up for the queen's arrival at the bridge. You will have a very good view from there, and be quite inconspicuous.'

'An what if she were to ask a question of us? I know nowt at all about bridge-building.'

'I'll lay odds you'll know a darn zight more un er does,' said Bidder, making them all laugh.

'I promise you, Kit,' said Robert, 'the queen is not going to engage you in conversation. Well, it is my hope she might deign to walk across and have a brief word with some of the men involved. If she should come anywhere near you, Kit, just be sure to be making a close study of her feet; that is tantamount to ducking out of her way whilst preserving the utmost courtesy and respect.' Bidder stood up and mimicked the action, to more laughter.

261

Issue resolved, the next half hour was spent in pleasant reminiscing about the old days. As they got up to leave, Robert wanted to ask Kit a question, but before he got the chance the old man said, 'I have summat for you,' and slipped out of the room.

'How is his health?' Robert inquired of the daughter-in-law. 'He seems spritely enough.'

'Oh, fit as a lop. I shouldn't be surprised if he sees us all out.' Robert recalled the old man saying something similar, the day he met him in Chesterfield.

Kit came back to the company carrying a miner's lamp; not a Davy but a Geordie lamp. 'You've seen this afore. Your dad give us it thirty year sin.'

Robert cradled the base of the lamp in his hand as he inspected it. He took note of the perforated metal plate and the series of inlet tubes inside the glass cylinder. 'This looks like a late prototype; might even be the very one Dad used for his demonstration at the Lit and Phil.'

'The same,' said Kit. 'Geordie asked us to keep it as a mark o friendship and for helping with the tests an such, but really I did nowt to help. It's you should have it, Bobby.' He made to deliver it fully into Robert's hand, but was resisted.

'No, Kit, certainly not. It was given, as you said, as a mark of friendship, and so it should be kept. Anyway, it is right that the lamp should stay in the hands of a pitman. If you are to bequeath it to anyone, may it be to your son, or to your grandson; that's how it should be.'

'I would like to have kept it in the family, true enough,' admitted Kit. 'Just thought...'

'Think nothing. Only of Geordie's wishes. And let it be.'

With that, Robert and Bidder left the Heppel home, and it was only when they were walking back along the narrow path that Robert realised he had forgotten to put his question to Kit.

'What was it?'

'Oh, I just wondered if he could remember where in the churchyard my mother was buried. Not to worry, I will look for it myself. If you don't mind helping, GP.'

'Glad to. Which way to the church?'

Skirting the outer wall of St Bartholomew's churchyard, Robert amused Bidder with his tale of the gravedigger he mistook for a ghost, but the mood became sombre as they walked through the gates and began to search among the tombstones for the name of Stephenson. They stayed together on the main path to the church door, then each took one of the paths either side of the door, moving gradually away from

262

one another as they continued the search. Robert's method was to ignore the larger, more ornate memorials; among the modest gravestones he concentrated on those areas of the ground where the inscriptions signified interments from the early years of the century. In between the adult graves he came across several tiny plots, which sparked a new thought that his baby sister must be buried here too. He wondered if she was alongside their mother or elsewhere; George had never mentioned it, and he could not remember ever visiting the graveside of either, though he recalled looking in vain with his old friend John Tate, and now here he was searching with another.

Every so often Robert would lift his head looking for Bidder, but his colleague seemed to be having no more success than he, passing tablet after tablet without a particular name attracting his notice. Eventually they met again by the south wall and, with a mutual shake of heads, walked back together to rest their legs inside the small church.

'I suppose there was no money for any sort of headstone,' Robert said. He fell silent after that, thinking, thinking, thinking of his wife memorialised in Hampstead, and of the family vault in Chesterfield. His eyes strayed to the floor of the chancel, as if he imagined his mother and sister lying under it. On the pew beside him Bidder shivered a little.

'I had forgotten how sunless this place is,' Robert acknowledged. 'Perhaps I should send them money for a new window. It has significance for me other than... I used to play flute in the orchestra here.' He gestured to the choir stalls, and conjured an image of himself there at service, oblivious of other associations, playing to please his new mama.

'Want to continue the zearch?' Bidder said at last.

'No, I don't think we will find anything. Instead, let me show you my first little school. It is just across the street from here.'

The Rutters' schoolrooms, however, had reverted to their former use as a private house. The man who opened the door told them that James Rutter, the son, had been dead these twenty years. Such education as could be found in the village was entirely in the hands of the church.

'I wonder if Dr Bruce is still alive,' Robert mused aloud, thinking of Percy Street even as the door closed on his earliest schoolday memory. 'Now, GP, would it tax your strength to walk back to Newcastle?'

'You're more like your dad than I uzed to credit,' said Bidder, just a hint of mild complaint in his tone. He meant more than in the challenge implicit in Robert's question; he had never known such restlessness in him.

The two friends returned to the city along the same route that schoolboy Robert used to take on his cuddy, and on his first trip with

Aunt Nelly the day his father started his tramp to Montrose. The railway tracks followed the lines of the old wagon way, and whenever a coal train passed by on its journey to the staiths Bidder joked that they should jump aboard one of the tubs and *ride eazy*. It was mid-afternoon by the time they arrived at Newcastle quayside. Rather than turn up Sandgate, they stayed by the river to take a closer look at the new bridge from below. One hundred and twenty feet up, the bridge commanded its position.

'She's by way of reprezenting what she does,' Bidder remarked.

'What do you mean?'

'Only that she's somewize like a long train of railway carriages, stretched across the river.'

Robert studied the structure anew, and appreciated Bidder's simile - there was a sense in which the six arches seemed invested with a latent energy, connected and ready to move. The stone piers, that he had previously thought of as giant legs planted firmly in the river bed, seemed by this new conceit more like great arms thrusting out from the water, their hands gripping the impatient bridge, restraining it. The image fed his condition of fevered calm, and redirected it. He was captivated by the dramatic execution of his own vision, and at once forgot his intention to complete the sentimental journey of his childhood.

'Let us go up there,' he said.

'Where? To the bridge?'

'In case it should break free before the morrow and ride off on some adventure down the railway line.'

'Thay, you're as mump aided as I be.'

'What?'

'Daft, I mean. Lead on, Chief.'

Bidder followed Robert up the bank and along the road to the site of the new Central Station. There was such a bustle of workmen and supervisors preparing for the queen's visit that no-one challenged the two men as they passed through and out along the side of the tracks to the railway bridge. At its centre they discovered a fifteen-feet high iron archway, newly constructed above the railway lines. It was secured to the guard rails on either side of the bridge; presumably a temporary addition for the sake of the royal opening. A single gull was perched up there, surveying the scene. Robert inspected the anchorage on the east side of the bridge, mindful of possible damage to his precious structure, and again Bidder thought of George, though he did not say it aloud. Apparently satisfied with the workmanship, Robert leaned across the bridge rail to stare at the black water below. Bidder peeked over the edge from a foot or so further back.

'Tharz a long way down,' he said redundantly.

Robert lifted his eyes and stared out over the water to the mouth of the river, then in the general direction of his old colliery home. Bidder watched him watching the horizon. He was in a state of some anxiety for Robert, though he could not quite put his finger on the reason, unless it was simply that his friend had not moved from his precarious position near the edge. They stood like this with only the wind for company, until Robert spoke up.

'You like the bridge, Bidder?'

'I do. May be your best yet.'

'May be my last. *If you would see his monument, look around.* You've been to St Paul's?'

'I have.'

Robert contemplated the Tyne; remembered the Thames, rank and mysterious on his first visit. Before Fanny. Before... almost everything.

'I am thinking of buying a boat. A yacht, I suppose. Something large enough to sail overseas. Perhaps you would like to travel with me.'

'Dreckly, yes, be a diversion. Where zull we go?'

'Some remote island. Somewhere the postman can't find us. We'll find somewhere peaceful and just drop anchor for a while.'

'Suits me, Chief.'

They returned to the silence of their individual thoughts until (heart-stopping shudder) the gull flapped its wings as it took off above them. The bird spread itself to follow the course of the river, dipping as it went. Robert watched it to a speck, then shifted his gaze to the Newcastle side. His eyes swept across the lantern spire of St Nicholas, the castle keep...

'I can't see Grey's Monument from here.'

Before his friend had time to protest, he climbed to the top of the iron rail, using the archwork for purchase, and held on, leaning boldly out to catch the sights of the city.

Bidder was alarmed. 'Have a care, Chief. Dun want you diving arf the bridge.'

'Don't worry, George. We Stephensons have a good head for heights.' He settled his back against the metal arch. 'Did I never tell you of my father's giant leap?'

'Can't zay you have. Why don't you come down from there and speak of it?'

'It was Kit Heppel told me the story,' said Robert, showing no inclination to move. 'They were both young pitmen then...' He was

265

interrupted by a shrill blast of steam. Beyond Bidder he saw a locomotive emerging from the station. It was not pulling coaches but service wagons - workers, no doubt, on maintenance or erection duties for the opening. Bidder, hearing the train behind him, stepped cautiously away from the track, gripped the bridge rail with a queasy sensation and tried not to look down.

'Come on Rob,' he pleaded. 'Iz like to shake you arf o there.'

Robert seemed to comply, moved his weight forward on his feet as if about to jump down from the rail, then recovered his position, seeking his balance as he watched the approach of the train. Unbidden imagination - in the moment of standing up, his mind leapt from young Geordie Stephenson to the navvy Powder to a copper-coloured Juan Bellinck at Vauxhall, *the genuine native Indian American*; Frances Sanderson watching with innocent enthusiasm. Robert stretched out both arms, in the manner of a tightrope walker.

The locomotive thundered by. He held his position. Workers sat on the flat-bed wagons, staring as at a frieze. A few cheered or jeered. Only when the train had crossed the entire span of bridge and rolled on into Gateshead did Robert let his arms drop and his body relax once more against the arch. He exhaled, and grinned at Bidder. 'Not a single vibration.' Tested his sole against the bridge rail. 'Not a tremor.'

He made an exultant jump off the rail and landed on both feet in front of Bidder. The impact of the landing jarred Old Bob's key from his top pocket. It bounced once on the safe side of the rail, dropped through the bridge with a couple of clinks, and was lost, given up to the River Tyne.

When Robert arrived at the same spot shortly before noon on the Friday, smartly dressed and accompanied from the Guildhall by the mayor of Newcastle and entourage, he found the scene at the crossing transformed. The metalwork of the temporary archway was almost hidden under a profusion of flowers and evergreens; at the top a crown of dahlias, surmounting the initials VR shaped out of wrought iron. An inscription underneath read *Welcome to both sides of the Tyne*. Banners and a union jack hung from the arch. The railway track on the western side of the bridge had disappeared under a crimson-covered platform, presently being muddied by five hundred pairs of boots and shoes of the assembled guests practising forbearance in the constant drizzle. Bidder was among them, with other senior representatives from the railway companies and contractors involved in the project. On his side of the track, Robert had already passed the line of delegated workmen, noticing Kit particularly by

266

a slight coming to attention as he walked by, and a bashful glance from the collier when he saw himself observed. Robert suppressed a greeting, not to embarrass him further.

The civic party from Gateshead met Robert's group at the centre of the bridge. While members crossed the track to the western side, where they politely jockeyed for position at the front of the stage and kept an ear open for news of the royal train, Robert stayed for a moment to look over the rail at the crowds below the bridge. Though the haze prevented him from seeing all the way down river, he had an impression of masses lining the banks on both sides. From there they could hope to catch only the most fleeting glimpse of the train and none at all of her Majesty. The Tyne was crowded with boats and ships that bobbed in cheerful defiance of the weather, decked in reds, blues and whites. Beyond the river, some of the factory chimneys had been newly painted, and it seemed as if there had been a general effort to curtail the smoke from the works. Nearer to the bridge, Robert could see people at all the windows of the elevated buildings on both banks, in the Moot Hall, the old castle, and even on the wet roof of the hotel at Gateshead station, near the rise where a detachment from the Royal Artillery was positioned with four of the twenty-one field pieces primed for the royal salute.

He felt a tap at his shoulder. Bob Hodgson, construction engineer for the bridge, joined him at the rail. Hodgson whispered, as if passing on confidential information. 'The police superintendent has just now told me their estimate of spectators. Well over sixty thousand, within the city precincts.'

'I am glad the rain has not put them off.'

'Perhaps it has - God knows how many more there might have been. They've not had a monarch to visit here since the first King Charles. Well done, Mr Stephenson; auspicious day. I am sure her Majesty will have much to say to you.'

'And to you Bob, I trust. Credit where it is due.'

'I hope to get the chance to speak to Prince Albert,' said Hodgson. 'I want to show him this.' From his pocket he produced a large nail, bent like a boy's fishhook.

'What is it? I mean, what does it signify?'

'A project free of accidents. You know we have lost no-one, in all the months of construction? Well, if it had not been for this nail we would have done. Matter of weeks ago, had a chap tip himself backwards just where they were putting the rail up - head first over the edge. Except this nail was sticking out from a piece of scaffolding, and it caught his trouser leg on the way down. Held him, hung upside down, until we could get a rope lowered and haul him to safety. Fortunate fellow, eh? I've put him in the line along there, just in case he's wanted to be spoken to.'

'The tale of the nail, eh? It will fascinate the prince, for sure,' said Robert. He thought of Tom One-Eyebrow, who fell to his death in Colombia, and wondered for the first time what family he might have left back home in Cornwall.

A whistle sounded, the signal that the royal train had passed through Heaton and was on its slow progress towards the bridge. The two men rejoined their civic hosts in front of the platform.

'Congratulations on the arch, by the way,' Robert said quietly. 'Nice touch.'

Long before the royal train appeared to the party gathered at the bridge, they could hear the cheers and applause building with the urge of a forest fire that no amount of rain could check, reaching an intensity under the roof of the new station, and setting off fresh conflagrations along both banks of the river below. Some of the cheers were squandered on the pilot engine, fronted with a crown of leaves and flowers, that emerged first onto the bridge and scurried across without stopping until it arrived at the station in Gateshead. A moment later, the crowd was silenced by a greater din - the first volley of the royal salute fired from the castle. It was answered from the Gateshead side, and repeated at three second intervals from either bank until all twenty-one guns were spent. The spectators stayed hushed - cowed almost, as if they were actually under attack - until the reverberation of the last shot faded, then their roar redoubled at the exact moment that the locomotive carrying the queen's colours rolled out of the station and onto the bridge.

Robert saw, as it passed him at the arch, that the engine was one of his own design. Someone had painted a large gold crown on the side of the firebox. There followed seven First-Class carriages of the royal suite, then the state carriage itself, distinguishable by the ventilator on its roof in the form of a crown as the badge of royalty. Robert mentally acknowledged the skill of the driver who executed the approach precisely to bring the royal carriage to a stop immediately beneath the triumphal archway. The usual squeak of steam and brakes was muffled by the excited cheers of the platform party, so that it seemed the train landed soft upon a cloud of goodwill.

He could see, inside the plate glass windows of the carriage, lavender silk drapes partly drawn aside to reveal royal hands resting on a satin-wood table in the centre. There was the small, slightly chubby right hand of the queen with what looked like a sapphire on her third finger, light blue sleeves above, and perhaps an edge of tartan shawl. Prince Albert opposite, hands folded together, sharp white cuffs under a black suit. Some movement of a human kind in the background; the children probably, eager to see or just restless with the journey.

The hub-bub on the bridge died down; the respective mayors stepped forward from the line Robert was in, and shuffled into position next to the door of the carriage, with a mutually inane smile like Bobchinsky and Dobchinksy in the Gogol play. Nothing else happened, until the prince consort's left hand lifted to draw back the drape on his side, and pull the sliding window about eight inches lower. Robert could see his face now, noted especially his longish nose and well-trimmed moustache, the mildness in his eyes as he watched the two officials through the window. Captain Weatherley, the Newcastle mayor, had something of a puppy-dog expression, awaiting a command from his queen. When it did not come, he glanced sideways at Prince Albert with a wordless appeal and received a nod, whereupon the mayor unrolled the parchment he was holding in his hand, planted his legs slightly apart as though to steady himself on a rolling ship, and began to read:

TO THE QUEEN'S MOST EXCELLENT MAJESTY.

The humble Address of the Mayor, Aldermen and Burgesses of Newcastle-upon-Tyne. May it please your Majesty - We, your Majesty's dutiful and loyal subjects, the mayor, aldermen and burgesses of Newcastle-upon-Tyne, respectfully tender to your Majesty, on the occasion of your first visit to the ancient town of Newcastle-upon-Tyne, the cordial and sincere expression of our loyalty and attachment. In past times the visits of the Sovereign to this town were for the purposes of war. We congratulate your Majesty on your visit being made under happier circumstances...

For the first part of this address, Prince Albert kept his eyes on the monarch, in deference to the speech being addressed to her, but Robert noticed how they later shifted to the interior of the carriage, and how his lips pursed, signs perhaps that the royal children might not be taking the speaker quite so seriously as he was taking himself. Happily the calligrapher had not been given space to make the declaration a long one and Captain Weatherley soon reached his conclusion:

We pray your Majesty may long live to reign over a happy and united people.

He looked up beaming from the manuscript, then bowed his head either to his sovereign or to his wider audience as they applauded politely. There was another pause while the mayor searched for clues as to what to do next; receiving none he took it in his head to improvise, rolling up the parchment and making as if to post it through the open section of the window in the direction of the queen. Prince Albert forestalled him, leaned towards the door and opened it before the scroll came through.

From nowhere, so it seemed, a servant in royal livery appeared on the platform outside the carriage to take the strain of the open door. Hodgson, next to Robert, essayed a sort of lopsided attention, feeling in his pocket for the lucky nail in anticipation of the royal approach. But the prince advanced no further than the open door, taking the parchment from the mayor with another nod, and passing it to his wife inside. He resumed his seat.

Robert could see more of Queen Victoria now, in profile, and the children inside - the Princess Royal, the Prince of Wales, and the six-year-old Princess Alice. All three were dressed in kilts of the same tartan as their mother's shawl, and all had fingers in absent exploration of mouths or noses as they tilted their heads to stare through the open doorway. The queen laid the scroll on the table, and the prince subtly moved it to the seat beside him just before a small wet hand reached out to pick it up. The mayor of Gateshead (Robert did not know his name) stepped forward with obvious pride, made an elaborate bow before the open carriage, and unrolled his parchment.

Robert studied the queen, or as much as he could see under her silk bonnet, as she attended to the second address. She could no longer be described as youthful; six children before the age of thirty must take their toll even with the best of medical care. She was a good deal plainer than the portraits he had seen, certainly rounder in the face, and her appearance at this angle did not flatter her nose, nor her chin which was decidedly in retreat from her lower lip. He was most concerned about the lack of expression in her blue eyes; she was facing the mayor, but seemed to be looking at nothing at all, like an ordinary woman in church thinking about the washing she had to do on the morrow. Granted the speech was not one to inspire, but Robert hoped she would show a little more animation should she speak more than a few words to him when they met. Otherwise he would not quite know what to say that would interest her.

We entreat your Majesty to be permitted to express the pleasure we experience in witnessing an instance of that high and truly royal determination of your Majesty to make yourself acquainted by actual observation and intercourse with the various portions of your Majesty's dominions, thereby strengthening more and more the bond of union so happily subsisting between the British people and their Sovereign by confirming it in person, and sealing it with a smile. And we fervently pray that your Majesty and your Majesty's Royal Consort and family may long enjoy the blessings of health, and the proud satisfaction of beholding on every side the grandeur of your empire and the happiness of your people.

Given under the common seal of the Mayor, Aldermen and Burgesses of the Borough of Gateshead, this 25th day of September, 1849.

There were not many full stops, but those few were ignored by the mayor until he reached the final one, which he reached with breathless gratitude. Having learned from the experience of his counterpart, he subsequently wasted no time in rolling up the parchment and handing it through the open door, not to the monarch but to her consort, who handed it to the queen, then retrieved it from the table to stow it out of the reach of inquisitive children. The mayor took a pace back, and the queen finally acknowledged the applause of the guests with a practised smile and a regal wave. Prince Albert motioned to the servant, who in turn made a signal to someone at the front of the train. Captain Weatherley was stepping forward again with an object in his hand just as the servant was closing the carriage door. Robert watched the mayor take a half turn back to the platform party, confusion on his face. Someone brushed past Robert and took Weatherley's elbow, at the same time ordered the servant to desist from closing the door. Robert recognized the newcomer as the Earl Grey. His lordship, with Weatherley still in his grip, had a whispered conversation with Prince Albert, who then disappeared from the carriage window. A few moments later, the crowd clapped wildly to see the young Prince of Wales appear in the doorway. Lord Grey manoeuvred Weatherley in front of the boy prince, and the mayor presented him with a silver paper cutter, which he immediately gave to his mama and scampered back inside. The queen beckoned the mayor to her and spoke a few words, which seemed to gratify him immensely. He stepped backwards, bowing furiously to the queen, as the servant, on instruction from the earl, resumed his closing of the carriage.

'God Save the Queen!' somebody shouted from the platform, and the cry became a chorus on the bridge, then on the banks below the bridge, then on the quayside as the royal train started up again and completed the crossing into Gateshead and southward. Sixty thousand voices roared on the family who had set not one foot on one inch of either town. There had been no official timekeeping of the royal visit, but by general consent it had lasted a little less than five minutes.

For the mayor Captain Weatherley it was the finest five minutes of his life. He recounted every moment of it to fellow members and guests as they began to disperse. He was particularly keen to seek out Robert Stephenson and pass on the queen's comments. 'It's a beautiful bridge, she told me; a beautiful bridge.'

*

271

A few months later, following her confinement for the birth of Prince Arthur and on her way to Holyrood, Her Royal Highness graciously agreed to be present at the official opening of the viaduct at Berwick, which was henceforth to be known as the Royal Border Bridge. It was on that occasion Robert Stephenson was offered a knighthood for his services to the country. He declined the honour, as his father had before him.

Epilogue

George Parker Bidder had been somewhat distracted, not to say discomposed, by the pictures in the hallway, and was thus the last of the chief mourners to leave 31 Gloucester Square and climb into the carriage immediately behind the waiting hearse. He joined the two Stephenson cousins, George and Robert, and fellow executor, Charles Parker. Before the hearse were the carriage that contained the civic delegation from Newcastle in full regalia and another with the mayor of Sunderland accompanied by Edward Pease's surviving son Joseph, also John Dixon and John Ellis. A further eleven carriages lined up behind.

Bidder had been at Robert's side almost constantly since he was taken ill aboard the *Titania* with the liver complaint that proved fatal, and Bidder had been the orchestrator behind the scenes of the practical arrangements for the funeral; keeping busy was his way of staving off despair over the loss of his great friend, and besides who was more acquainted than he with the network of relationships, personal and professional, that made up the life to be celebrated as much as the death to be mourned on this day?

Just before eleven o' clock, the cortège left the square. The blinds of all the houses had been pulled down in respect, and the only sounds were the occasional shiver of a harness, the rhythmic clip-clop of hooves on cobbles. Six horses pulled the hearse, four drew each of the mourning coaches. The procession slowly followed the route of Robert's habitual walk, across Bayswater Road and into Hyde Park through the Victoria Gate. The hawkers and street performers that usually populated the area around the gate were conspicuous by their absence. No place today for the girl who once danced a silent hornpipe for the gentleman's delight.

It had not been a simple matter to obtain permission for the funeral train to pass through Hyde Park, for no precedent existed. Charles Manby, the Honorary Secretary of the Institution of Civil Engineers, had been prevailed upon to write to the Duke of Cambridge in his capacity as the Ranger of Hyde Park, and the Duke had felt the need to refer the request for the queen's approval. Her Majesty acknowledged the high position that Mr Stephenson had occupied and the world-wide reputation he had won for himself, and considered that his funeral, though strictly speaking private as conducted by his friends, partook of the character of a public ceremony; moreover, being anxious to show that she fully shared with the public the loss which the country had sustained by his death, she could not hesitate for a moment in giving her sanction to the course which his Royal Highness the Ranger had recommended.

Bidder was glad of it. Nothing was more appropriate than that his friend, who had loved the open air so much, should be led in peace under trees and by water. The Serpentine seemed cleaner now, with the new pumping station installed. (Hawksley, the engineer, was one of those who awaited their arrival at Dean's Yard.) This part of his final journey was a reminder, too, of Robert's close involvement with the Great Exhibition, though the Crystal Palace had long since removed to Sydenham. Prince Albert had been generously appreciative of his work as a Commissioner.

At the statue of Achilles the procession wheeled right and headed sedately towards the Apsley House exit from the park. The spirit of the Iron Duke was there in full *hauteur*, though his body was lying next to Nelson's in St Paul's. George Hudson had long ago vacated his house on the far side of the street, living now in virtual penury on the other side of the Channel.

Bidder had not failed to notice how people had gathered in numbers at strategic points on the way from Gloucester Square, but that did not prevent his astonishment when the cortège left the tranquillity of the park to make its way past the Wellington Arch into Grosvenor Place. The entire length of the street was filled on both sides by a mass of soberly-dressed spectators, five or six deep, yet the silence was as profound as though the whole of London were deserted. There was barely a movement but for the lifting of hats and the bowing of heads as the hearse passed by, and so it continued all along Victoria Street too and into the enclosure of Dean's Yard. It was almost noon and Bidder knew that respects were being paid simultaneously in Whitby, Sunderland, Tynemouth, North Shields, Gateshead and especially in Newcastle, where a fifteen-hundred strong workforce from Robert Stephenson and Company would even now be marching to a memorial service at the church of St Nicholas.

In considering the eminently supported application for the sepulture of Robert Stephenson in Westminster Abbey, the dean and chapter had been at pains to point out that the great west door of the abbey receives the mortal remains only of monarchs and nobles. Accordingly, when the hearse of the untitled engineer arrived at its destination, the coffin was lifted and carried through the cloisters by a distinguished group of pall-bearers led by the Marquis of Chandos, and met at a side door by the dean and clergy, attended by the choir. The assemblage of official mourners followed the casket through the side door, turned left into the aisle and processed the length of the nave - the organist, Mr Turle, accompanying the choir as it chanted offices for the burial of the dead. There was a pause to allow guests to take the seats that had been allocated them, joining a congregation that had somehow swelled to three thousand, though only two thousand tickets of invitation had been issued.

For Robert's friend Bidder, much of the ensuing service was lost among his emotions. The readings, intended to uplift, brought him low. The music of Croft and Purcell washed over like an ocean that threatened to drown him, robbing him of breath. He caught at phrases: *Man that is born of woman; Thou knowest, Lord, the secret of our hearts; I said I will take heed to my ways;* and, as the body was consigned to the grave, *I heard a voice from heaven...*

The ceremony concluded with a benediction by the dean. Bidder sat in place, trying to recover his composure, while the people around him filed slowly out. Eventually, even the organ had stopped playing, and he was left alone in the quiet and chill of the great church. He knew he had duties yet to be performed. People would be waiting for him; but still Bidder found it hard to leave. He walked to the centre of the nave, to the stone in the floor below which his friend's body was interred. It was, as yet, unmarked. Kneeling down, Bidder stared at the spot for a minute, while he reached for the contemplative calm he had been unable to find during the service. Just as he made to rise and depart at last, he noticed the inscription on the adjoining stone. It read, *Thomas Telford, 1834.*

'Well, Chief,' Bidder spoke aloud, 'you do not rest zolitary after all, for yere's some worthy company, perhaps. Farewell dear Robert. I leave thee to God and good neighbours.' He laid his hand on the stone, but could find no comfort there.

THE END

Biography

David Williams grew up as one of seven children in a mining community in the North East of England, a childhood he has written about with humour and affection in his popular collection of short stories *We Never Had It So Good*, published by Zymurgy.

While pursuing a varied career in teaching, the arts, marketing and training, David has also been a prolific free-lance writer, with many plays broadcast by the BBC, books and plays published by top education publishers in the UK, Australia, Germany and Scandinavia, and many credits as a writer and format creator for popular TV and radio quiz and game shows. He has written and produced educational and training videos, DVDs and software. He is a member of the Society of Authors and NAWE. He often performs at public readings, workshops and seminars. He writes stories and articles for magazines such as *The Author* and *The New Writer* and has a regular blog *Writer in the North*.

David's first novel was *11:59*, a contemporary thriller published by Wild Wolf. It was a semi-finalist in the 2010 Amazon Breakthrough Novel Award, which annually attracts 10,000 entries worldwide. *Publishers Weekly* described it as: 'One taut little thriller...A near-cinematic stylist, the author deftly sustains the tension right up until the final segment...a sterling example of astute character studies melded with highly topical concerns.'

David also reached the semi-final of the 2011 Amazon Breakthrough Novel Award with this novel. 'One day I hope to win it!' he says.

David Williams has been married to schooldays sweetheart Paula 'for years and years'. They have three grown-up children and a growing band of grandchildren. The drama in their life comes from following the fortunes, on and off the field, of their local football team, Newcastle United.

Lightning Source UK Ltd.
Milton Keynes UK
UKOW03f1531230414

230468UK00001B/25/P